2018

中国国际收支报告
China's Balance of Payments Report

国家外汇管理局国际收支分析小组
BOP Analysis Group
State Administration of Foreign Exchange

中国金融出版社
China Financial Publishing House

责任编辑：张翠华
责任校对：孙　蕊
责任印制：程　颖

图书在版编目（CIP）数据

2018 中国国际收支报告 / 国家外汇管理局国际收支分析小组编 . —北京：中国金融出版社，
2019.7

ISBN 978-7-5220-0183-8

Ⅰ . ① 2…　Ⅱ . ①国…　Ⅲ . ①国际收支—研究报告—中国—2018　Ⅳ . ① F812.4

中国版本图书馆 CIP 数据核字（2019）第 146356 号

2018 中国国际收支报告

2018 Zhongguo Guoji Shouzhi Baogao

出版
发行　**中国金融出版社**

社址　北京市丰台区益泽路 2 号
市场开发部　（010）63266347，63805472，63439533（传真）
网上书店　http://www.chinafph.com　（010）63286832，63365686（传真）
读者服务部　（010）66070833，62568380
邮编　100071
经销　新华书店
印刷　天津银博印刷集团有限公司
尺寸　210 毫米 ×285 毫米
印张　14.25
字数　218 千
版次　2019 年 7 月第 1 版
印次　2019 年 7 月第 1 次印刷
印数　1-2000
定价　80.00 元
ISBN　978-7-5220-0183-8
如出现印装错误本社负责调换　联系电话：(010) 63263947

国家外汇管理局
国际收支分析小组人员名单

组　　长：潘功胜

副组长：郑　薇　宣昌能　张　新　陆　磊

审　　稿：孙天琦　刘　斌　叶海生　徐卫刚　王　晖

统　　稿：王春英　周　济　贾　宁　赵玉超　胡　红　韩　健

执　　笔：

第一部分：李　萌　刘立中　管恩杰

第二部分：邬　烨　高　畅　胡　红　贺　萌　李玲青

第三部分：杨　灿

第四部分：乔林智　张洪诚

第五部分：赵玉超

专　　栏：杨　茜　林　萌　马玉娟　贺　萌　陈　丰

附录整理：刘立中

英文翻译：胡　红　王　亮　高　铮　杨　灿　贺　萌　刘立中

英文审校：Nancy Hearst（美国哈佛大学费正清东亚研究中心）

Contributors to this Report

Head
Pan Gongsheng

Deputy Head
Zheng Wei   Xuan Changneng   Zhang Xin   Lu Lei

Readers
Sun Tianqi   Liu Bin   Ye Haisheng   Xu Weigang   Wang Hui

Editors
Wang Chunying   Zhou Ji   Jia Ning   Zhao Yuchao   Hu Hong   Han Jian

Authors
Part One: Li Meng   Liu Lizhong   Guanenjie
Part Two: Wu Ye   Gao Chang   Hu Hong   He Meng   LiLingqing
Part Three: Yang Can
Part Four: Qiao Linzhi   Zhang Hongcheng
Part Five: Zhao Yuchao
Boxes: Yang Qian   Lin Meng   Ma Yujuan   He Meng   Chen Feng

Appendix: Liu Lizhong

Translators: Hu Hong   Wang Liang   Gao Zheng   Yang Can   He Meng
Liu Lizhong

Proofreader: Nancy Hearst (Fairbank Center for East Asian Research, Harvard
University)

内容摘要

2018 年，全球经济继续扩张但增长势头放缓，国际金融市场波动性有所加大。我国经济运行总体平稳，人民币对美元汇率双向波动，在全球货币中表现相对稳健。

2018 年，我国国际收支延续基本平衡。经常账户保持在合理的顺差区间，全年顺差 491 亿美元，占 GDP 的比重为 0.4%。其中，货物和服务贸易合计顺差 1 029 亿美元，占 GDP 的比重为 0.8%，贸易收支更加平衡。第二季度起经常账户恢复顺差，第二至第四季度顺差逐季增加，分别为 53 亿美元、233 亿美元和 546 亿美元。非储备性质的金融账户保持顺差，全年顺差 1 306 亿美元。其中，直接投资顺差 1 070 亿美元，仍是较稳定的顺差来源；证券投资顺差 1 067 亿美元，创历史新高，主要体现了资本市场进一步开放的效果；其他投资逆差 770 亿美元，在双向波动中保持基本稳定。总体来看，以中长期投资和资产配置为目的的资本流入仍占主导，我国对外投资保持理性。2018 年，交易形成的外汇储备资产小幅增长、基本稳定，说明我国国际收支继续呈现自主平衡格局。2018 年末，我国对外金融资产和负债较 2017 年末分别增长 2.5% 和 2.9%，对外净资产 2.13 万亿美元，增长 1.4%。

2019 年，我国将继续推动经济高质量发展和全方位对外开放，有助于夯实国际收支平稳运行的基础。预计我国国际收支将延续经常账户基本平衡、跨境资本流动总体稳定的发展格局。下一步，外汇管理部门将坚持稳中求进的工作总基调，深化外汇管理改革，推动金融市场双向开放，服务国家全面开放新格局。同时，坚持底线思维，防范跨境资本流动风险，保障外汇储备安全、流动、保值增值，维护国家经济金融安全。

Abstract

In 2018 the global economy continued to expand even though the speed slowed down. Furthermore, volatility in the international financial market strengthened China's economy and generally remained stable. The RMB exchange rate fluctuated in both directions against the USD but remained relatively steady among global currencies.

China's balance of payments maintained a basic equilibrium in 2018. The current account remained within a reasonable surplus range. In 2018 the current account surplus was USD 49.1 billion, accounting for 0.4 percent of GDP. Trade in goods and services posted a surplus of USD 102.9 billion, accounting for 0.8 percent of GDP, which was generally more balanced. In the second quarter, the current account returned to a surplus. The current account surplus grew from the second to the fourth quarter, at USD 5.3 billion, USD 23.3 billion, and USD 54.6 billion respectively. The non-reserve financial account continued its surplus of USD 130.6 billion. Direct investments posted a surplus of USD 107.0 billion, which was still considered a stable surplus. Portfolio investments posted a surplus of USD 106.7 billion, reaching a historic high level. This revealed the effects of the further opening of the capital market. In general, capital inflows for mid-to long-term investments and assets allocations remained dominant and outward investments continued to be rational. In 2018 reserve assets from transactions grew slightly and remained stable. China's balance of payments is independently able to maintain an equilibrium. At the end of 2018, China's external financial assets and liabilities both increased, up by 2.5 percent and 2.9 percent respectively from the end of 2017. External net assets registered USD 2.13 trillion, up 1.4 percent.

In 2019 China will promote strategic high-quality development and an opening up on all fronts, which will strengthen the basic foundation for stable balance-of-payments operations. We expect that China's balance of payments will maintain a basic equilibrium and cross-border capital flows will remain stable. The foreign-exchange management authorities will pursue the underlying principle of making progress while ensuring stability, deepen the foreign-exchange management reform, and boost the opening up of the financial market, to serve China's fully open strategy. Meanwhile, we will insist on maintaining a bottom line, defend against risks associated with cross-border capital flows, and ensure the security, liquidity, and preservation of the foreign-exchange reserves to safeguard the economic and financial security of the country.

目　录

表

Content

Box

Chart

Table

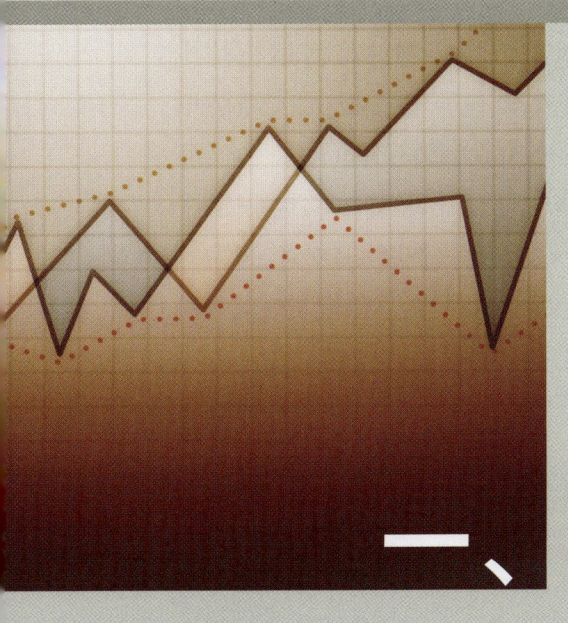

一、国际收支概况

（一）国际收支运行环境

2018 年，我国国际收支面临的内外部经济金融环境复杂多变。全球经济延续增长态势，但不确定因素较多，增幅有所放缓。国内经济运行总体平稳，为国际收支基本平衡奠定了良好的经济基础。

世界经济复苏有所放缓。2018 年，发达经济体和新兴市场经济体经济运行均出现分化。美国经济第三、第四季度已经有所放缓，失业率低位下行；欧元区经济增长势头放缓，德国第三季度 GDP 环比收缩 0.2%，为 2015 年以来首次负增长，通胀水平整体温和；日本经济增速持续降低，第一、第三季度环比出现萎缩，通胀水平依然疲软；受脱欧不确定性影响，英国经济持续低速增长，第一季度 GDP 增速为六年来最低水平；新兴市场经济体表现继续分化，总体上处于经济企稳和恢复的状态，但部分国家受到金融市场动荡、高失业率等因素拖累（见图 1-1）。

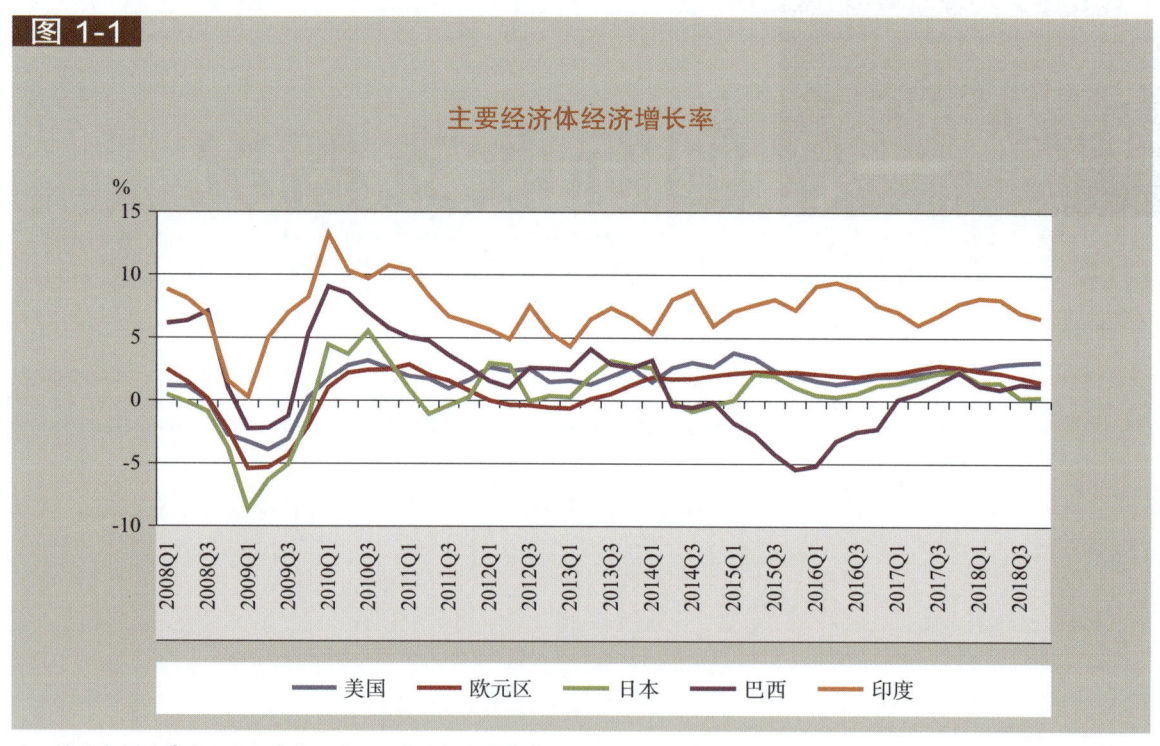

图 1-1

主要经济体经济增长率

注：美国数据为季度环比折年率，其他经济体数据为季度同比。
数据来源：环亚经济数据库。

全球货币政策持续分化。美联储全年加息四次，联邦基金利率由年初的1.25%~1.50% 上调至 2.25%~2.50%，同时持续推进缩表计划。欧央行 2018 年维持主要政策利率不变，并宣布 2019 年夏天之前不会改变，月度资产购买规模逐步削减，并在 2018 年底结束。日本央行保持极低的利率水平，并继续维持各类资产购买规模不变。英格兰银行 2018 年 8 月 2 日议息会议上调基准利率 25 个基点至 0.75%，此后继续维持基准利率与资产购买规模不变。新兴市场经济体货币政策分化，但面对全球金融环境收紧及本币贬值压力，多家央行选择加息或偏中性的货币政策立场。俄罗斯、印度、土耳其、阿根廷、墨西哥等央行采取措施收紧货币政策，以应对汇率贬值、资本外流和通胀压力等问题。另外，为促进经济增长，韩国、巴西等央行保持相对宽松的货币政策立场。

国际金融市场波动加大。2018 年，受贸易摩擦、美联储加息及全球经济周期可能见顶的影响，国际金融市场波动加大。美元指数较上年末上涨 4.4%，欧元、英镑贬值；主要发达经济体股市出现下跌，美国道琼斯工业平均指数、欧元区斯托克 50 指数分别下跌 6.0% 和 14.0%。内外因素触发部分新兴市场经济体金融市场动荡，部分新兴经济体货币一度大幅走低，出现汇市、债市和股市共振下跌现象，JP Morgan 新兴市场货币指数（EMCI）和 MSCI 新兴市场股指全年跌幅超过 10% 和 16%。2018 年国际大宗商品走势疲弱，S&P GSCI 商品价格指数下跌 15.4%（见图 1-2 和图 1-3）。

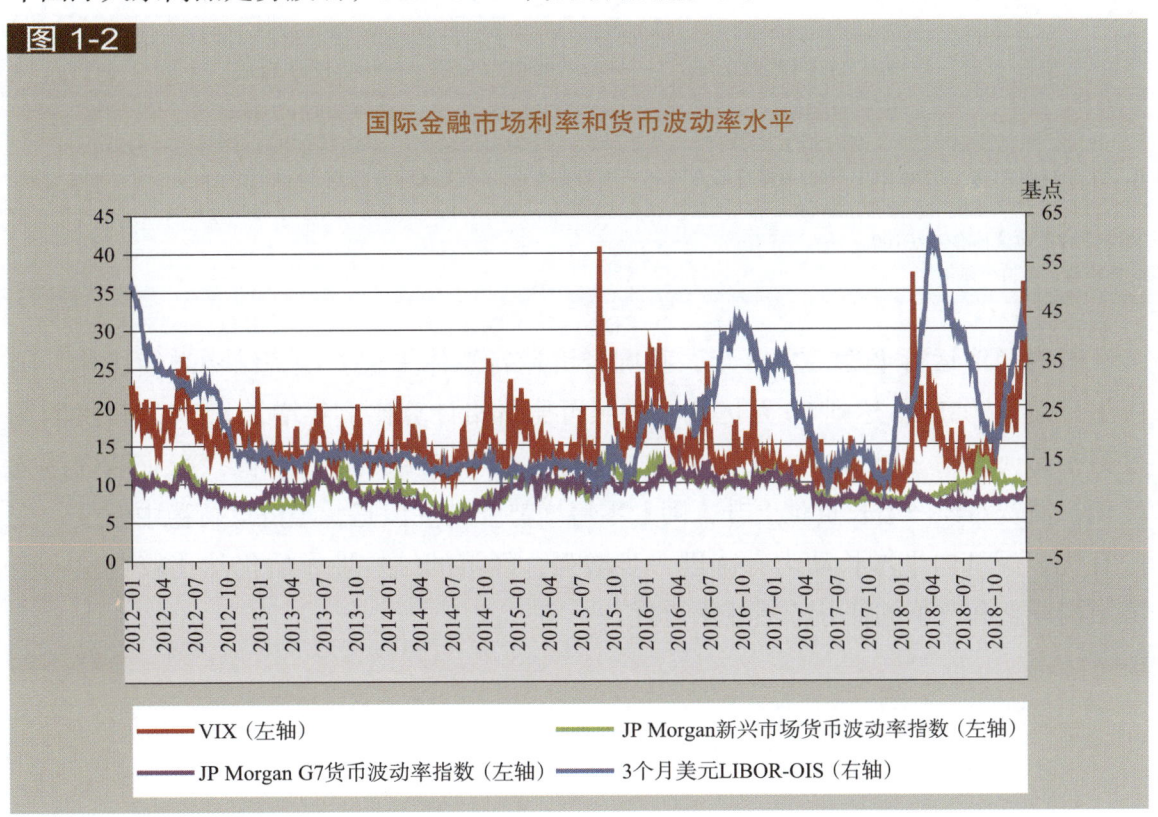

图 1-2

国际金融市场利率和货币波动率水平

数据来源：彭博资讯。

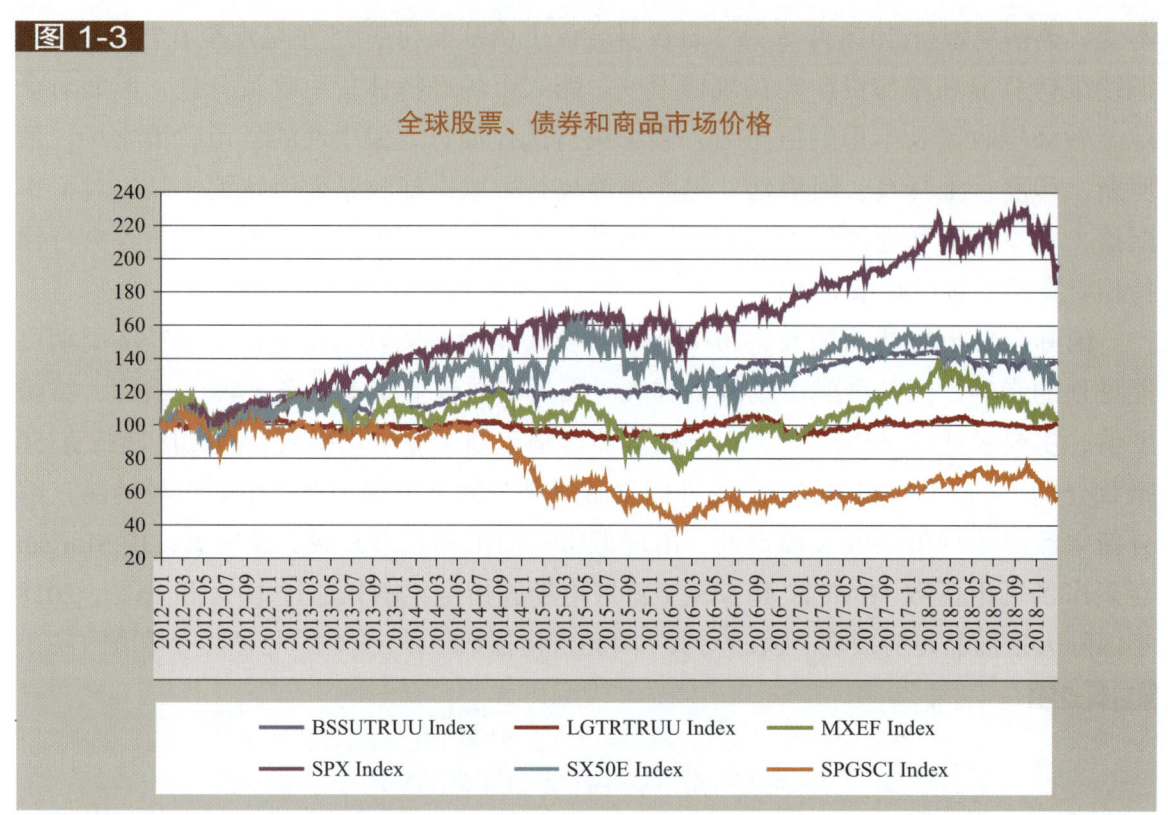

图 1-3

全球股票、债券和商品市场价格

注：BSSUTRUU 和 LGTRTRUU 分别为彭博巴克莱新兴市场和发达国家主权债券指数，MXEF 为 MSCI 新兴市场股指，SPX 为美国标准普尔 500 股指，SX50E 为欧元区斯托克 50 股指，SPGSCI 为标准普尔 GSCI 商品价格指数，并将各指数 2012 年的年初值标准化为 100。
数据来源：彭博资讯。

　　国内经济运行平稳。2018 年，我国经济运行总体平稳，经济结构继续优化。国内生产总值（GDP）达到 90 万亿元，按照可比价格计算比上年增长 6.6%，居民消费价格指数（CPI）上涨 2.1%（见图 1-4)，工业、服务业生产总体平稳，产业结构持续优化，消费对经济增长贡献上升，网上零售增势强劲。但是，经济运行稳中有变、变中有忧，经济内生增长动力有待进一步增强，经济的结构性矛盾仍然比较突出，经济结构调整和改革的任务依然任重道远。

图 1-4

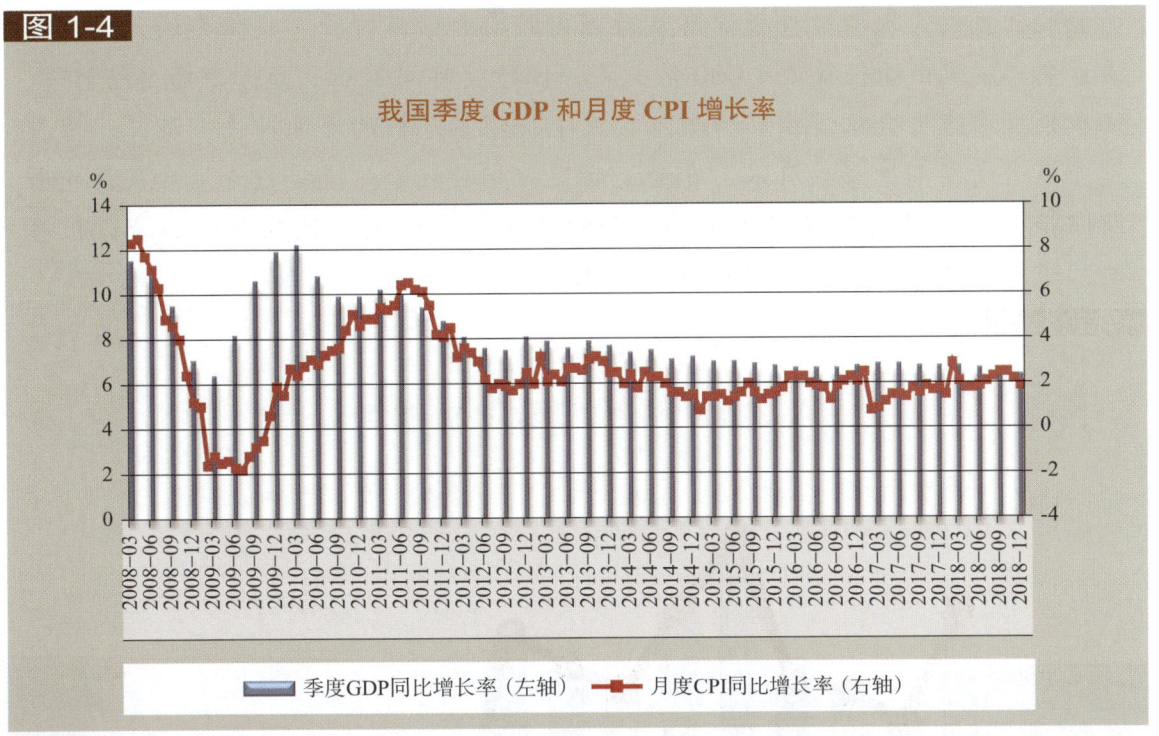

我国季度 GDP 和月度 CPI 增长率

数据来源：国家统计局。

专栏 1

全球跨境资本流动稳定性特点及启示

　　近十年来，在影响全球跨境资本流动稳定性的各种渠道中，银行渠道发挥关键性作用。当发生外部负面冲击时，无论发达国家还是新兴市场，其境内的外资均主要通过银行渠道流出，以缩减跨境借贷为主要形式。总结经验，在当前我国跨境资本流动"宏观审慎＋微观监管"两位一体的管理框架下，维持稳健的银行体系，关注外部风险敞口，有助于维护我国经济金融安全。

　　银行渠道是跨境资本流动的关键渠道，对保持跨境资本稳定格局至关重要。在 2008 年国际金融危机中，银行渠道资本流动对各国的冲击远大于证券投资和直接投资渠道。其一，银行渠道的资金流出主要体现在跨境借贷的大幅萎缩，资金流出呈现幅度大、速度快、持续时间长的特点。如 2008 年第三季度前，发达国家的银行渠道资金流入量维持在每季度 1 万亿美元以上。雷曼破产后，银行渠道的资金迅速转为流出，峰值超过每季度 2 万亿美元。2009 年第三季度后，全球避险情绪有所缓解，但银行渠道资金流入量持续萎缩，并显著低于危机前水平。其二，证券投资渠道呈现较强的顺周期性。证券投资渠道资金流出主要体现在境外投资者减持国内股票和债券资产。危机期间，新兴市场资金季度流出峰值接近 1 000 亿美元，但持续时间较短。随着市场情绪好转，证券投资渠道资金从流出转为流入，完全抵消了危机的负面冲击。其三，直接投资渠道受周期性影响有限，资金流动变化相对较小。直接投资资金关注中长期回报，主要受结构性因素影响，如竞争力、产业链、税收制度和地理位置等，受周期性影响较小（见图 C1-1 和图 C1-2）。

图 C1-1

境外资金流入发达国家境内情况

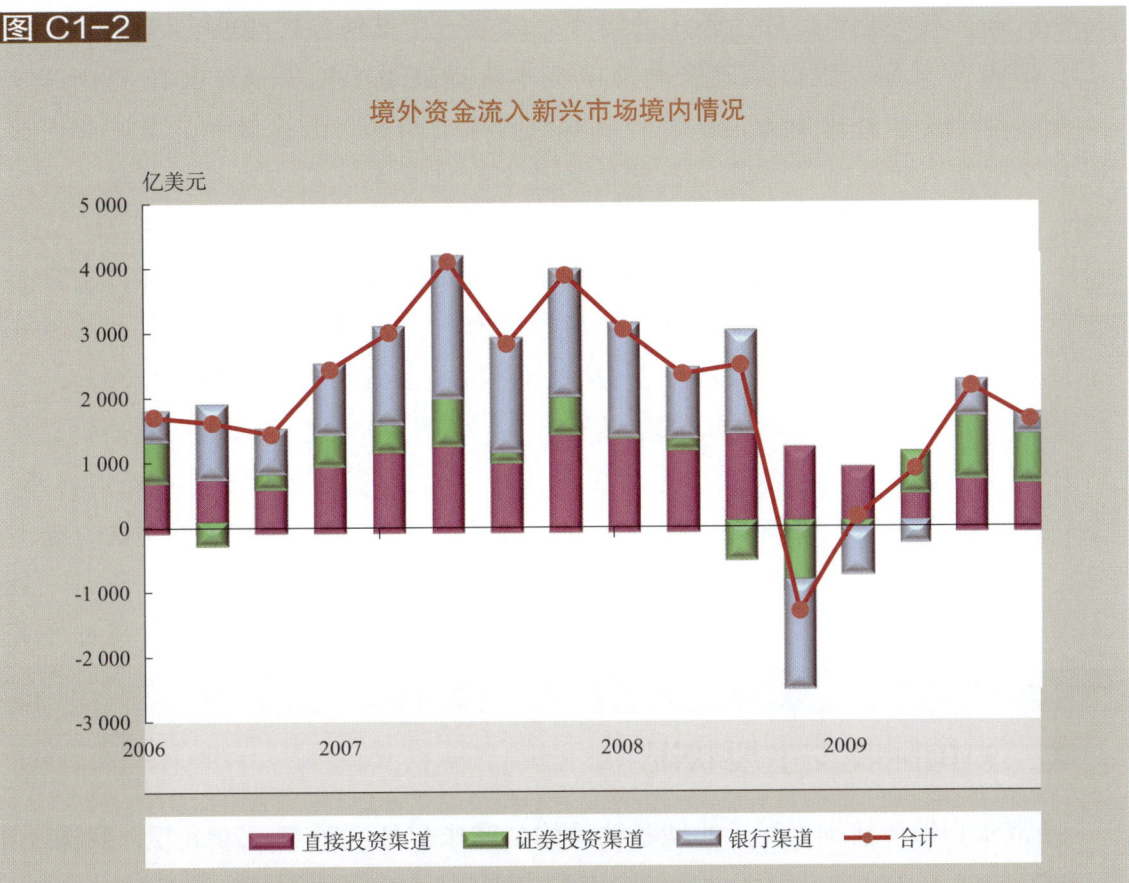

图 C1-2

境外资金流入新兴市场境内情况

图例：
- 直接投资渠道
- 证券投资渠道
- 银行渠道
- 合计

注：基于各国国际收支平衡表季度数据整理 ①。新兴市场数据不涵盖中国。
数据来源：国际货币基金组织。

　　当银行渠道资金持续流出时，证券投资和直接投资渠道在发达国家和新兴市场中的作用略有不同。发达国家的证券投资渠道资金流入恢复较快，对银行渠道资金的持续流出起到部分抵消作用。而新兴市场的直接投资渠道保持季均约 1 000 亿美元的资金流入，是跨境资本流动中更为重要的缓冲因素。

　　新兴市场国内银行与企业行为的自我强化加剧了美元短缺，引发连锁反应。以韩国为例，国内银行的美元负债在 2008 年国际金融危机前远超美元资产，债务到期需要不断借入美元。而国内进出口企业单边看涨韩元，持有较多美元贷款，中小企业普遍通过外汇衍生工具押注韩元相对美元升值，同样积累大量美元债务。危机时，全球避险情绪加剧，美元融资成本攀升，跨境借贷萎缩，国内银行间市场极度缺少美元。银行停止向企业拆借，企业只能出售资产获取美元，加剧国内资产和汇率下跌，导致境外投资者进一步减持韩国股票和

① 图中数据仅考虑境外主体的资金流入境内市场的情况，不考虑境内主体对境外的投资。数据为负值表示境外主体的资金从境内市场撤回。发达国家和新兴市场资金额为各国简单加总数，未做抵消处理。证券投资渠道不包含衍生品投资和银行相关投资；银行渠道为其他投资项，扣除贸易信贷和政府部门资金变动，加入银行投资股票和债券资产变动。

债券资产，引发连锁反应。韩元实际有效汇率一度下跌接近40%。

2010 年至今，银行渠道仍是跨境资本流动最重要的渠道。2015 年新兴市场面临跨境资本流出压力，银行和证券投资渠道均转为资金流出，其中银行渠道资金流出最为显著，季度流出峰值接近 800 亿美元。而直接投资渠道维持了稳定的资金流入，起到了缓冲作用。

当前，我国跨境资本流动实施"宏观审慎＋微观监管"两位一体的管理框架，其中银行渠道是宏观审慎管理的重要内容。历史经验表明，从银行体系和监控外部风险敞口两方面来增强我国应对外部冲击的能力，有助于维护经济金融安全。一方面，维持稳健的银行体系，保障银行系统充裕的外币流动性，可对外部冲击引发的流动性紧张起到缓冲作用，保持跨境资本流动的稳定格局。另一方面，在逆周期市场化调节跨境资本流动时，应加大对外部风险敞口的关注，如汇率对冲比例、外汇杠杆等，以防止银行或企业盲目扩大外汇敞口，放大外部冲击。同时，引导企业合理运用外汇衍生产品，防范隐性杠杆攀升和异常跨境资本流动。

（二）国际收支主要状况

经常账户保持基本平衡，非储备性质的金融账户延续顺差。 2018 年，我国经常账户顺差 491 亿美元；非储备性质的金融账户顺差 1 306 亿美元（见表 1-1）。

表 1-1　我国国际收支差额主要构成

单位：亿美元

项　　目	2013 年	2014 年	2015 年	2016 年	2017 年	2018 年
经常账户差额	1 482	2 360	3 042	2 022	1 951	491
与 GDP 之比	1.5%	2.3%	2.7%	1.8%	1.6%	0.4%
非储备性质的金融账户差额	3 430	−514	−4 345	−4 161	1 095	1 306
与 GDP 之比	3.6%	−0.5%	−3.9%	−3.7%	0.9%	1.0%

数据来源：国家外汇管理局、国家统计局。

货物贸易更趋平衡。 按国际收支统计口径[①]，2018 年，我国货物贸易出口 24 174 亿美元，较上年增长 9%；进口 20 223 亿美元，增长 16%；顺差 3 952 亿美元，下降 17%（见图 1-5）。

[①] 国际收支统计口径的货物贸易与海关统计口径的主要差异在于：一是国际收支中的货物只记录所有权发生了转移的货物（如一般贸易、进料加工贸易等贸易方式的货物），所有权未发生转移的货物（如来料加工或出料加工贸易）不纳入货物贸易统计，而纳入服务贸易统计；二是计价方面，国际收支统计要求进出口货值均按离岸价格记录，海关出口货值为离岸价格，进口货值为到岸价格，因此国际收支统计从海关进口货值中调出国际运保费支出，并纳入服务贸易统计；三是补充部分进出口退运等数据；四是补充了海关未统计的转手买卖下的货物净出口数据。

图 1-5

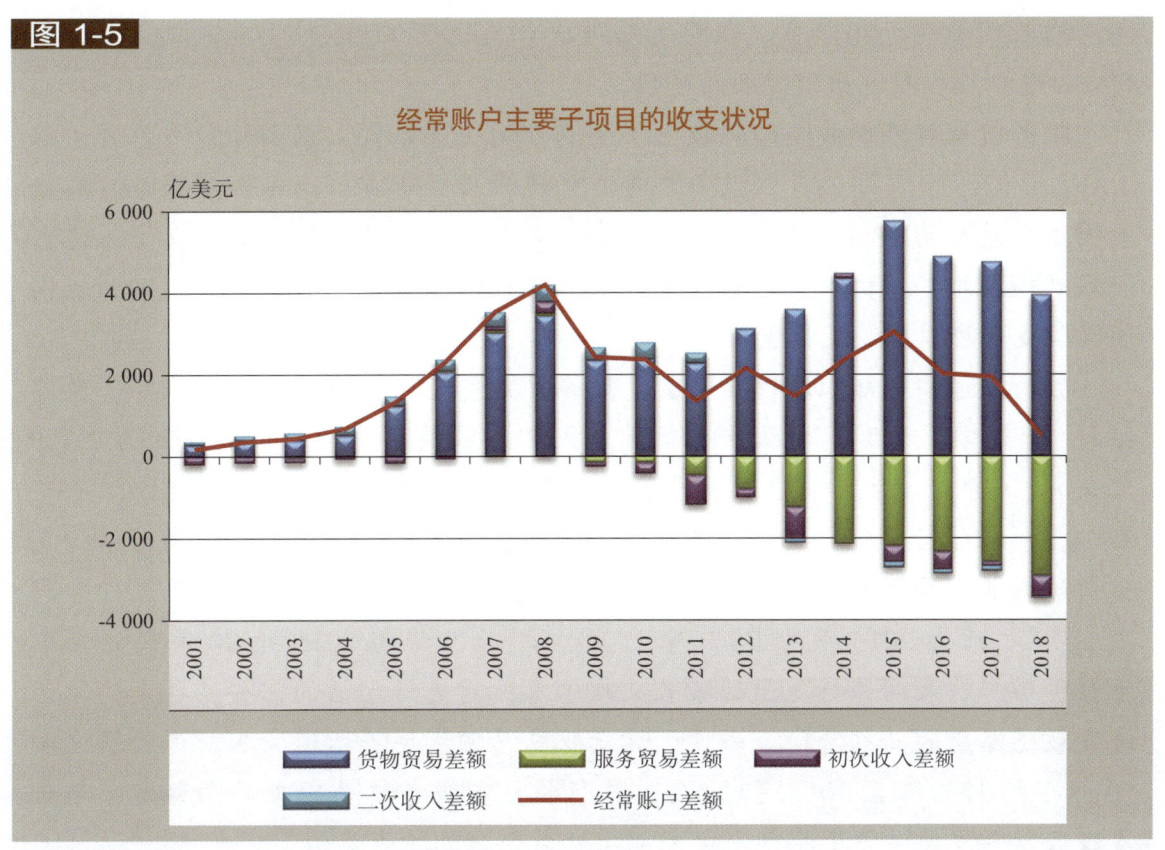

经常账户主要子项目的收支状况

亿美元

图例：货物贸易差额　服务贸易差额　初次收入差额　二次收入差额　经常账户差额

数据来源：国家外汇管理局。

服务贸易逆差平稳增长。2018 年，服务贸易收入 2 336 亿美元，较上年增长 10%；支出 5 258 亿美元，增长 11%；逆差 2 922 亿美元，增长 13%（见图 1-5）。其中，运输逆差 669 亿美元，增长 20%；旅行逆差 2 370 亿美元，增长 8%。

专栏 2

提升我国服务业竞争力　优化服务贸易收支结构

21 世纪以来，我国服务贸易进入快速发展时期。2018 年，我国服务贸易进出口连续 5 年保持全球第二位。随着国民收入水平的提高，旅行支出大幅上升，但国内高附加值服务业尚待发展，服务贸易逆差自 2014 年以来一直在 2 000 亿美元以上，2018 年逆差达 2 922 亿美元。当前，服务贸易在全球贸易体系中地位日益提高，提升我国服务业竞争力、优化服务贸易收支结构，对维护我国国际收支平衡具有重要意义。

一、我国服务贸易发展现状

我国服务业占国内生产总值（GDP）比重持续上升，服务贸易进出口规模持续增长，连续 5 年保持全球第二位。2001 年以来，我国服务贸易进出口规模年均增长约 14%。2018 年，服务贸易进出口总规模 7 594 亿美元，较上年增长 11%，进口规模超过出口规模的 2 倍。

服务贸易对维护我国国际收支平衡的作用更加重要。据国际货币基金组织 (IMF) 数据，2017 年，我国服务贸易逆差规模居全球首位，占全球服务贸易逆差国逆差总额的 38%。近年来，我国货物贸易顺差收窄，但服务贸易逆差达到一定规模后增幅放缓。未来如果服务贸易逆差保持平稳或有所改善，将为我国国际收支平衡提供稳定性支撑。

旅行、运输和知识产权使用费是服务贸易逆差的主要项目。2018 年，我国旅行 (含留学、旅游、就医等)、运输、知识产权使用费项下逆差分别为 2 370 亿美元、669 亿美元和 302 亿美元，对服务贸易逆差贡献度分别达 81%、23% 和 10%。以旅行为例，随着我国经济持续增长与国民收入的不断提高，旅行支出快速增长，显著高于旅行收入。2018 年我国旅行支出为 2 773 亿美元，与同期 GDP 之比由 2013 年的 1.3% 升至 2%，增长态势与 20 世纪 90 年代的日本十分类似，这表明旅行支出的增长反映了人民对美好生活的需要，也是开放经济发展道路上的必经阶段。当前，旅行收支总额和逆差增速放缓，逆差增速由 2015 年的 12% 降至 2018 年的 8%，旅行收支占服务贸易比重趋向稳定，与日本服务贸易发展过程中旅行支出大幅上升后企稳的特点类似。

二、我国服务业竞争力提升的重点领域与发展

旅游、教育等高附加值服务业发展空间广阔。2017 年，全球服务贸易顺差前五大经济体主要顺差项目集中于旅游、教育、金融服务等高附加值行业。受国内消费升级影响，我国出境旅游、留学和就医需求显著上升。从旅游人数来看，2018 年出入境旅游人数差距较小，分别为 1.5 亿和 1.4 亿人次[①]，但出入境旅游消费金额差距较大，因此可进一步挖掘 "入境游" 高附加值行业的发展空间，将低附加值服务出口向高附加值服务出口转化，优化旅游产品结构，提升国内旅游消费品质，大幅改善旅行项下收支逆差。

运输等传统服务业提升潜力巨大。国际运输业竞争激烈、市场集中度高，排名前五位的海运公司市场占有率近 70%。我国仅有一家海运企业进入前 5 名，占全球市场份额的 10% 左右。受进口较快增长影响，运输支出持续增加，2018 年运输项下进口 1 092 亿美元。但承运人往往为外方指定的外运公司，我国运输企业发展受限，2018 年运输出口仅为 423 亿美元。2017 年我国货物贸易收支总额近 4 万亿美元，在全球货物贸易收支总额中占比超过 20%，因此可考虑充分利用贸易大国的优势，借助运输与贸易相辅相成的关系，加强海运企

—————————————
① 数据来源：中华人民共和国文化和旅游部官网。

业与货主间的密切合作，拓展运输服务网络，提高我国运输业竞争力，进一步带动我国对外贸易蓬勃发展。

技术产品出口有较大发展空间。 2018 年，知识产权使用费进出口分别为 358 亿美元和 56 亿美元，较上年分别增加 70 亿美元和 8 亿美元，结合我国在全球产业链中的分工，我国技术进口主要集中在通讯和汽车等行业。我国技术产品开发起步较晚，早期阶段借助引入的高新技术促进生产经营，形成技术出口红利仍需一定时间。目前我国企业整体技术水平正在不断提升，2018 年我国研发支出占 GDP 的比重达到 2.18%，依托大数据、物联网、云计算等新技术，提升自身的核心竞争力，帮助企业建立技术自主培育体系，增强技术产品自主创新能力，降低对外依赖度，以科技带动贸易产业向前发展，将是落实供给侧结构性改革、推动国民经济高质量发展的重要体现。

服务贸易在全球经济中作用日趋凸显，在全球价值链体系中也占据重要地位。 因此，进一步推动我国服务业开放与发展，优化资源配置，提高服务业经营效率和服务质量，提升国际竞争力，不仅有助于我国适应对外开放新格局，也是供给侧结构性改革的应有之意。

初次收入[①]**呈现逆差。** 2018 年，初次收入项下收入 2 348 亿美元，较上年下降 18%；支出 2 862 亿美元，下降 4%；逆差 514 亿美元。其中，雇员报酬顺差 82 亿美元，投资收益逆差 614 亿美元（见图 1-5）。从投资收益看，2018 年我国对外投资的收益为 2 146 亿美元，外国来华投资的利润利息、股息红利等合计 2 760 亿美元。

二次收入逆差收窄。 2018 年，二次收入项下收入 278 亿美元，较上年下降 1%；支出 302 亿美元，下降 25%；逆差 24 亿美元，较上年减少 80%（见图 1-5）。

直接投资顺差扩大。 按国际收支统计口径[②]，2018 年，直接投资顺差 1 070 亿美元，较上年扩大 2.9 倍（见图 1-6）。其中，我国对外直接投资（资产净增加）965 亿美元，较上年下降 30%；境外对我国直接投资（负债净增加）2 035 亿美元，增长 23%。

证券投资顺差显著上升。 2018 年，证券投资顺差 1 067 亿美元，较上年增长 2.6 倍（见图 1-6）。其中，我国对外证券投资（资产净增加）535 亿美元，下降 44%；境外对我国证券投资（负债净增加）1 602 亿美元，增长 29%。

其他投资转为逆差。 2018 年，贷款、贸易信贷等其他投资逆差 770 亿美元，

① 国际货币基金组织《国际收支和国际投资头寸手册》(第六版) 将经常项下的"收益"名称改为"初次收入"，将"经常转移"名称改为"二次收入"。
② 国际收支统计口径的直接投资与商务部统计口径的主要差异在于，国际收支统计采用资产负债原则编制和列示，商务部直接投资数据采用方向原则编制和列示，两者对反向（逆向）投资和联属企业间投资的记录原则不同。此外，国际收支统计中的直接投资负债与商务部来华直接投资的差异还在于，直接投资负债包括外商直接投资企业的未分配利润、已分配未汇出利润、盈余公积、股东贷款、金融机构吸收外资等内容。

2017 年为顺差 519 亿美元（见图 1-6）。其中，我国对外其他投资（资产净增加）1 984 亿美元，较上年增长 97%；境外对我国的其他投资（负债净增加）1 214 亿美元，下降 21%。

图 1-6

资本和金融账户主要子项目的收支状况

亿美元

■ 直接投资差额　　■ 证券投资差额　　■ 其他投资差额

数据来源：国家外汇管理局。

储备资产基本稳定。2018 年，我国交易形成的储备资产（剔除汇率、价格等非交易价值变动影响）增加 189 亿美元。其中，交易形成的外汇储备增加 182 亿美元（见图 1-7）。截至 2018 年末，我国外汇储备余额 30 727 亿美元，较 2017 年末下降 672 亿美元，主要受汇率、价格等非交易价值变动影响。

图 1-7

外汇储备资产变动额

亿美元

数据来源：国家外汇管理局。

表 1-2　中国国际收支平衡表　　　　　　　　　　　　　　　　　　　　　　　　单位：亿美元

项　　　目	行次	2017 年	2018 年
1. 经常账户	1	**1 951**	**491**
贷方	2	27 450	29 136
借方	3	−25 499	−28 645
1.A 货物和服务	4	**2 170**	**1 029**
贷方	5	24 293	26 510
借方	6	−22 123	−25 481
1.A. a 货物	7	**4 759**	**3 952**
贷方	8	22 162	24 174
借方	9	−17 403	−20 223
1.A. b 服务	10	**−2 589**	**−2 922**
贷方	11	2 131	2 336
借方	12	−4 720	−5 258
1.A. b.1 加工服务	13	**179**	**172**
贷方	14	181	174
借方	15	−2	−3
1.A. b.2 维护和维修服务	16	**37**	**46**
贷方	17	60	72

项　目	行次	2017 年	2018 年
借方	18	−23	−25
1.A. b.3 运输	19	**−560**	**−669**
贷方	20	373	423
借方	21	−933	−1 092
1.A. b.4 旅行	22	**−2 193**	**−2 370**
贷方	23	386	404
借方	24	−2 579	−2 773
1.A. b.5 建设	25	**36**	**49**
贷方	26	123	136
借方	27	−86	−86
1.A. b.6 保险和养老金服务	28	**−74**	**−66**
贷方	29	41	49
借方	30	−115	−116
1.A. b.7 金融服务	31	**18**	**12**
贷方	32	34	33
借方	33	−16	−21
1.A. b.8 知识产权使用费	34	**−239**	**−302**
贷方	35	48	56
借方	36	−287	−358
1.A. b.9 电信、计算机和信息服务	37	**75**	**65**
贷方	38	269	300
借方	39	−194	−235
1.A. b.10 其他商业服务	40	**169**	**191**
贷方	41	593	662
借方	42	−424	−470
1.A. b.11 个人、文化和娱乐服务	43	**−20**	**−24**
贷方	44	8	10
借方	45	−27	−34
1.A. b.12 别处未提及的政府服务	46	**−18**	**−27**
贷方	47	17	18
借方	48	−35	−45
1.B 初次收入	49	**−100**	**−514**
贷方	50	2 876	2 348
借方	51	−2 976	−2 862
1.B.1 雇员报酬	52	**149**	**82**
贷方	53	217	181
借方	54	−68	−99

续表

项　目	行次	2017 年	2018 年
1.B.2 投资收益	55	**−254**	**−614**
贷方	56	2 652	2 146
借方	57	−2 906	−2 760
1.B.3 其他初次收入	58	**4**	**18**
贷方	59	7	21
借方	60	−3	−3
**　1.C 二次收入**	61	**−119**	**−24**
贷方	62	282	278
借方	63	−400	−302
1.C.1 个人转移	64	−25	−4
贷方	65	70	62
借方	66	−95	−66
1.C.2 其他二次收入	67	−93	−20
贷方	68	212	216
借方	69	−305	−236
2. 资本和金融账户	70	**179**	**1 111**
2.1 资本账户	71	**−1**	**−6**
贷方	72	2	3
借方	73	−3	−9
2.2 金融账户	74	**180**	**1 117**
资产	75	−4 239	−3 721
负债	76	4 419	4 838
**　2.2.1 非储备性质的金融账户**	77	**1 095**	**1 306**
资产	78	−3 324	−3 532
负债	79	4 419	4 838
**　　2.2.1.1 直接投资**	80	**278**	**1 070**
**　　　2.2.1.1.1 直接投资资产**	81	**−1 383**	**−965**
2.2.1.1.1.1 股权	82	−1 363	−790
2.2.1.1.1.2 关联企业债务	83	−20	−175
2.2.1.1.1.a 金融部门	84	−178	−208
2.2.1.1.1.1.a 股权	85	−176	−200
2.2.1.1.1.2.a 关联企业债务	86	−2	−8
2.2.1.1.1.b 非金融部门	87	−1 205	−757
2.2.1.1.1.1.b 股权	88	−1 186	−590
2.2.1.1.1.2.b 关联企业债务	89	−18	−167
**　　　2.2.1.1.2 直接投资负债**	90	**1 661**	**2 035**
2.2.1.1.2.1 股权	91	1 406	1 544

项　目	行次	2017 年	2018 年
2.2.1.1.2.2 关联企业债务	92	255	491
2.2.1.1.2.a 金融部门	93	121	176
2.2.1.1.2.1.a 股权	94	90	149
2.2.1.1.2.2.a 关联企业债务	95	32	26
2.2.1.1.2.b 非金融部门	96	1 539	1 859
2.2.1.1.2.1.b 股权	97	1 316	1 395
2.2.1.1.2.2.b 关联企业债务	98	223	465
2.2.1.2 证券投资	99	**295**	**1 067**
2.2.1.2.1 资产	100	**−948**	**−535**
2.2.1.2.1.1 股权	101	−328	−177
2.2.1.2.1.2 债券	102	−620	−358
2.2.1.2.2 负债	103	**1 243**	**1 602**
2.2.1.2.2.1 股权	104	362	607
2.2.1.2.2.2 债券	105	881	995
2.2.1.3 金融衍生工具	106	**4**	**−62**
2.2.1.3.1 资产	107	15	−48
2.2.1.3.2 负债	108	−12	−13
2.2.1.4 其他投资	109	**519**	**−770**
2.2.1.4.1 资产	110	**−1 008**	**−1 984**
2.2.1.4.1.1 其他股权	111	0	0
2.2.1.4.1.2 货币和存款	112	−571	−731
2.2.1.4.1.3 贷款	113	−435	−818
2.2.1.4.1.4 保险和养老金	114	0	−6
2.2.1.4.1.5 贸易信贷	115	−194	−653
2.2.1.4.1.6 其他	116	191	224
2.2.1.4.2 负债	117	**1 527**	**1 214**
2.2.1.4.2.1 其他股权	118	0	0
2.2.1.4.2.2 货币和存款	119	1 079	514
2.2.1.4.2.3 贷款	120	501	321
2.2.1.4.2.4 保险和养老金	121	7	2
2.2.1.4.2.5 贸易信贷	122	−12	408
2.2.1.4.2.6 其他	123	−47	−31
2.2.1.4.2.7 特别提款权	124	0	0
2.2.2 储备资产	125	**−915**	**−189**
2.2.2.1 货币黄金	126	0	0
2.2.2.2 特别提款权	127	−7	0
2.2.2.3 在国际货币基金组织的储备头寸	128	22	−7

项　　目	行次	2017 年	2018 年
2.2.2.4 外汇储备	129	−930	−182
2.2.2.5 其他储备资产	130	0	0
3. 净误差与遗漏	131	**−2 130**	**−1 602**

注：1. 本表根据《国际收支和国际投资头寸手册》(第六版) 编制。

2. "贷方"按正值列示，"借方"按负值列示，差额等于"贷方"加上"借方"。本表除标注"贷方"和"借方"的项目外，其他项目均指差额。

3. 本表计数采用四舍五入原则。

数据来源：国家外汇管理局。

（三）国际收支运行评价

　　我国国际收支延续基本平衡。经常账户继续处于合理的顺差区间，2018 年顺差 491 亿美元，与 GDP 之比为 0.4%，经常账户更趋平衡主要体现了国内制造业转型、消费需求增加和升级的结果，对全球经济再平衡也具有重要贡献。非储备性质的金融账户保持顺差，在一些新兴经济体出现本币大幅贬值和资本外流的背景下，2018 年我国非储备性质的金融账户顺差 1 306 亿美元，连续第二年呈现净流入。总体来看，虽然外部环境复杂严峻，但人民币汇率双向浮动弹性增强，国际收支自主平衡的能力进一步提升，我国交易形成的外汇储备资产保持基本稳定 (见图 1-8)。

图 1-8

我国国际收支主要结构

亿美元

图例：
经常账户差额
非储备性质的金融账户差额
外汇储备资产变动

数据来源：国家外汇管理局。

经常账户收支状况合理稳健。一是经常账户主要项目结构合理。2018 年，我国货物和服务贸易合计顺差 1 029 亿美元，差额与 GDP 之比为 0.8%，是 1994 年以来的最低值，贸易收支更加平衡；初次收入逆差 514 亿美元，差额与 GDP 之比为 -0.4%，属于近十年的平均水平（见图 1-9）。二是经常账户差额逐季改善。2018 年第一季度，我国经常账户逆差 341 亿美元，差额与 GDP 之比为 -1.1%；第二至第四季度，经常账户转为顺差 53 亿美元、233 亿美元和 546 亿美元，与 GDP 之比分别回升至 0.2%、0.7% 和 1.5%。当前我国经常账户收支已经到了比较均衡的区间，不同时期出现小幅顺差或逆差都属于基本平衡范畴。

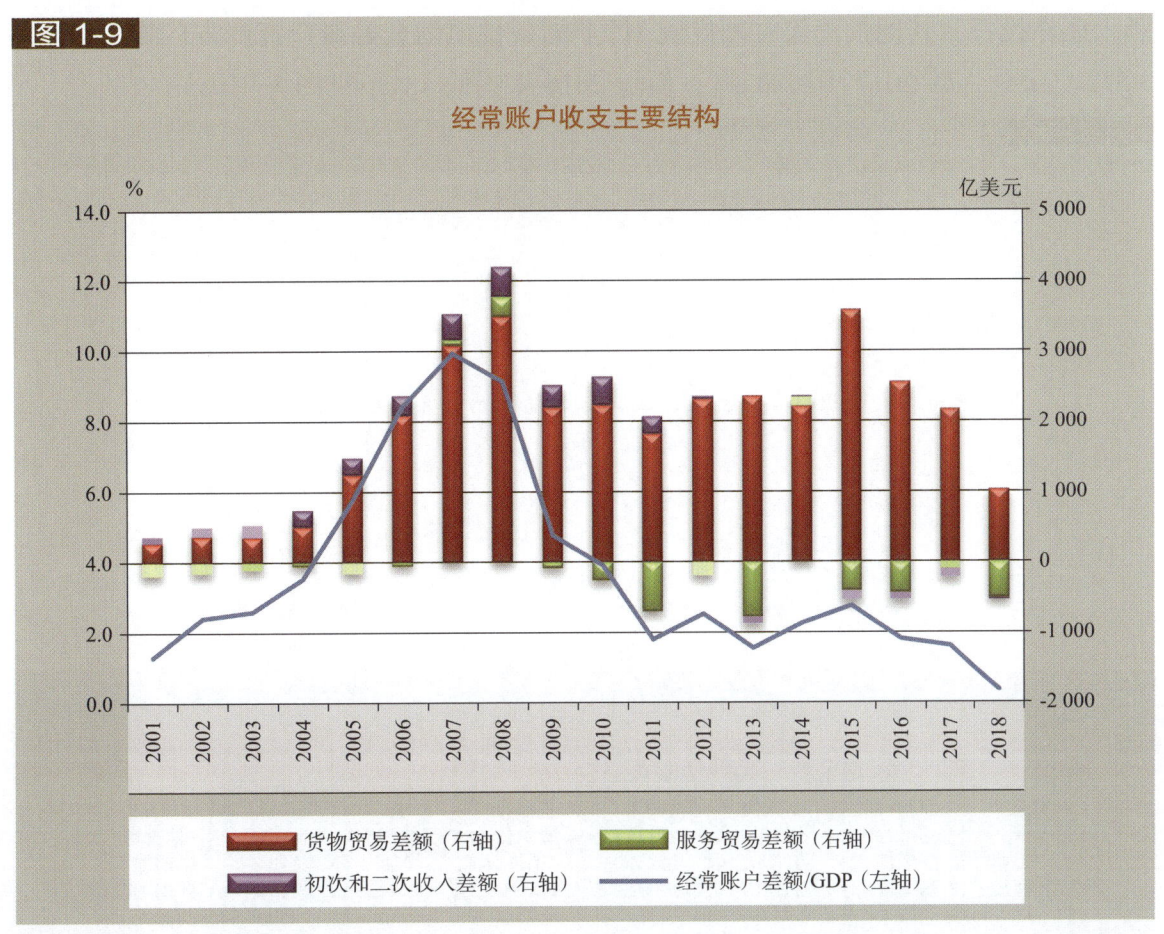

图 1-9

经常账户收支主要结构

数据来源：国家外汇管理局、国家统计局。

非储备性质的金融账户结构进一步优化。**一是**具有中长期投资性质的直接投资仍是较为稳定的顺差来源。2018 年，我国国际收支口径的直接投资净流入 1 070 亿美元，在 2016 年短暂逆差后已连续两年保持顺差。**二是**资本市场对外开放效果显著。2018 年，证券投资净流入 1 067 亿美元，达到历史最高水平，其中很大一部分是来自境外央行的投资，中长期资产配置需求较高。**三是**其他投资的稳定性有所提高。2018 年，在依旧复杂严峻的外部环境下，其他投资逆差 770 亿美元，远低于 2015 年和 2016 年每年三四千亿美元的逆差规模，说明市场主体跨境融资的调整更趋理性。

对外和来华双向投资平稳增长。**一是**外来投资持续增长，我国仍是外资主要投资目的地之一。2018 年，外国来华直接投资、证券投资和其他投资等外来投资（即非储备性质的金融账户负债方）累计净增加 4 838 亿美元，连续第三年回升，规模已恢复至历史较高水平，既体现了我国推动高水平对外开放、持续改善营商环境的政策效果，也说明我国能够为国际资本公平竞争提供足够广阔的空间。**二是**对外投资合理增长，市场主体对外投资和配置资产步伐理性有序。2018 年，我国对外直接投资、证券投资和其他投资等对外投资（即非储备性质的金融账户资产方）累计净增加3 532 亿美元，较 2017 年增加 6%，但较 2016 年仍低 48%（见图 1-10）。

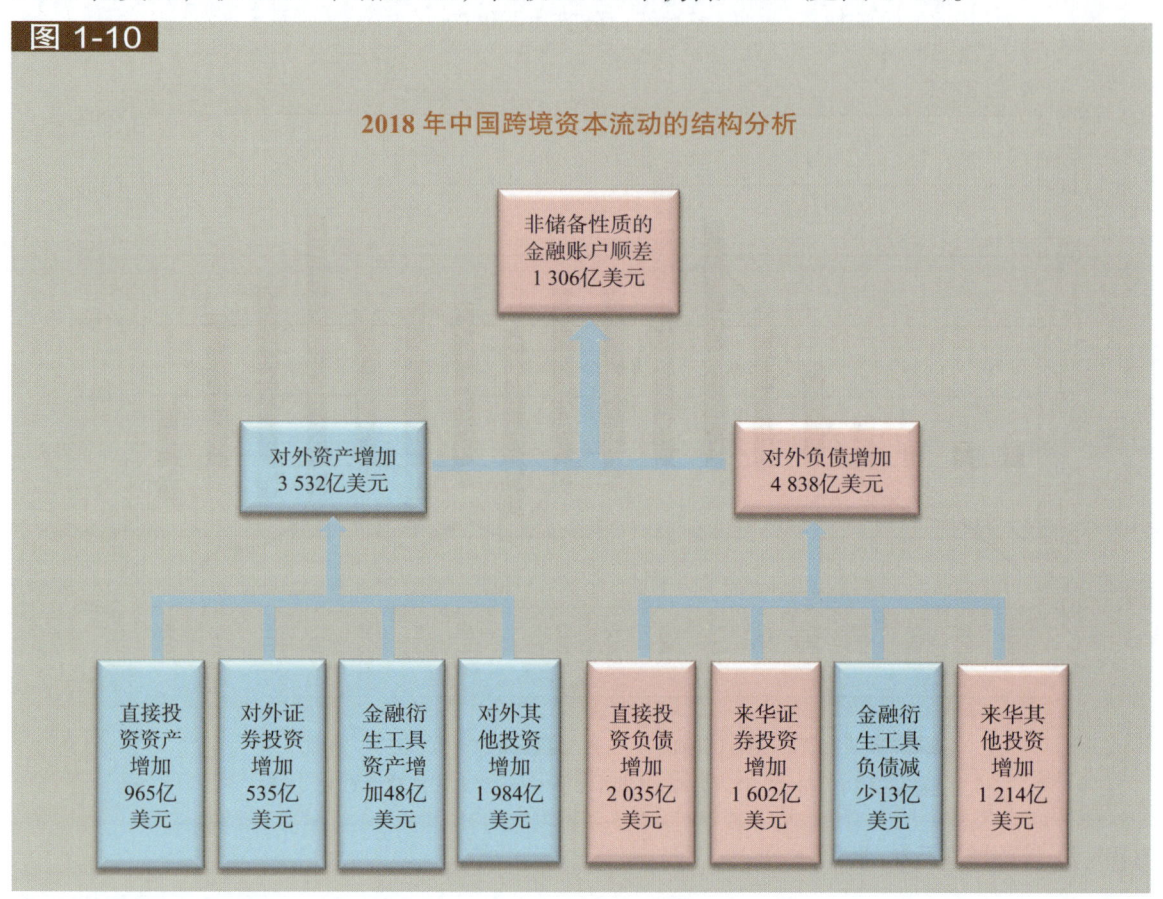

图 1-10

2018 年中国跨境资本流动的结构分析

数据来源：国家外汇管理局。

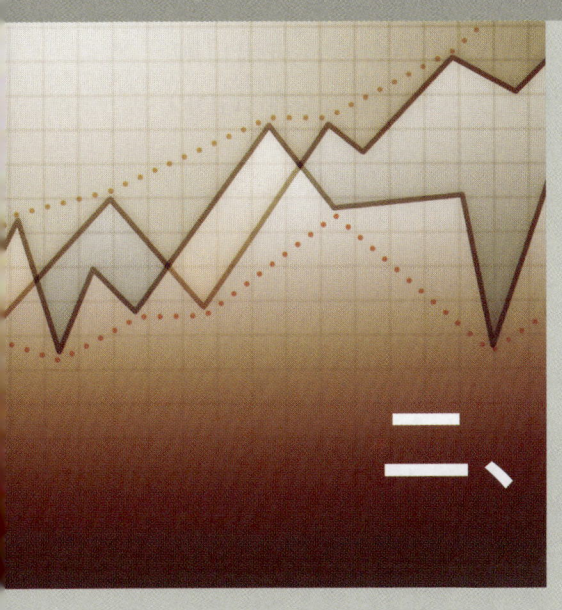

二、国际收支主要项目分析

（一）货物贸易

货物贸易进出口更趋平衡，贸易依存度保持稳定。 在全球贸易环境更趋复杂的情况下，我国对外贸易保持总体平稳、稳中有进。据海关统计，2018 年，我国进出口总额达 4.6 万亿美元，较上年增长 13%，增速较上年同期加快 1.1 个百分点。其中，出口增长 10%，提高 2 个百分点；进口增长 16%，下降 0.3 个百分点；进出口顺差 3 511 亿美元，较上年下降 16%。2018 年，我国外贸依存度（即进出口总额 /GDP）为 33.9%，与上年基本持平（见图 2-1）。

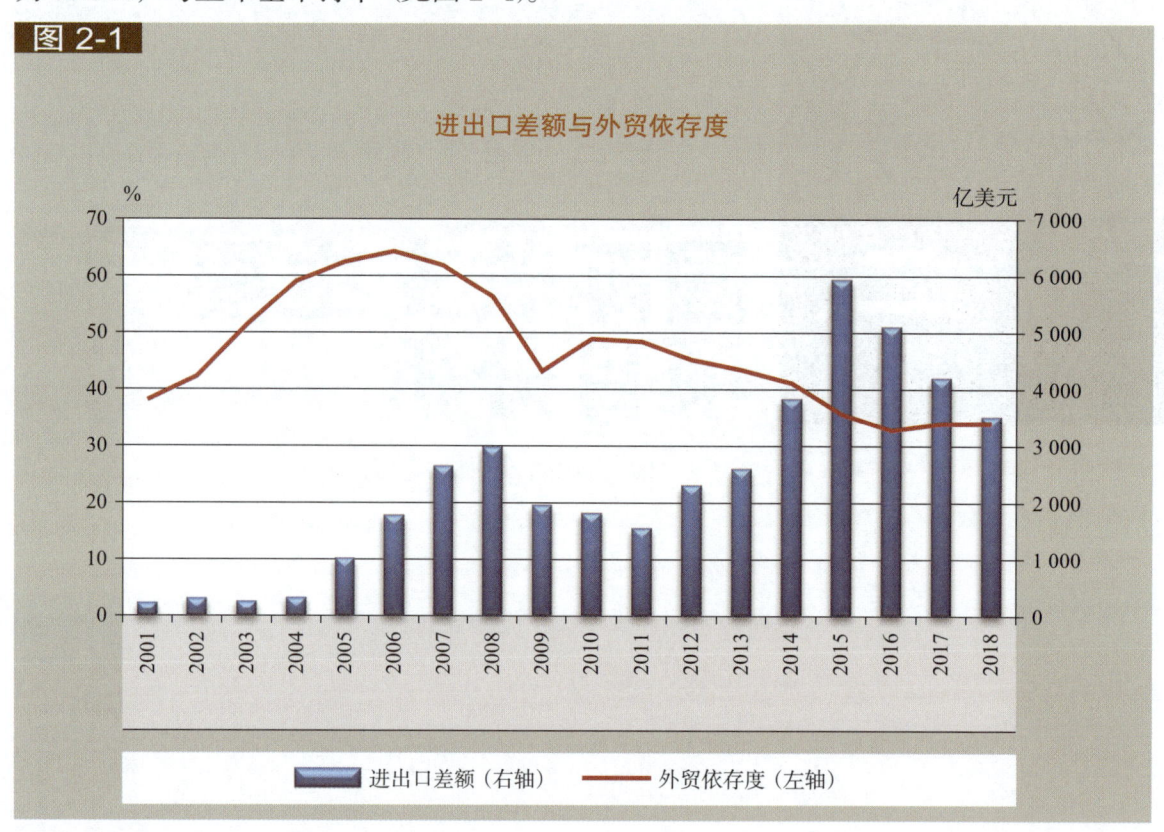

图 2-1

进出口差额与外贸依存度

数据来源：海关总署、国家统计局。

出口结构优化，进口量价齐升。 2018 年，我国高新技术产品合计出口 7 469 亿美元，较上年增长 12%，占我国出口总值的三成，比 2017 年提升 1 个百分点。同期，作为劳动密集型典型产品的纺织纱线、服装、玩具、鞋、帽合计出口 3 227 亿美元，占出口总量的 13%，比上年下降 1 个百分点（见图 2-2）。根据海关统计（人民币计价），2018 年，进口数量指数上升 6.4%，进口价格指数上升 6.1%。据此测算，2018年进口数量变化对进口增长的贡献为 51%，价格变化贡献为 49%。其中，2018 年原油进口量增长 10%，进口金额上升 47%，对进口增长的贡献率为 26%，是带动我国进口上升的重要因素。

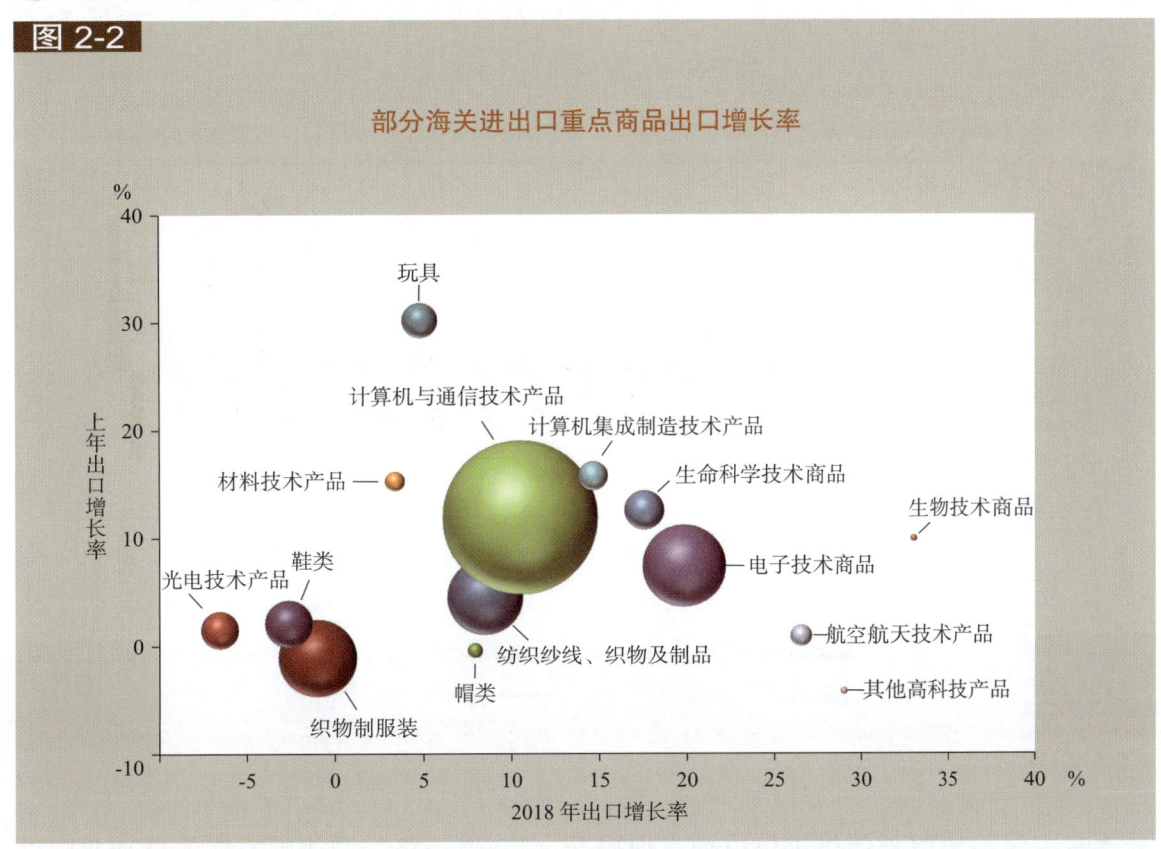

图 2-2

部分海关进出口重点商品出口增长率

注：1. 图中劳动密集型商品包括纺织纱线、服装、玩具、鞋、帽等 5 类，高科技商品包括生命科学技术商品、电子技术商品、生物技术商品、计算机与通信技术产品等 9 类。2. 气泡图横轴和纵轴分别为 2018 年和 2017 年该种类别商品出口增长率，气泡大小为 2018 年该类商品出口绝对金额。
数据来源：海关总署。

民营企业进出口增长动能较强，外资企业顺差略有收窄。 2018 年，民营企业进出口 1.8 万亿美元，增长 16%，占我国进出口总值的 38%，比上年提高 1.2 个百分点，对外贸进出口增长的贡献度接近五成，进出口顺差 5 288 亿美元，较上年增长 5 个百分点。外商投资企业进出口总值 1.97 万亿美元，增长 7%，占比 43%。其中，外商投资企业出口 10 360 亿美元，增长 6%，进口 9 321 亿美元，增长 8%，进出口顺差 1 040 亿美元，收窄 10%。同期，国有企业进出口总值为 8 046 亿美元（见图 2-3）。

图 2-3

按贸易主体货物贸易差额构成

数据来源：海关总署。

我国对主要贸易伙伴进出口均实现提升，"一带一路"沿线国家成为拉动我国外贸发展的新动力。2018 年，我国对美国、欧盟、日本的进出口增速分别为 9%、11% 和 8%，三个地区进出口之和占进出口总值的 36%；与东盟、非洲国家的进出口增速分别为 14% 和 20%，较上年上升 1.2 个和 7.3 个百分点，两个地区进出口之和占进出口总值的 17%，较上年占比提高 0.4 个百分点。同期，我国对"一带一路"沿线国家进出口增速为 16%，比我国对全球进出口增速高 3.7 个百分点（见图 2-4）。

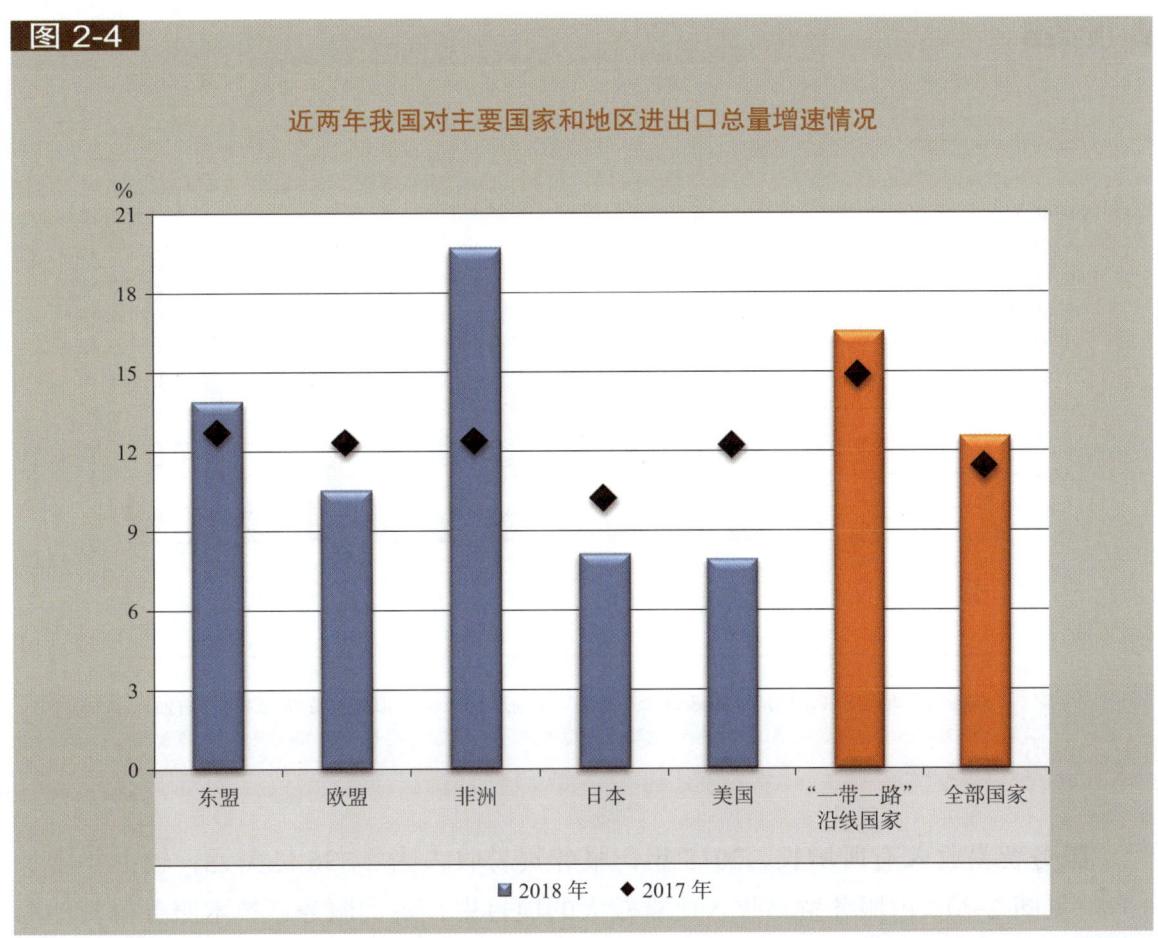

图 2-4

近两年我国对主要国家和地区进出口总量增速情况

数据来源：海关总署。

（二）服务贸易

服务贸易规模保持增长趋势。 2018 年，我国服务贸易收支总额 7 594 亿美元，较上年增长 11%，服务贸易与货物贸易总额的比例为 17%（见图 2-5）。其中，其他商业服务收入金额最高，为 662 亿美元；旅行支出最高，为 2 773 亿美元。

图 2-5

货物贸易和服务贸易收支总额比较

亿美元

货物贸易（左轴）　　服务贸易（左轴）　　服务贸易/货物贸易（右轴）

数据来源：国家外汇管理局。

服务贸易收入有所增长。 2018 年，服务贸易收入为 2 336 亿美元，较上年增长 10%（见图 2-6）。占服务贸易收入比重较大的项目中，咨询服务、技术服务等其他商业服务收入增长 12%，占比 28%；运输收入增长 13%，占比 18%；旅行收入由上年的下降 13% 转为上升 5%，占比 17%。新兴服务如电信、计算机和信息服务与知识产权使用费等收入均较上年增长，我国服务贸易结构不断优化。

服务贸易支出保持增长。 2018 年，服务贸易支出 5 258 亿美元，较上年增长 11%。占服务贸易支出比重较大的项目中，旅行支出增长 8%，占比 53%；运输支出增长 17%，占比 21%。知识产权使用费支出增长较快，为 358 亿美元，增长 24%。

图 2-6

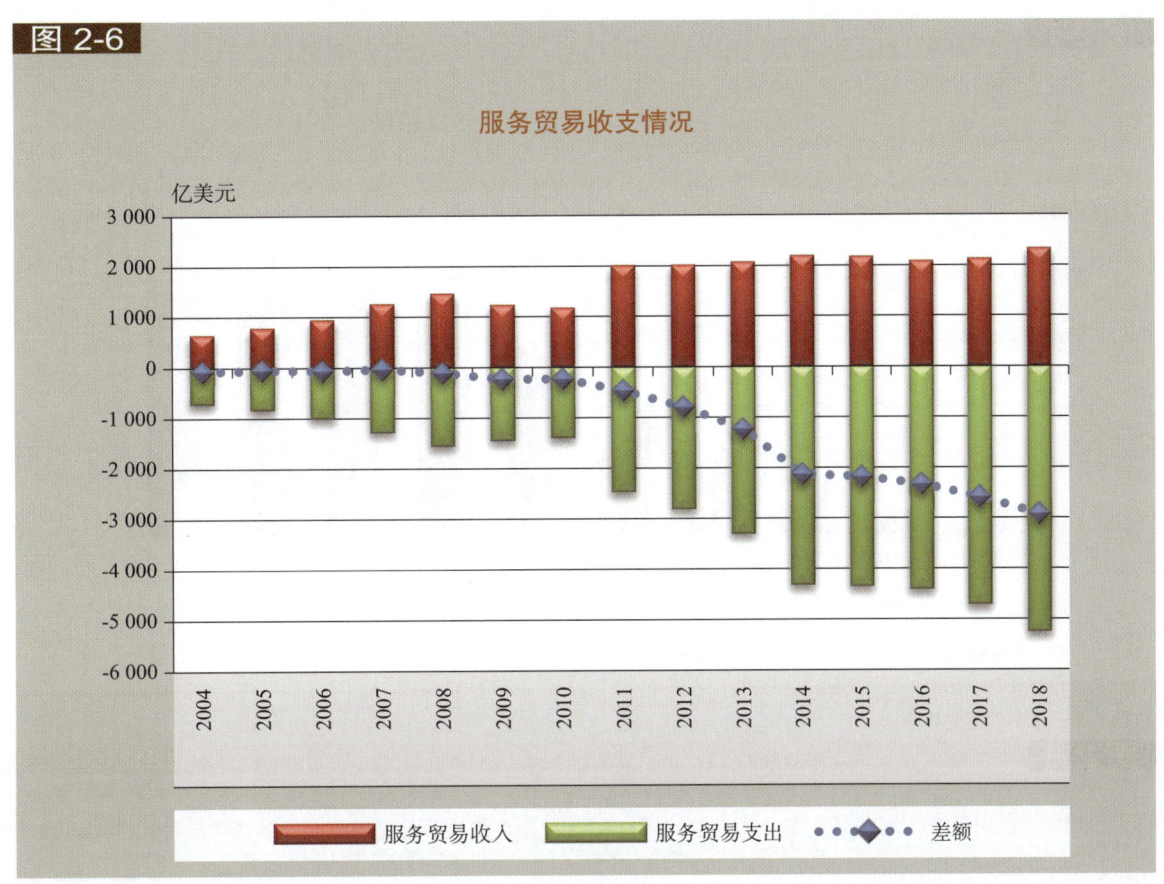

服务贸易收支情况

数据来源：国家外汇管理局。

　　服务贸易逆差继续扩大。2018 年，服务贸易逆差为 2 922 亿美元，较上年增长 13%。旅行仍为服务贸易逆差主要来源（见图 2-7），2018 年逆差 2 370 亿美元，小幅增长 8%。随着我国对外开放程度的深入，出国旅游、留学需求基本稳定，带动旅行逆差渐趋平稳。排名第二的是运输，2018 年逆差 669 亿美元，增长 20%；第三是知识产权使用费，逆差 302 亿美元，增长 26%。

　　服务贸易国别集中度较高。2018 年，我国服务贸易前十大伙伴国（地区）依次为中国香港、美国、日本、德国、英国、新加坡、韩国、澳大利亚、加拿大和俄罗斯，合计规模达 5 286 亿美元，占总服务贸易规模的 70%。除对新加坡为小额顺差外，我国对其余九个主要贸易伙伴国（地区）的服务贸易均呈逆差。其中，对美国、中国香港、日本、澳大利亚、加拿大、德国、英国、俄罗斯的逆差均超百亿美元规模（见图 2-8）。

数据来源：国家外汇管理局。

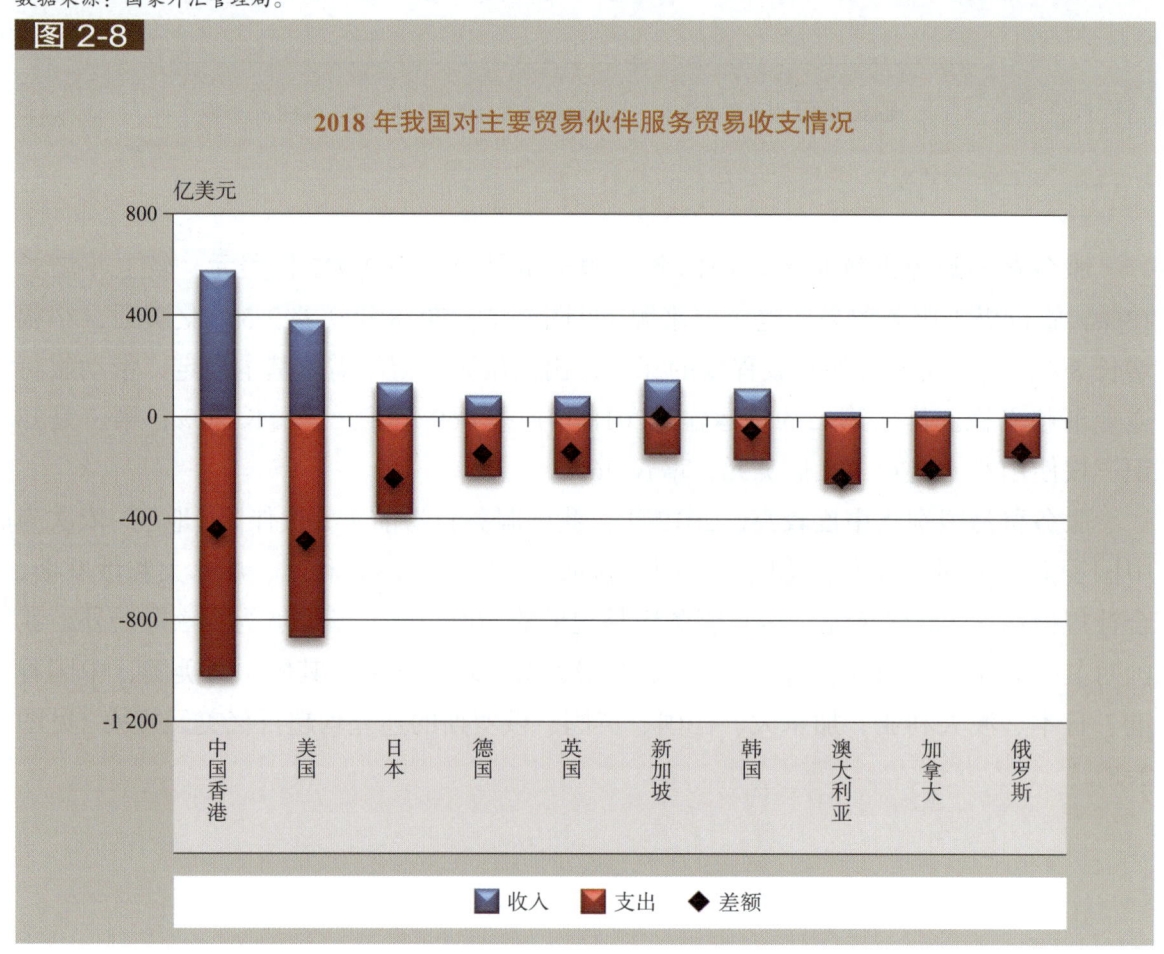

数据来源：国家外汇管理局。

专栏 3

我国知识产权使用费对外支出位居世界前列

国际收支统计显示,1997 年以来①,我国知识产权使用费对外支出逐年增长,2018 年达 358 亿美元,年均增长 22%,这一方面体现了我国经济发展和产业升级对先进技术的客观需求;另一方面反映了我国高度重视知识产权保护,尊重"创新"的市场价值。同时,我国知识产权研发也取得长足进步,知识产权使用费收入呈现快速增长。

我国知识产权使用费支出已居世界前列,并成为服务贸易第三大逆差项目。2018 年,我国知识产权使用费对外支出 358 亿美元,较上年增长 24%;收入 56 亿美元,增长 16%;逆差 302 亿美元,增长 26%(见图 C3-1),是位列旅行、运输之后的第三大服务贸易逆差项目,占服务贸易整体逆差的 10%,这主要是该项对外支出较收入增长更快所致。根据国际货币基金组织统计,2018 年前三季度,中国知识产权使用费支出 277 亿美元,远高于日本、德国,位列世界第四,约占同期全球支出总额的 7%(见图 C3-2)。

我国知识产权进口主要是引进先进技术和特许权,以计算机、通信、汽车类企业为主要使用者,以美国、德国和日本为主要伙伴国。根据《服务贸易统计手册(2010)》,知识产权使用费可具体细分为五项:特许和商标使用费、研发成果使用费、复制或分销计算机软件许可费、复制或分销视听及相关产品许可费、其他知识产权许可费。我国 2018 年知识产权使用费支出,从细项看,逾八成用于进口国外科研成果和特许权;从企业行业看,排名前三的分别是"计算机、通信和其他电子设备制造业""汽车制造业"以及"铁路、船舶、航空航天和其他运输设备制造业",其支出合计占比逾四成;从伙伴国看,美国、德国及日本位列前三。知识产权进口特点反映了我国经济发展和转型升级中对先进技术的需求,也反映了我国知识产权保护意识和保护力度的提升。

---

① 1997 年,我国国际收支平衡表中知识产权使用费从零到有。

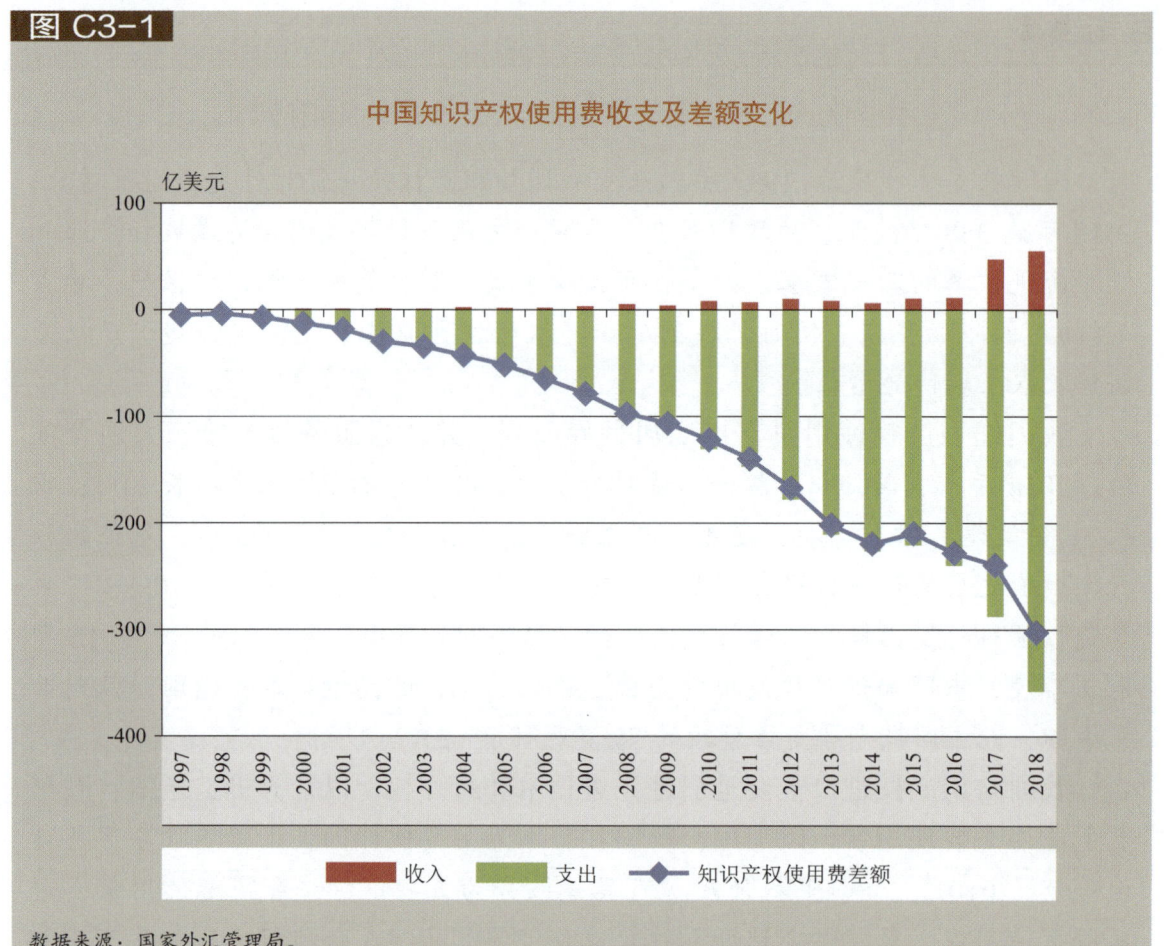

图 C3-1

中国知识产权使用费收支及差额变化

数据来源：国家外汇管理局。

　　我国知识产权使用费收入也呈现快速增长，企业创新能力提升。1997—2018 年，我国知识产权使用费收入从 1 亿美元增加到 56 亿美元，年均增长 25%。2018 年前三季度，我国该项收入全球排名第十一位，较 2007 年排名前进十二位。这表明中国企业开始重视并加大研发投入，不断提升自身技术和品牌附加值，助力相关产业升级。

图 C3-2

2018 年前三季度全球知识产权使用费支出排名前十位的国家

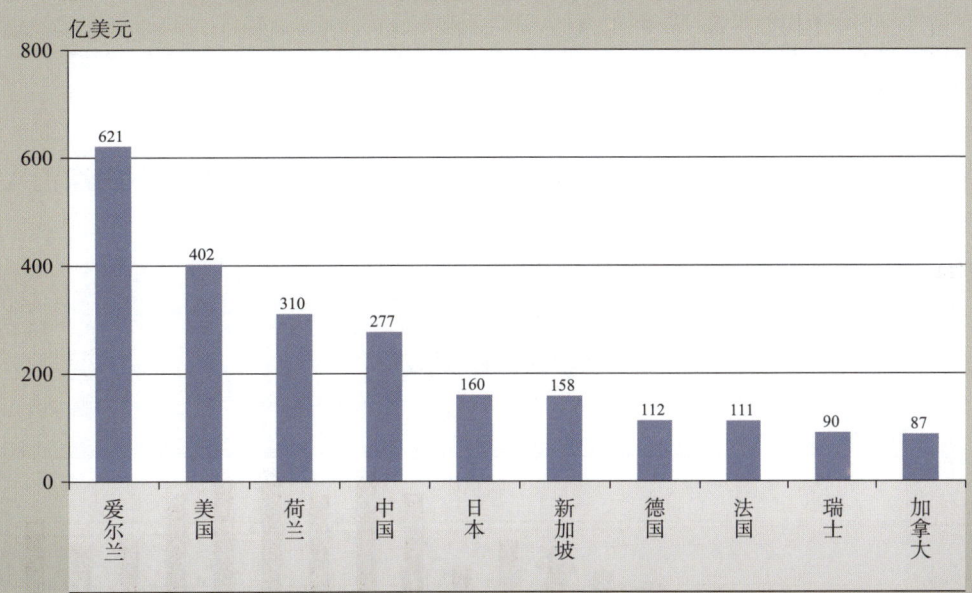

数据来源：国际货币基金组织。

图 C3-3

2018 年前三季度全球知识产权使用费收入排名前十一位的国家

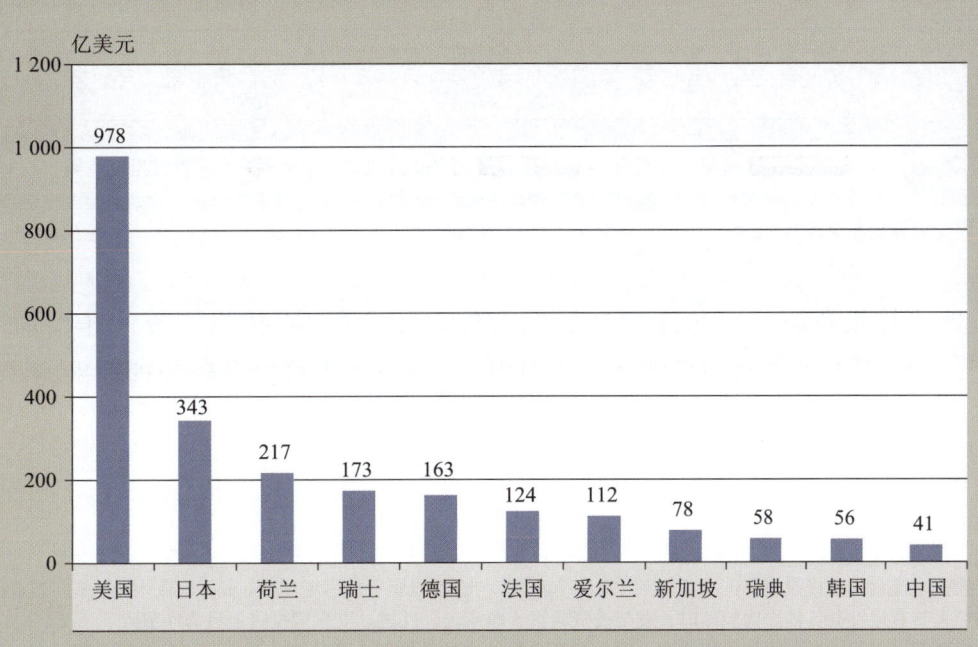

数据来源：国家外汇管理局。

经过 20 年的发展，我国知识产权使用费收入和支出水平均大幅增长，但较高的逆差表明我国已经成为知识产权大国但还不是强国，研发与创新仍在路上。长期坚持并加强知识产权保护不但能够提高中国在国际知识产权领域的声誉，更能促进中国经济高质量发展。

（三）直接投资

直接投资呈现较大净流入①。2018 年，我国国际收支口径的直接投资净流入 1 070 亿美元（见图 2-9），较上年增长 2.9 倍。

图 2-9

直接投资基本情况

亿美元

图例：■ 来华直接投资　■ 对外直接投资　●●● 直接投资差额

数据来源：国家外汇管理局。

对外直接投资减少。2018 年，我国对外直接投资（直接投资资产净增加②）965 亿美元，较上年减少 30%（见图 2-10），国内企业对外直接投资较为理性平稳。

---

① 直接投资净流动指直接投资资产净增加额（资金净流出）与直接投资负债净增加额（资金净流入）之差。当直接投资资产净增加额大于直接投资负债净增加额时，直接投资项目为净流出。反之，则直接投资项目为净流入。

② 直接投资资产以我国对外直接投资为主，但也包括少量境内外商投资企业对境外母公司的反向投资等。直接投资资产交易净增加，在国际收支平衡表中为负值，表示净流出。

图 2-10

对外直接投资状况

数据来源：国家外汇管理局。

　　从投资形式看，对外股权和债权直接投资一降一升。**一是**对外股权投资 790 亿美元，较上年减少 42%。表明受国际环境不稳定、不确定因素增多影响，境内企业对外长期投资和资产配置趋于谨慎。**二是**对境外关联公司贷款 175 亿美元，较上年增长较快，反映境内主体资产配置偏好向跨境借贷转换。

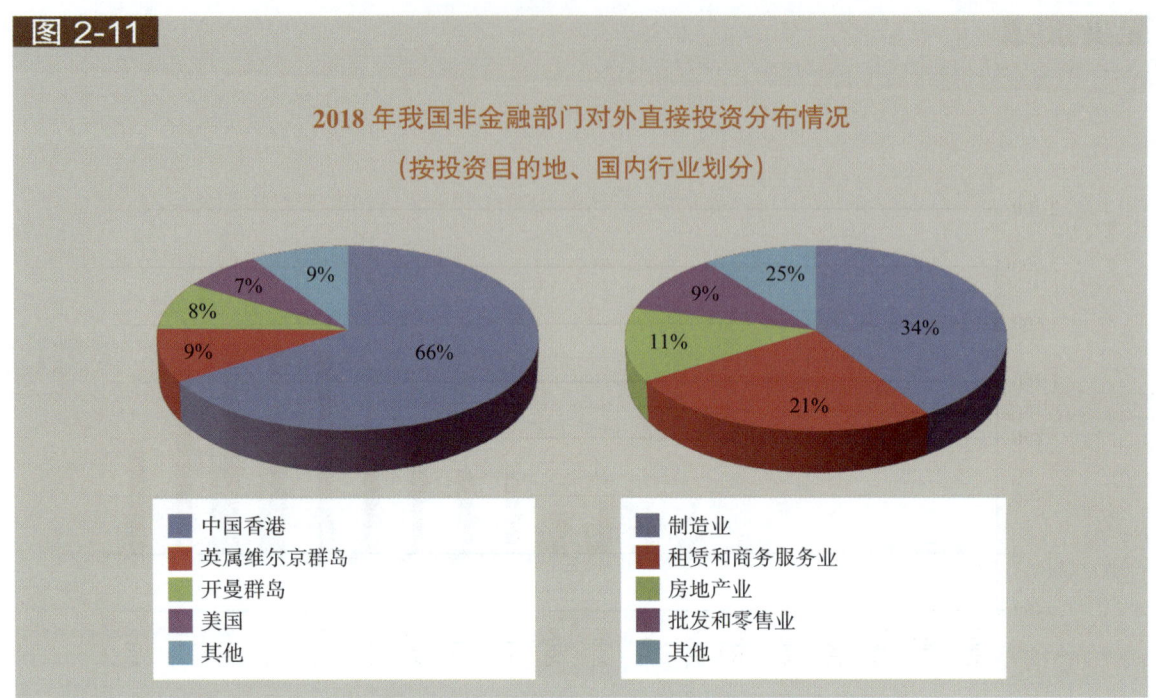

图 2-11

2018 年我国非金融部门对外直接投资分布情况
（按投资目的地、国内行业划分）

左图图例：
- 中国香港
- 英属维尔京群岛
- 开曼群岛
- 美国
- 其他

左图数据：66%、9%、8%、7%、9%

右图图例：
- 制造业
- 租赁和商务服务业
- 房地产业
- 批发和零售业
- 其他

右图数据：34%、21%、11%、9%、25%

数据来源：国家外汇管理局。

　　分部门看，我国非金融部门和金融部门对外直接投资一降一升。**一是**非金融部门对外直接投资 757 亿美元，较上年减少 37%，主要是新增股权投资和收益再投资合计回落五成，而对外债权投资增长 8 倍。中国香港、英属维尔京和开曼群岛等资金进出管理相对宽松的地区继续成为较多境内企业"走出去"的首站目的地。在国内"走出去"的行业中，制造业继续保持首位，占比为 34%（见图 2-11）。**二是**金融部门对外直接投资 208 亿美元，较上年增长 17%，逾八成来自银行部门。

　　外国来华直接投资继续保持较大规模。2018 年，外国来华直接投资净流入（直接投资负债净增加①）2 035 亿美元，较上年增长 23%，净流入规模为近三年最高值。

　　从投资形式看，来华股权和债权直接投资均增长。**一是**来华股权投资净流入 1 544 亿美元，较上年增长 10%（见图 2-12）。其中，资本金形式的股权投资上半年较快增长，下半年虽然流入趋缓，但仍超过上年同期水平。来华股权投资总体维持在较高水平，表明外资仍保持对我国经济发展前景的信心。**二是**接受境外关联公司贷款 491 亿美元，增长 92%，分季度看，第一季度和第二季度呈现较大净流入，第三季度和第四季度净流入规模明显回落，反映外商投资企业利用国内和国际两个市场、两种资源方面较为灵活。

---

　　①　直接投资负债以吸收来华直接投资为主，也包括少量境外子公司对境内母公司的反向投资等。直接投资负债交易净增加，在国际收支平衡表中为正值，表示净流入。

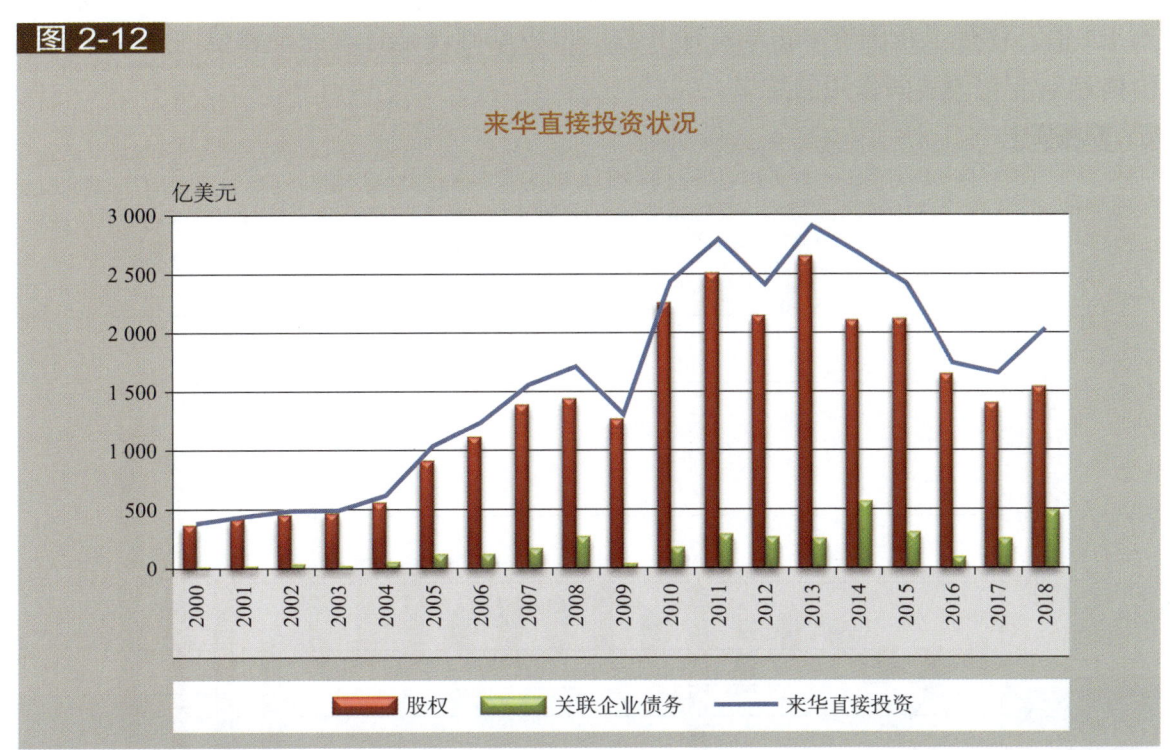

图 2-12

来华直接投资状况

亿美元

数据来源：国家外汇管理局。

　　分部门看，我国非金融部门和金融部门吸收来华直接投资均有所上升。**一是**我国非金融部门吸收来华直接投资净流入 1 859 亿美元，较上年增长 21%，占来华直接投资净流入的九成。2018 年，制造业吸收直接投资占整个非金融部门的 19%，与上年基本持平，引资规模较上年增长近 4 成，持续多年稳居吸引来华直接投资最多的行业前两位。租赁和商业服务业成为我国非金融部门吸收直接投资最多的行业，占比 22%。同时，对我国非金融部门直接投资最多的国家 / 地区是中国香港，占比逾七成，其次是开曼群岛、新加坡和韩国，三国（地区）合计占比 11%。**二是**我国金融部门吸收来华直接投资净流入 176 亿美元，增长 45%，主要为银行业和保险业等收益再投资较多。

（四）证券投资

　　证券投资总体呈现较大规模净流入。2018 年，我国证券投资项下净流入（净负债增加①）1 067 亿美元，较上年多流入 2.6 倍（见图 2-13）。从交易项目看，股权投资和债券投资净流入均增多，其中股权投资净流入增长更为显著。2018 年，股权投资净流入 430 亿美元，较上年多流入 12 倍，债券投资净流入 637 亿美元，较上年多流

_____

① 在国际收支平衡表中为正数，表示净流入。

入 1.4 倍，体现了我国资本市场有序开放、市场基础设施日臻完善和境内外金融资产价格相对变化等共同作用的结果。

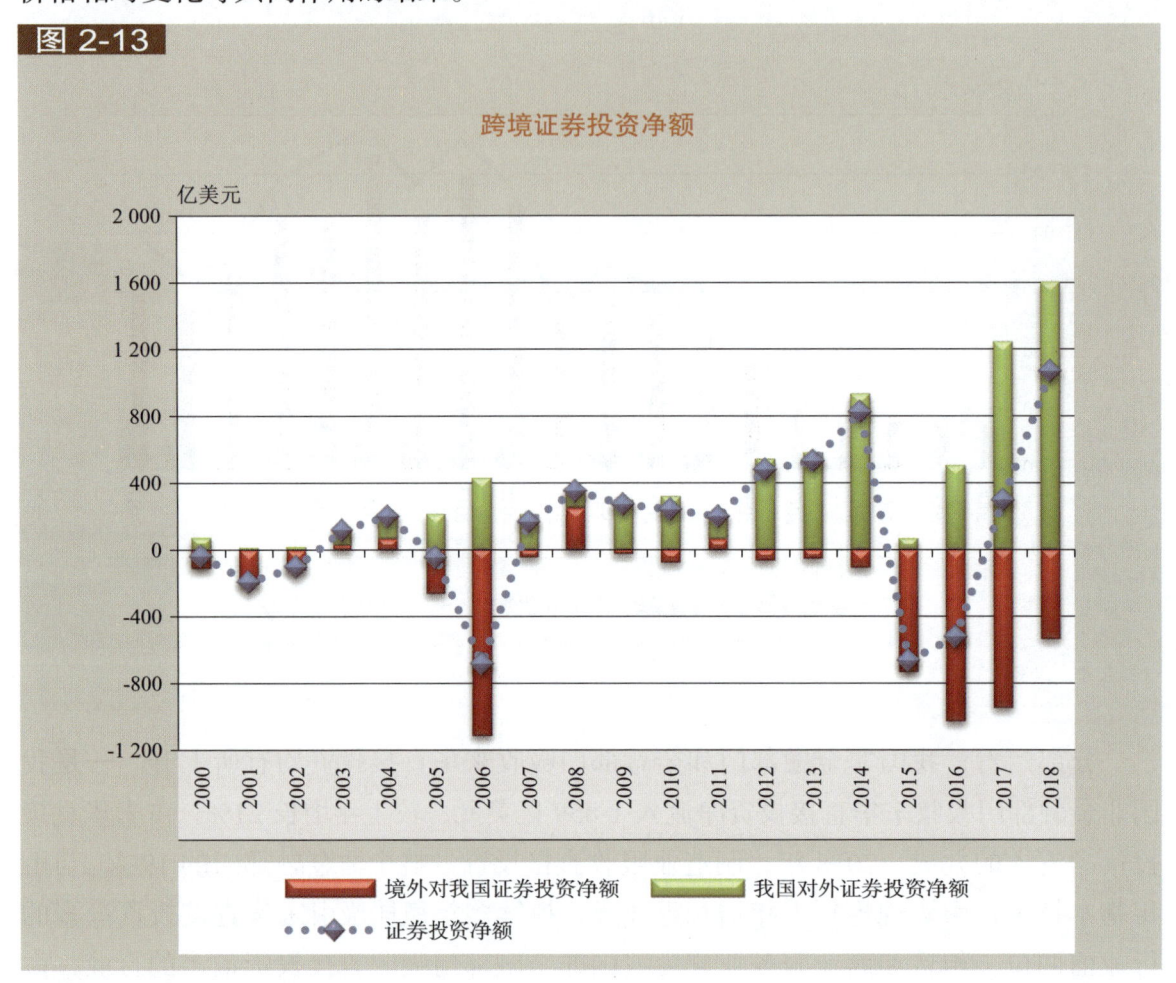

图 2-13

跨境证券投资净额

亿美元

图例：
- 境外对我国证券投资净额
- 我国对外证券投资净额
- 证券投资净额

注：我国对外证券投资正值表示减持对外股权或债券，负值表示增持对外股权或债券；境外对我国证券投资正值表示增加对国内股权或债权投资，负值表示减少对国内股权或债权投资。

数据来源：国家外汇管理局。

我国对境外证券投资下降。 2018 年，我国对外证券投资净流出（资产净增加①）535 亿美元，较上年下降 44%。其中，股权投资 177 亿美元，下降近五成；债券投资 358 亿美元，下降约四成，主要是由于境内金融机构对境外债券市场的投资放缓，以及我国居民跨境配置境外股票资产的需求减弱。分季度看，第一季度对外证券投资 335 亿美元，第二至第四季度分别回落为 43 亿美元、92 亿美元和 66 亿美元。

从对外证券投资的渠道看，**一是** 境内银行等金融机构对外证券投资合计净购买境外证券 366 亿美元，下降约五成；**二是** 我国居民通过"港股通"和"基金互认"等渠道净购买境外证券类资产 85 亿美元，下降 78%；**三是** 我国居民购买非居民境内发

---

① 国际收支平衡表中为负数，表示净流出（资产增加）。

行债券 72 亿美元，增长 1.5 倍；**四是**合格境内机构投资者（QDII 及 RQDII）投资非居民发行的股票和债券合计 35 亿美元，下降 23%。此外，减持境外银行承兑远期信用证（附汇票）23 亿美元，较上年少减持近七成。

境外对我国证券投资净流入上升。2018 年，境外对我国证券投资净流入（负债净增加[①]）1 602 亿美元，较上年增长 29%。其中，境外对我国股权投资净流入 607 亿美元，增长近七成；债券投资净流入 995 亿美元，增长 13%。这说明我国证券市场吸引力不断提升，境外投资者参与的积极性和便利度显著提高，也体现了 A 股纳入明晟（MSCI）新兴市场指数等积极信号的影响。分季度看，前三季度境外对我证券投资延续 2017 年下半年以来的趋势，保持高位净流入，分别为 438 亿美元、652 亿美元和 431 亿美元，第四季度有所回落，为 81 亿美元。

从境外对我国证券投资的主要渠道看，**一是**境外机构投资境内证券市场 962 亿美元，增长 79%，主要是境外央行增持我国政府发行的债券；**二是**通过"沪股通"和"深股通"渠道流入资金 447 亿美元，增长八成；**三是**非居民购买我国居民机构境外发行的股票、债券 274 亿美元，其中以我国居民机构在香港上市发行的 H 股为主，下降 38%。此外，银行承兑远期信用证（附汇票）形成资金净流出 80 亿美元。

（五）其他投资

其他投资总体呈现逆差。2018 年，我国其他投资项下净流出（净资产增加）770 亿美元，而上年为净流入（净负债增加）519 亿美元（见图 2-14）。其中，货币和存款净流出 217 亿美元；贷款净流出 497 亿美元；贸易信贷净流出 245 亿美元；其他应收应付表现为净流入 193 亿美元。

我国对境外其他投资增加。2018 年，我国对外其他投资净流出 1 984 亿美元，较上年增长 97%。其中，对境外贷款增加 818 亿美元，主要是银行对境外子行和分支机构的贷款；在境外存款增加 731 亿美元，反映了境内主体积极参与国际经济活动的效果。同时，在出口增长的带动下，出口应收等贸易信贷资产增加了 653 亿美元。而其他应收资产则表现为下降 224 亿美元。

[①] 国际收支平衡表中为正数，表示净流入（负债增加）。

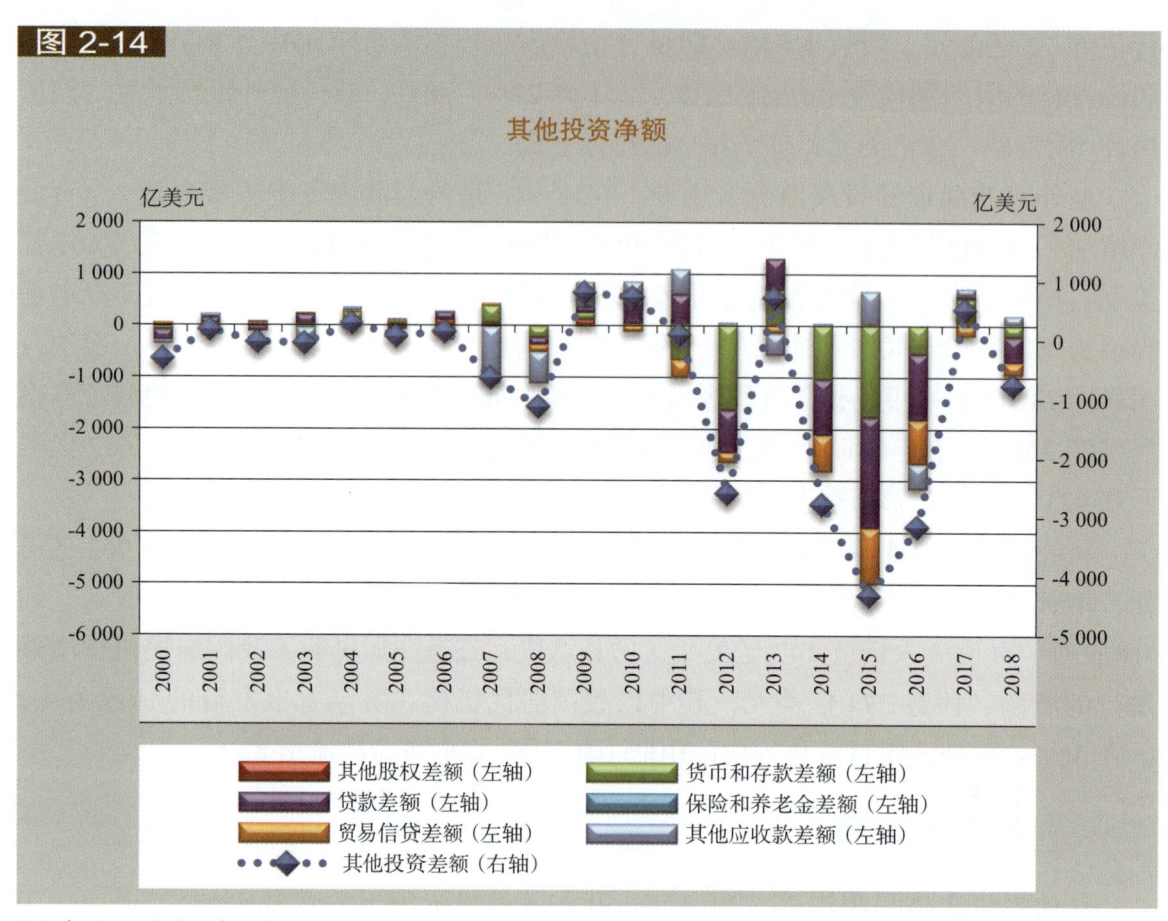

图 2-14

其他投资净额

数据来源：国家外汇管理局。

　　吸收其他投资净流入有所下降。2018 年，我国吸收其他投资净流入 1 214 亿美元，较上年减少 21%。其中，借入贷款 321 亿美元，较上年减少 36%，说明我国企业根据市场环境变化主动调整了跨境贷款规模；吸收货币和存款增加 514 亿美元，外币和人民币存款分别增加 362 亿美元和 152 亿美元；贸易信贷负债增加 408 亿美元，上年为减少 12 亿美元，主要是由于 2018 年进口较上年增长 16%，使进口应付款增加较快；其他应付负债减少 31 亿美元，较上年下降 34%。

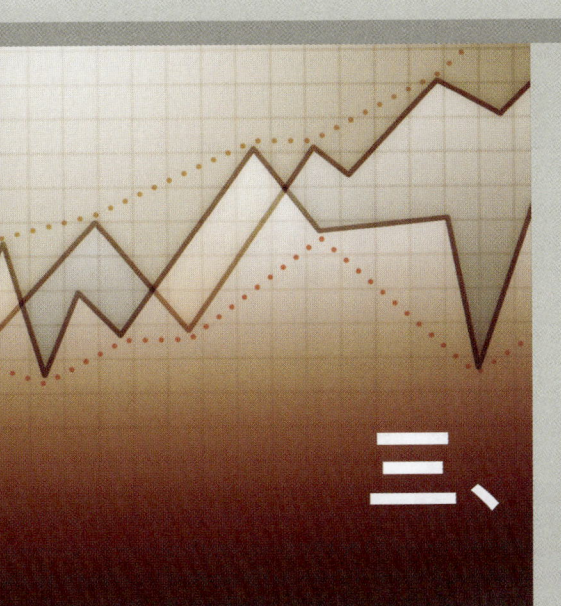

三、国际投资头寸状况

对外金融资产和负债①均有所增长。2018 年末，我国对外金融资产 73 242 亿美元，较上年末（下同）增长 2.5%；对外负债 51 941 亿美元，增长 2.9%；对外净资产为 21 301 亿美元，增长 1.4%（见图 3-1）。

图 3-1

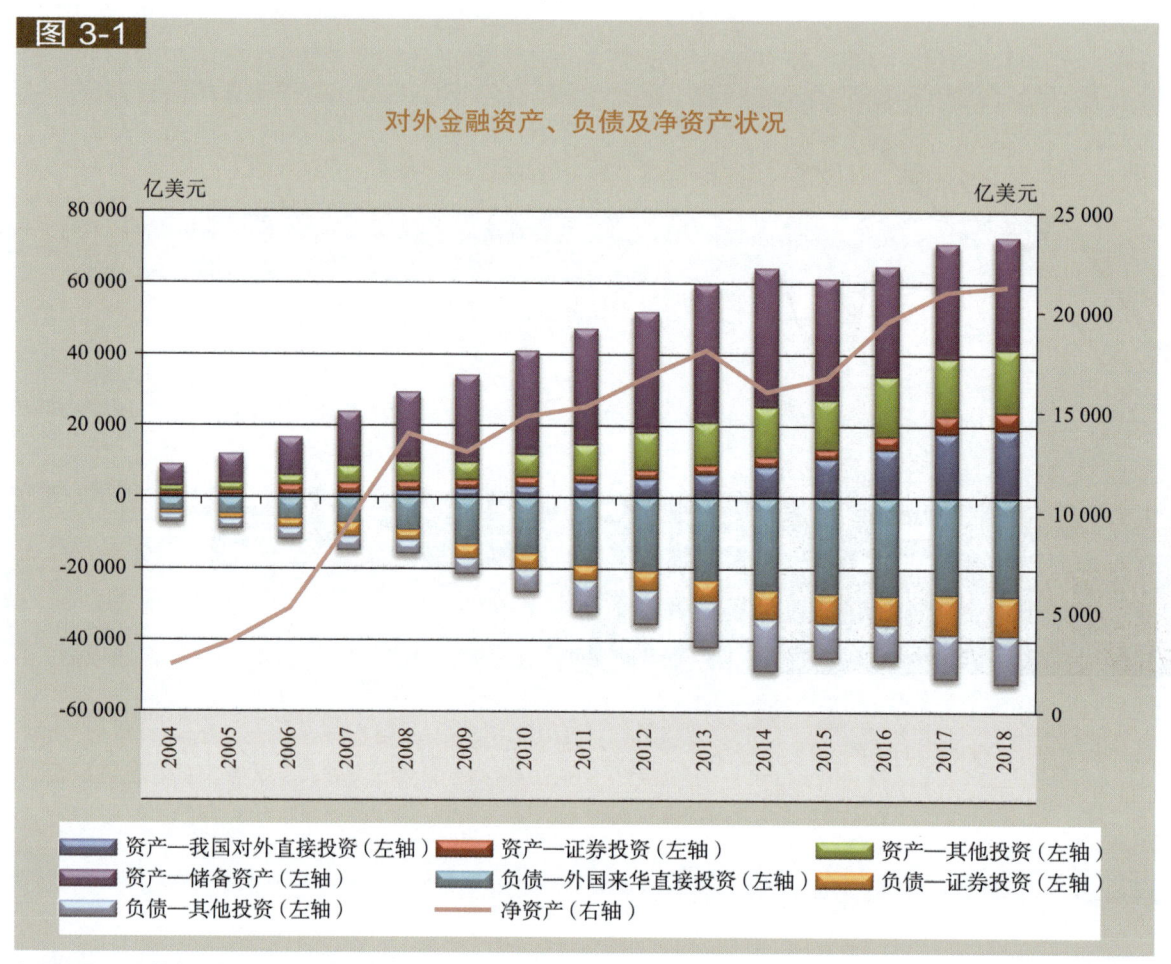

对外金融资产、负债及净资产状况

数据来源：国家外汇管理局。

对外资产中储备资产仍居首位，但民间部门持有占比不断上升。2018 年末，我国对外金融资产中，国际储备资产余额为 31 680 亿美元，较上年末下降 2.1%，其中由交易引起的储备资产余额增加 189 亿美元，由汇率及价格等非交易因素引起的储备资产余额减少 868 亿美元。储备资产占我国对外金融资产总额的 43%，继续占据对外资产首位，但比重较上年末下降 2 个百分点，为 2004 年公布国际投资头寸数据以来的最低水平；直接投资资产 18 990 亿美元，占资产总额的比重为 26%，提高 0.6

---

① 对外金融资产和负债包括直接投资、证券投资及存贷款等其他投资。之所以对外直接投资属于金融资产范畴，是因为境内投资者持有的是境外被投资企业的股权，这与证券投资中的股权投资无本质区别，只是直接投资通常持股比例较高，意在影响或控制企业的生产经营活动。反之，外来直接投资则属于对外金融负债范畴，也是境外投资者对外商投资企业的权益。

个百分点；证券投资资产 4 980 亿美元，占比 7%；金融衍生工具资产 62 亿美元，占比 0.1%；存贷款等其他投资资产 17 530 亿美元，占比 24%，提高 1.5 个百分点（见图 3-2）。

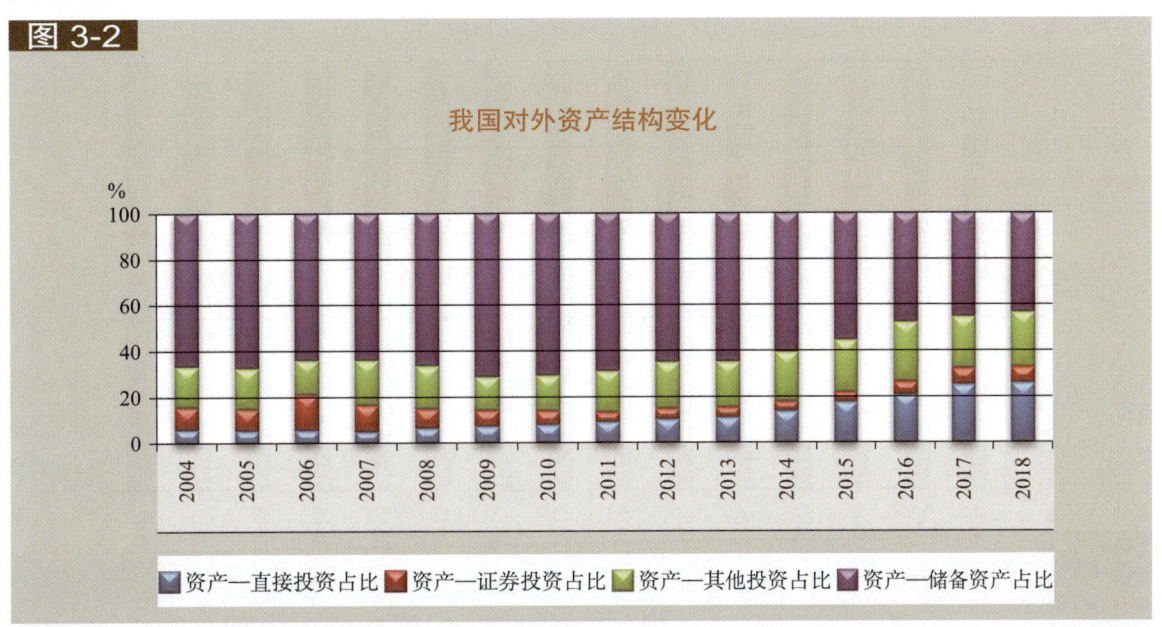

图 3-2

我国对外资产结构变化

数据来源：国家外汇管理局。

对外负债仍以外国来华直接投资为主，来华债券投资等占比增加。2018 年末，我国对外负债中，外国来华直接投资 27 623 亿美元①，较上年末增长 1.3%，继续位列对外负债首位，占比 53%，下降 0.8 个百分点；证券投资项下的债券负债 4 122 亿美元，占比 8%，上升 1.3 个百分点；存贷款等其他投资负债 13 294 亿美元，占比 26%，上升 1.4 个百分点（见图 3-3）。

---

① 外国来华直接投资存量包括我国非金融部门和金融部门吸收来华直接投资存量，以及境内外母子公司间贷款和其他债务性往来，并反映了价值重估因素的影响。

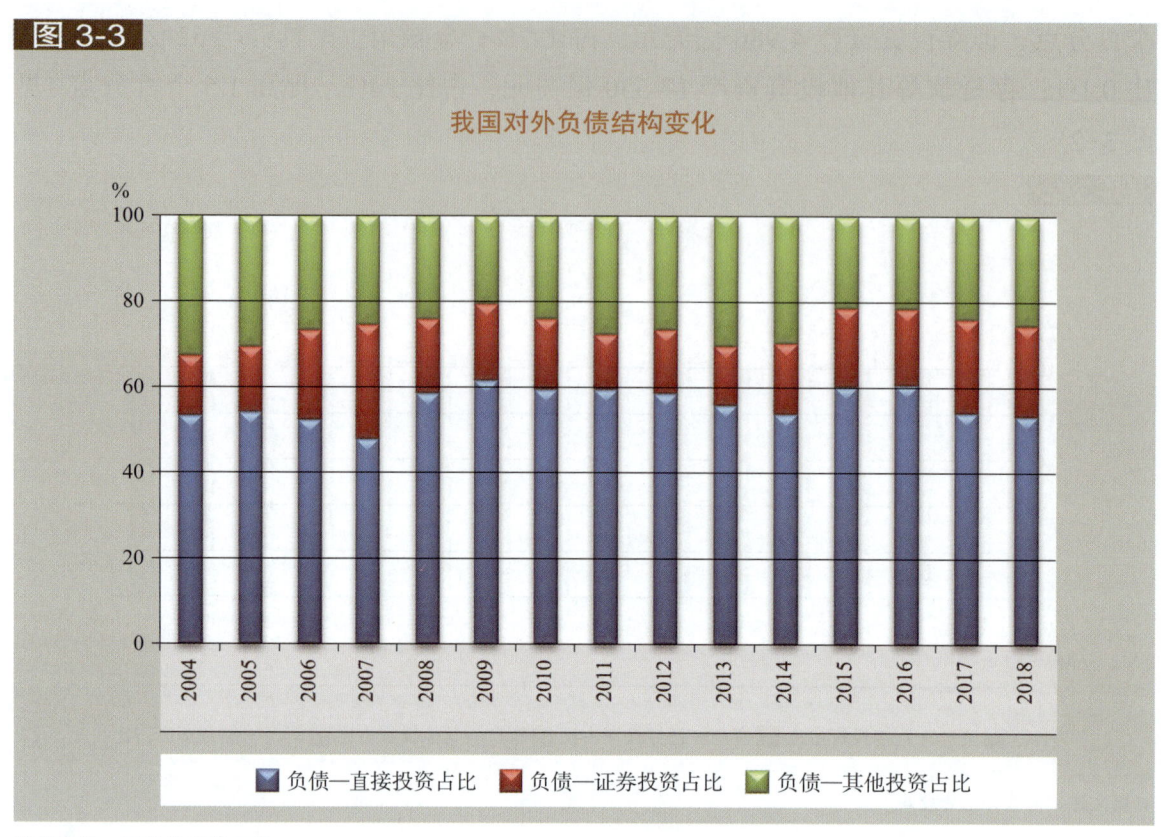

图 3-3

我国对外负债结构变化

■ 负债—直接投资占比　　■ 负债—证券投资占比　　■ 负债—其他投资占比

数据来源：国家外汇管理局。

投资收益差额延续逆差。2018 年，我国国际收支平衡表中投资收益为逆差 614 亿美元。其中，我国对外投资收益收入 2 146 亿美元，较上年下降 19%；对外负债收益支出 2 760 亿美元，下降 5%；二者年化收益率差异为 −2.4 个百分点，较上年扩大 0.2 个百分点（见图 3-4）。我国对外金融资产负债结构是投资收益差额为负的决定因素。2018 年末，我国对外金融资产中储备资产占比超四成，因主要为流动性较强的资产，2005 年至 2018 年我国对外金融资产年平均投资收益率为 3.3%；我国对外负债中外来直接投资占比过半，因股权投资属于长期、稳定的投资，投资回报一般高于其他形式资产，2005 年至 2018 年我国对外负债年平均投资收益率为 6.0%。来华直接投资资金持续流入并保持较高的投资收益率，说明我国长期投资环境对于境外投资者仍具有较大的吸引力。

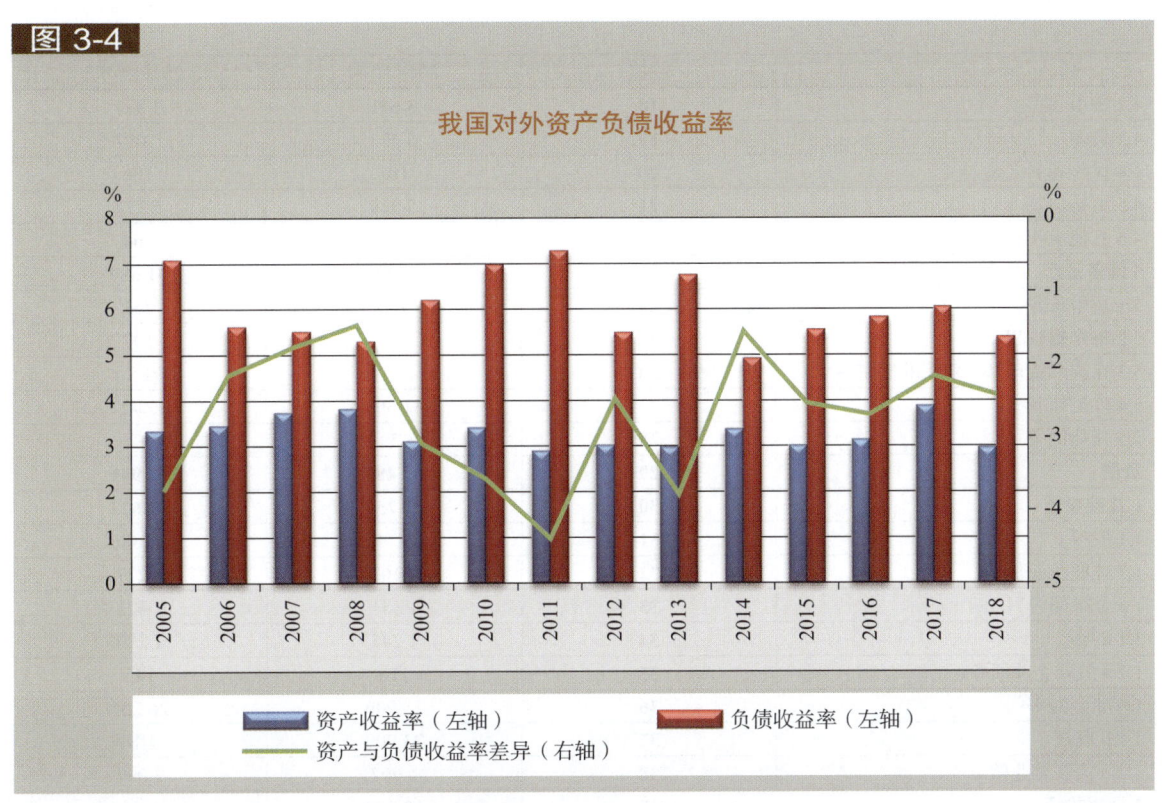

图 3-4

我国对外资产负债收益率

资产收益率（左轴）　　　　负债收益率（左轴）
资产与负债收益率差异（右轴）

注：① 资产（或负债）收益率 = $\dfrac{\text{年度投资收益收入（或支出）}}{\text{（上年末＋本年末对外资产（或负债）存量）/2}}$

② 资产负债收益率差异 = 资产收益率 − 负债收益率
数据来源：国家外汇管理局。

表 3-1　中国国际投资头寸表　　　　　　　　　　　　　单位：亿美元

项　　目	行次	2017 年末	2018 年末
净头寸 ①	1	21 007	21 301
资产	2	71 488	73 242
1 直接投资	3	**18 090**	**18 990**
1.1 股权	4	15 590	16 316
1.2 关联企业债务	5	2 501	2 674
1.a 金融部门	6	2 371	2 518
1.1.a 股权	7	2 276	2 416
1.2.a 关联企业债务	8	95	102
1.b 非金融部门	9	15 719	16 472
1.1.b 股权	10	13 314	13 900
1.2.b 关联企业债务	11	2 405	2 572
2 证券投资	12	**4 925**	**4 980**
2.1 股权	13	2 977	2 700
2.2 债券	14	1 948	2 279
3 金融衍生工具	15	**59**	**62**
4 其他投资	16	**16 055**	**17 530**
4.1 其他股权	17	54	54

① 净头寸是指资产减负债，"+"表示净资产，"−"表示净负债。本表记数采用四舍五入原则。

续表

项　　目	行次	2017 年末	2018 年末
4.2 货币和存款	18	3 611	3 937
4.3 贷款	19	6 373	7 097
4.4 保险和养老金	20	101	106
4.5 贸易信贷	21	5 319	5 972
4.6 其他应收款	22	597	364
5 储备资产	23	**32 359**	**31 680**
5.1 货币黄金	24	765	763
5.2 特别提款权	25	110	107
5.3 在国际货币基金组织的储备头寸	26	79	85
5.4 外汇储备	27	31 399	30 727
5.5 其他储备	28	5	−2
负债	29	**50 481**	**51 941**
1 直接投资	30	**27 257**	**27 623**
1.1 股权	31	25 150	25 386
1.2 关联企业债务	32	2 107	2 237
1.a 金融部门	33	1 351	1 422
1.1.a 股权	34	1 241	1 277
1.2.a 关联企业债务	35	110	145
1.b 非金融部门	36	25 906	26 201
1.1.b 股权	37	23 909	24 109
1.2.b 关联企业债务	38	1 997	2 092
2 证券投资	39	**10 994**	**10 964**
2.1 股权	40	7 623	6 842
2.2 债券	41	3 370	4 122
3 金融衍生工具	42	**34**	**60**
4 其他投资	43	**12 197**	**13 294**
4.1 其他股权	44	0	0
4.2 货币和存款	45	4 365	4 833
4.3 贷款	46	3 922	4 169
4.4 保险和养老金	47	100	109
4.5 贸易信贷	48	3 523	3 931
4.6 其他应付款	49	188	154
4.7 特别提款权	50	100	97

数据来源：国家外汇管理局。

专栏 4

我国银行业对外资产负债结构分析

　　2018 年末，我国银行业对外资产和对外负债规模较上年末有所增长，对外净负债规模较上年末下降。其中，对外资产 11 164 亿美元①，增长 12%，占我国

---

① 所用数据来自国家外汇管理局《对外金融资产负债及交易统计制度》采集的数据。我国已于 2015 年底参加国际清算银行的国际银行业统计，并按照其要求分季度报送我国银行业的对外资产负债情况，基于 2018 年 12 月末报送数据进行分析。

对外金融资产存量①的 15%；对外负债 12 976 亿美元，增长 1%，占我国对外负债存量的 25%；对外净负债 1 812 亿美元，下降 36%。

对外金融资产中存贷款占比逾七成，债券资产与股权等其他资产占比相当。我国银行业对境外发放贷款和在境外存款占对外资产比重超过七成，为 8 315 亿美元，较上年末增长 11%，其中主要是对境外发放的贷款；投资境外债券 1 365 亿美元，增长 17%，占比 12%，增速较 2017 年有所放缓；对外股权和金融衍生品等其他投资资产 1 485 亿美元，增长 12%，占比略高于债券资产。

对外负债中存贷款占比过半，股权等其他负债规模及占比均有所下降，债券负债与上年基本持平。我国银行业吸收境外存款和接受境外贷款 7 287 亿美元，较上年末增长 5%，占比过半，其中主要是从境外非金融部门获得的存款；对外债券负债 1 848 亿美元，增长 0.5%，占比 14%；股权和金融衍生品等其他投资负债 3 841 亿美元，下降 5%，占银行业对外负债的三成（见图 C4-1）。

图 C4-1

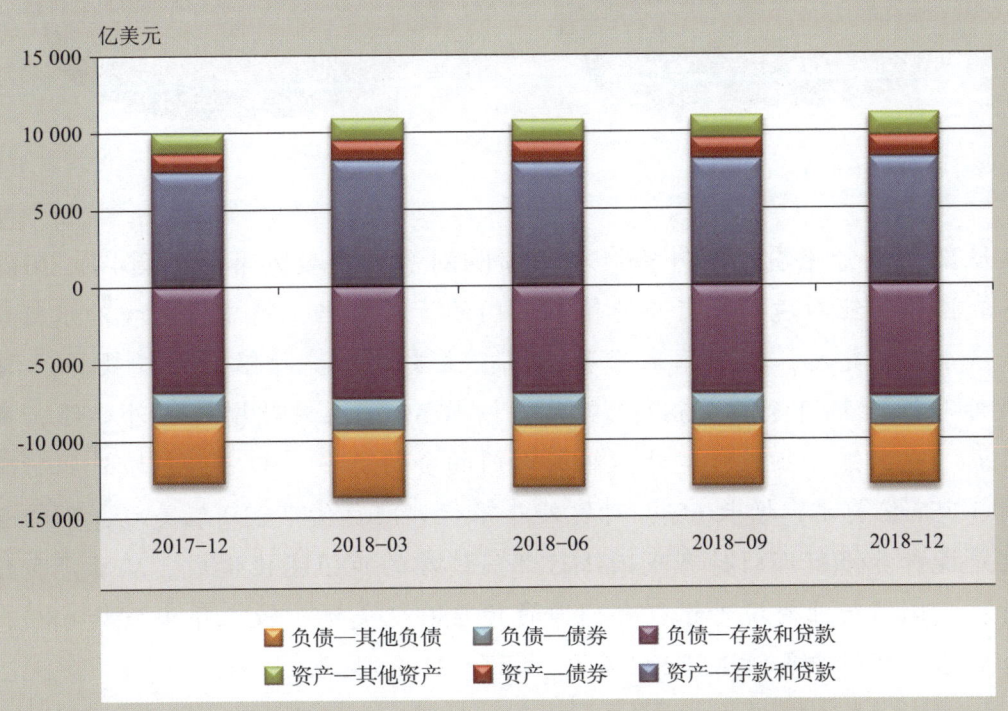

银行业对外金融资产负债结构

数据来源：国家外汇管理局。

从币种结构来看，外币呈现对外净资产，人民币呈现对外净负债。2018 年

---

① 对外资产存量规模含储备资产，若扣除储备资产，银行业对外资产占比为 27%。

末，银行业对外美元资产在银行业总对外资产中占比最大，为 7 759 亿美元，较上年末增长 15%，主要来自增持美元债券和股票等其他资产；人民币资产占比次之，为 1 214 亿美元，增长 3%，主要来自于增持人民币债券资产；其他外币资产 2 192 亿美元，共占比两成。银行业对外负债中美元负债占主导，为 5 052 亿美元，增长 7%；人民币负债占三成，为 4 061 亿美元，增长 1%；其他外币负债合计占比三成，为 3 863 亿美元。从资产负债净额看，我国对外人民币净负债 2 847 亿美元，与上年末持平；对外外币净资产 1 035 亿美元，上年末为净资产 35 亿美元（见图 C4-2）。

图 C4-2

银行业对外金融资产和负债币种结构

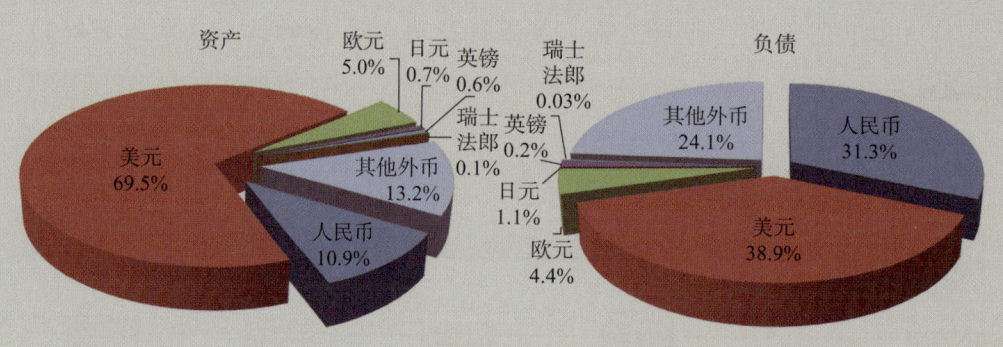

数据来源：国家外汇管理局。

从部门划分来看，对外资产和负债的对手方主要为非银行部门。2018 年末，我国银行业对境外银行与非银行部门的资产相当，其中，对境外银行部门资产 5 477 亿美元，较上年末增长 20%，主要是对境外银行存贷款资产增加；对境外非银行部门资产 5 687 亿美元，增长 5%，主要是增持境外非银行部门的债券。我国银行业吸收境外非银行部门的负债更多。其中，对境外银行部门负债 5 757 亿美元，增长 6%；对境外非银行部门负债 7 219 亿美元，下降 2%，主要是境外非银行部门持有我国银行部门债券的市值变化造成。从资产负债净额看，我国银行业对境外银行部门净负债 280 亿美元，较上年末下降 68%；对境外非银行部门净负债 1 532 亿美元，下降 21%（见表 C4-1）。

表 C4-1　2018 年末我国银行业对外资产负债结构

单位：亿美元

项　目		资　产		负　债		净资产
		金额	占比	金额	占比	金额
按工具类型分	存贷款	8 315	74%	7 287	56%	1 027
	债券	1 365	12%	1 848	14%	−483
	其他	1 485	13%	3 841	30%	−2 356

续表

项 目		资 产		负 债		净资产
		金额	占比	金额	占比	金额
按对手方部门划分	银行部门	5 477	49%	5 757	44%	−280
	非银行部门	5 687	51%	7 219	56%	−1 532
按币种分	人民币	1 214	11%	4 061	31%	−2 847
	美元	7 759	69%	5 052	39%	2 707
	欧元	561	5%	571	4%	−10
	日元	74	1%	146	1%	−71
	英镑	70	1%	21	0%	49
	其他	1 486	13%	3 125	24%	−1 639
合 计		**11 164**	**100%**	**12 976**	**100%**	**−1 812**

数据来源：国家外汇管理局。

从国家和地区分布来看，对外资产和负债的对手方主要为发达国家（地区）及离岸中心。我国银行业对外金融资产投向前三位国家（地区）依次是：对中国香港资产 3 347 亿美元，对美国 1 232 亿美元，对英国 440 亿美元，合计占总对外资产的 45%。我国银行业对外负债来源前三位国家（地区）依次是：对中国香港负债 6 918 亿美元，对新加坡负债 1 074 亿美元，对中国台湾负债 775 亿美元，合计占总对外负债的 67%（见图 C4-3）。

图 C4-3

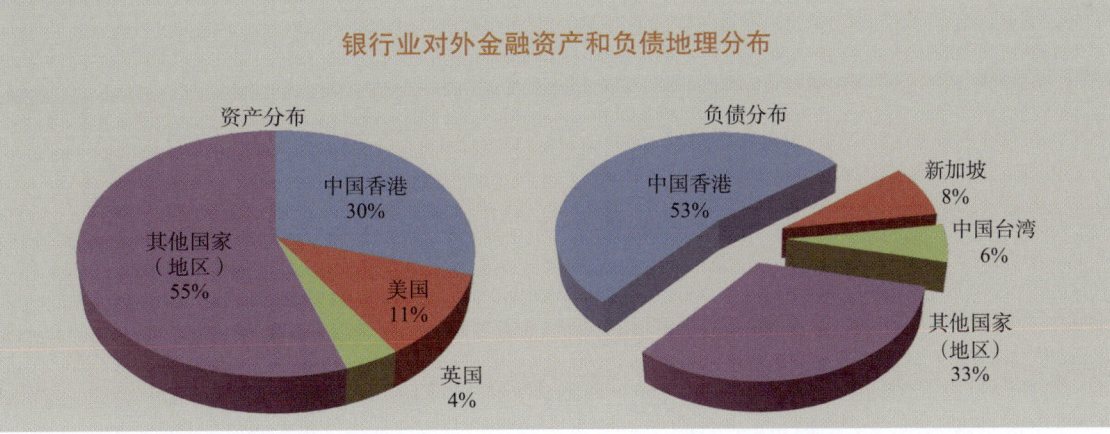

银行业对外金融资产和负债地理分布

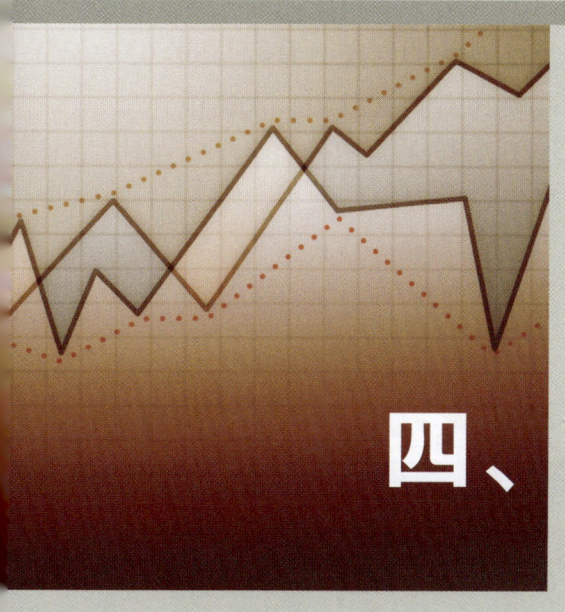

四、外汇市场运行与人民币汇率

（一）人民币汇率走势

人民币对美元汇率保持相对稳定。2018 年 12 月末，人民币对美元汇率中间价为 6.8632 元 / 美元，较上年末贬值 4.79%，境内市场（CNY）和境外市场（CNH）即期交易价累计均贬值 5.33%（见图 4-1），境内外市场日均价差 102 个基点，低于上年全年日均价差（ 130 个基点）。从全年看，在美元升值的背景下，人民币对美元跌幅与欧元、英镑等发达国家货币相当，远低于绝大多数新兴市场货币对美元跌幅，人民币在全球货币体系中成为较稳定的货币之一。

图 4-1

2018 年境内外人民币对美元即期汇率走势

数据来源：中国外汇交易中心、路透数据库。

人民币对其他主要货币有升有贬。2018 年末，人民币对欧元、日元、英镑、澳元、加元汇率中间价分别为 7.8473 元 / 欧元、6.1887 元 / 100 日元、8.6762 元 / 英镑、4.8250 元 / 澳元和 5.0381 元 / 加元，分别较上年末贬值 0.57%、贬值 6.47 %、升值 1.19%、升值 5.55 % 和升值 3.23%（见图 4-2）。

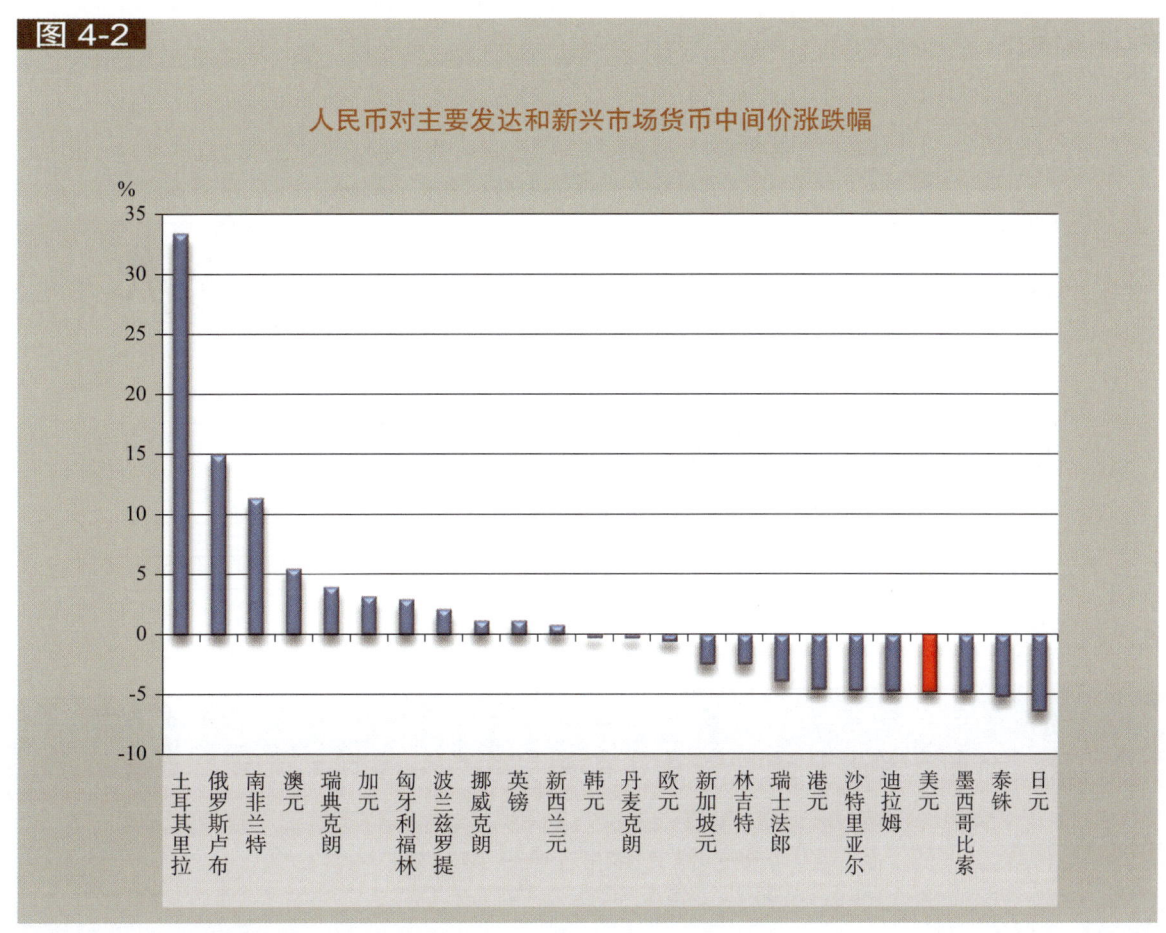

图 4-2

人民币对主要发达和新兴市场货币中间价涨跌幅

数据来源：中国外汇交易中心。

　　人民币对一篮子货币基本稳定。根据中国外汇交易中心的数据，2018 年末 CFETS 人民币汇率指数、参考 BIS 货币篮子和 SDR 货币篮子的人民币汇率指数分别为 93.28、96.78 和 93.14，分别较上年末贬值 1.66%、升值 0.89% 和贬值 2.97%。

　　根据国际清算银行（BIS）的数据，2018 年人民币名义有效汇率累计升值 1.2%，扣除通货膨胀因素的实际有效汇率累计升值 1.1%（见图 4-3）；自 2005 年人民币汇率形成机制改革以来，人民币名义和实际有效汇率累计分别升值 38.1% 和 47.2%。

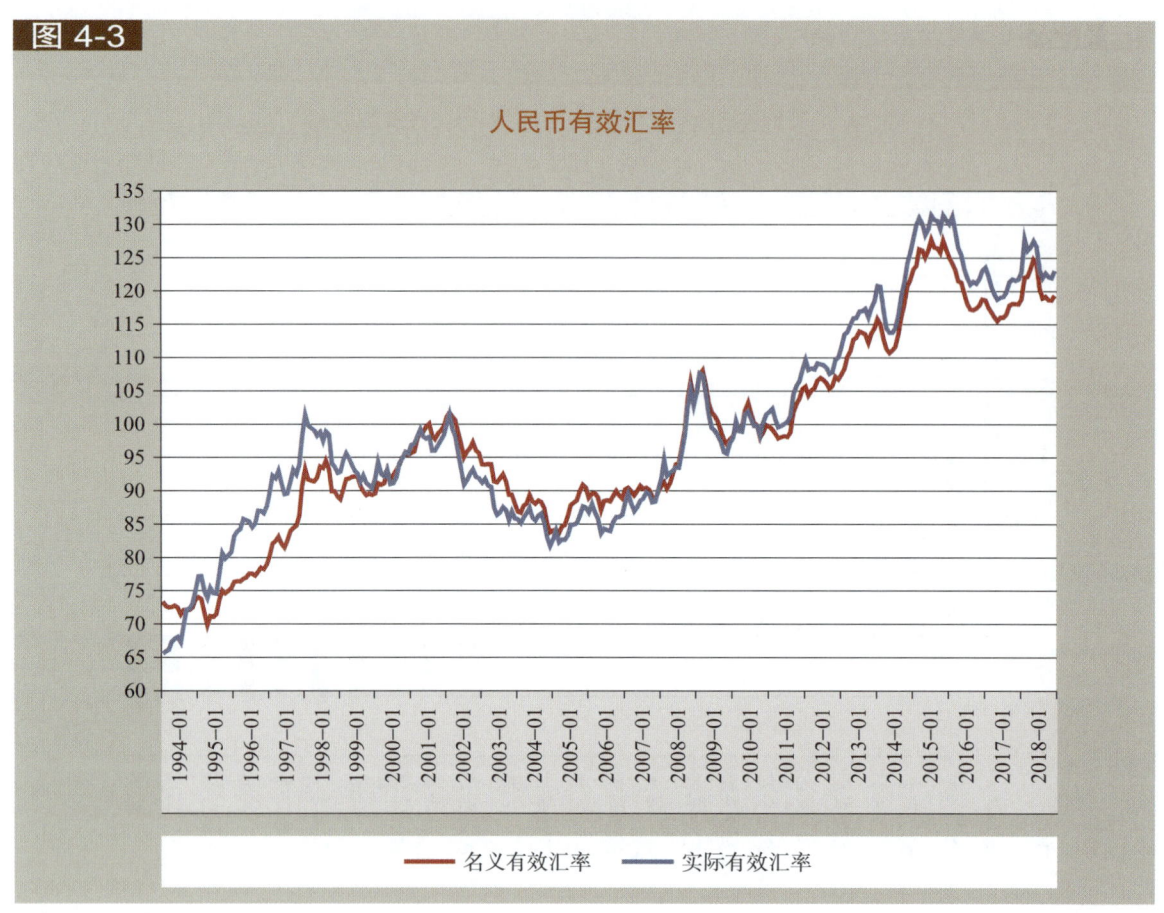

图 4-3

人民币有效汇率

名义有效汇率　　实际有效汇率

数据来源：国际清算银行。

人民币汇率双向波动弹性增强。2018 年，人民币对美元汇率收盘价年内波幅达到 11.3%，较上年明显增加。一方面，国内经济继续企稳，经济结构持续优化，跨境资本流动总体稳定，在基本面上为人民币汇率提供了支持。另一方面，受中美贸易摩擦、美元加息、利差收窄等因素影响，汇率机制日趋灵活的人民币顺应市场变化，呈现有涨有跌的正常波动。

2018 年末，境内外市场人民币对美元汇率 1 年期历史波动率分别为 4.3% 和 5.4%，较年初分别上升 1.2 个和 1.7 个百分点；期权市场隐含波动率分别为 5.2% 和 6.1%，较年初分别上升 1.2 个和 0.6 个百分点（见图 4-4），人民币汇率弹性与主要发达国家货币日益接近。

图 4-4

境内外市场人民币对美元汇率 1 年期波动率

历史波动率

期权隐含波动率

数据来源：彭博资讯。

　　期权市场显示人民币汇率预期稳定。 2018 年末，境内外风险逆转指标（看涨美元 / 看跌人民币期权与看跌美元 / 看涨人民币期权的波动率之差）分别为 0.92% 和 0.93%，均较上年末略有上升，但 11 月以来持续下降（见图 4-5）。从全年看，境内外期权风险逆转指标呈现先降后升再降的波动走势，但是全年高点远低于历史高位，显示汇率预期稳定。

图 4-5

境内外人民币对美元期权市场 1 年期风险逆转指标

图例： 境外   境内

数据来源：彭博资讯。

（二）外汇市场交易

2018 年，人民币外汇市场累计成交 29.07 万亿美元（日均 1 196 亿美元），较上年增长 20.7%（图 4-6）。其中，银行对客户市场和银行间外汇市场分别成交 4.23 万亿美元和 24.85 万亿美元①；即期和衍生产品分别成交 11.06 万亿美元和 18.01 万亿美元（见表 4-6），衍生产品在外汇市场交易总量中的比重升至 61.9%，交易产品构成进一步接近全球外汇市场状况（见图 4-7）。

即期外汇交易平稳增长。 2018 年，即期市场累计成交 11.06 万亿美元，较上年增长 16.6%。在市场分布上，银行对客户即期结售汇（含银行自身，不含远期履约）累计 3.43 万亿美元，较上年增长 11.0%；银行间即期外汇市场累计成交 7.63 万亿美元，较上年增长 19.3%，其中美元交易份额为 96.8%。

---

① 银行对客户市场采用客户买卖外汇总额，银行间外汇市场采用单边交易量，以下同。

图 4-6

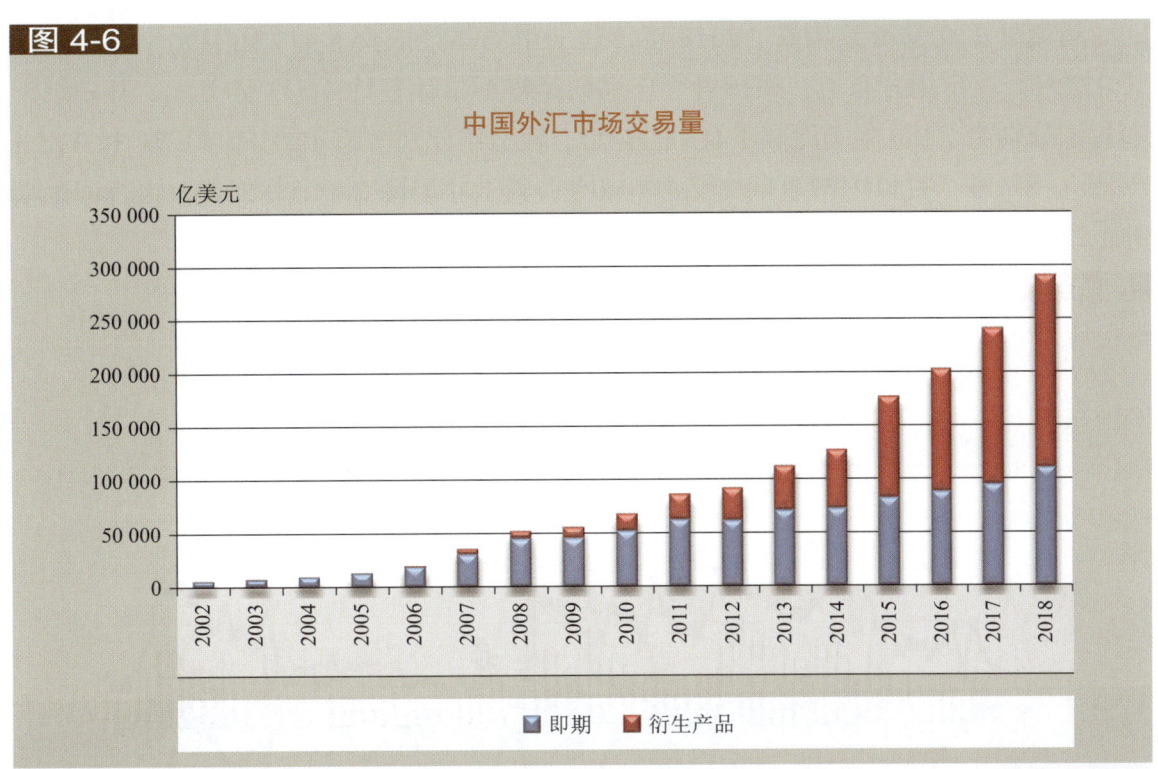

中国外汇市场交易量

亿美元

图例：即期　衍生产品

数据来源：国家外汇管理局、中国外汇交易中心。

图 4-7

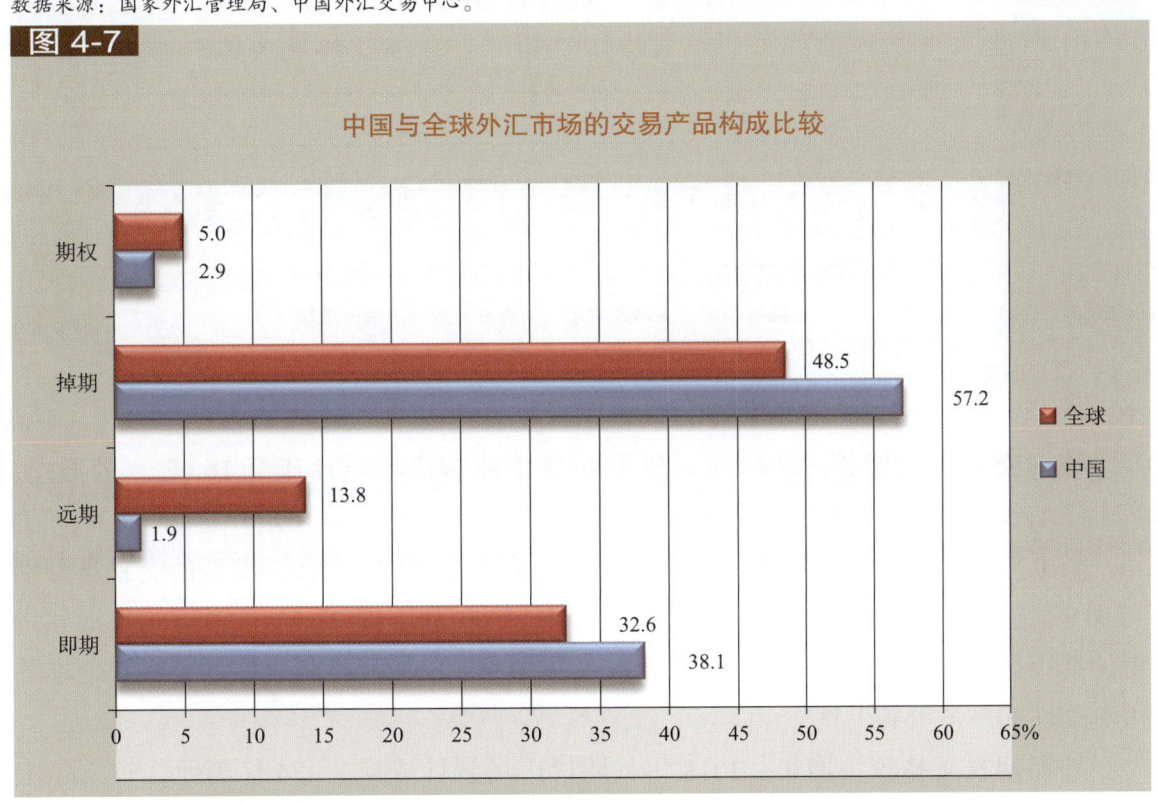

中国与全球外汇市场的交易产品构成比较

产品	全球	中国
期权	5.0	2.9
掉期	48.5	57.2
远期	13.8	1.9
即期	32.6	38.1

注：中国为 2018 年数据，全球为国际清算银行 2016 年 4 月调查数据。

数据来源：国家外汇管理局、中国外汇交易中心、国际清算银行。

远期外汇交易继续增长。2018 年，远期市场累计成交 5 419 亿美元，较上年增长 27.2%。在市场分布上，银行对客户远期结售汇累计签约 4 543 亿美元，其中结汇和售汇分别为 2 130 亿美元和 2 413 亿美元，较上年分别增长 40.9%、43.7% 和 38.5%（见图 4-8），6 个月以内的短期交易占 65.0%，较上年下降 2.0 个百分点；银行间远期外汇市场累计成交 875 亿美元，较上年下降 15.3%。

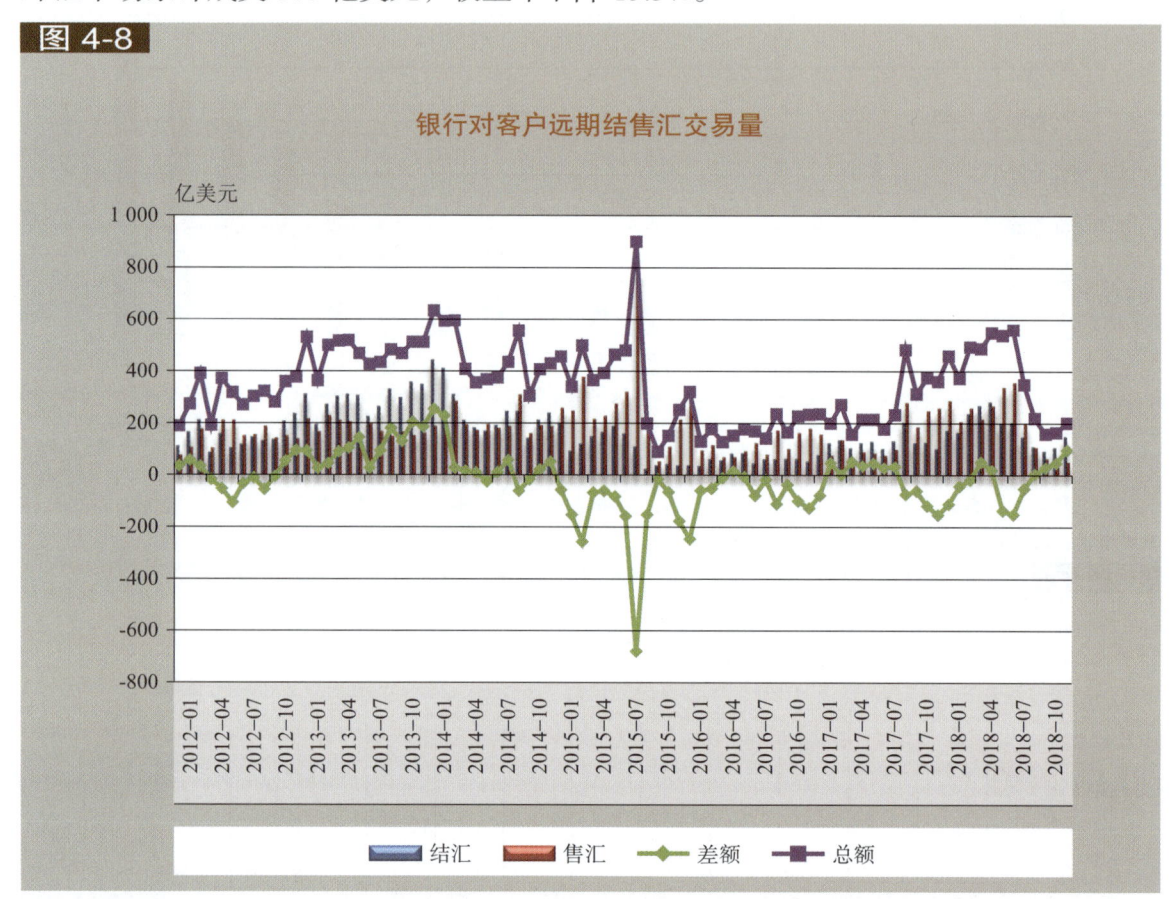

图 4-8

银行对客户远期结售汇交易量

数据来源：国家外汇管理局。

掉期交易持续增长。2018 年，外汇和货币掉期市场累计成交 16.62 万亿美元，较上年增长 22.6%。在市场分布上，银行对客户外汇和货币掉期累计签约 1 036 亿美元，较上年上升 0.4%，其中近端结汇 / 远端购汇和近端购汇 / 远端结汇的交易量分别为 919 亿美元和 117 亿美元，较上年分别增长 5.7% 和下降 28.1%；银行间外汇和货币掉期市场累计成交 16.51 万亿美元，较上年增长 22.6%，掉期交易是银行管理本外币流动性的一个重要工具。

外汇期权交易较快增长。2018 年，期权市场累计成交 8 474 亿美元，较上年上升 40.7%。在市场分布上，银行对客户期权市场累计成交 2 363 亿美元，较上年增长

2.4%；银行间外汇期权市场累计成交 6 111 亿美元，较上年增长 64.6%。

　　外汇市场参与者结构基本稳定。银行自营交易延续主导地位（见图 4-9），2018
年银行间交易占整个外汇市场的比重从 2017 年的 83.9% 上升至 84.8%；非金融客户
交易的比重从 15.3% 下降至 14.4%，跨境人民币结算业务发展产生的替代效应可能是
一个重要原因；非银行金融机构交易的市场份额为 0.8%，与 2016 年和 2017 年基本
一致，非银行金融机构在我国外汇市场的参与度仍有限。

图 4-9

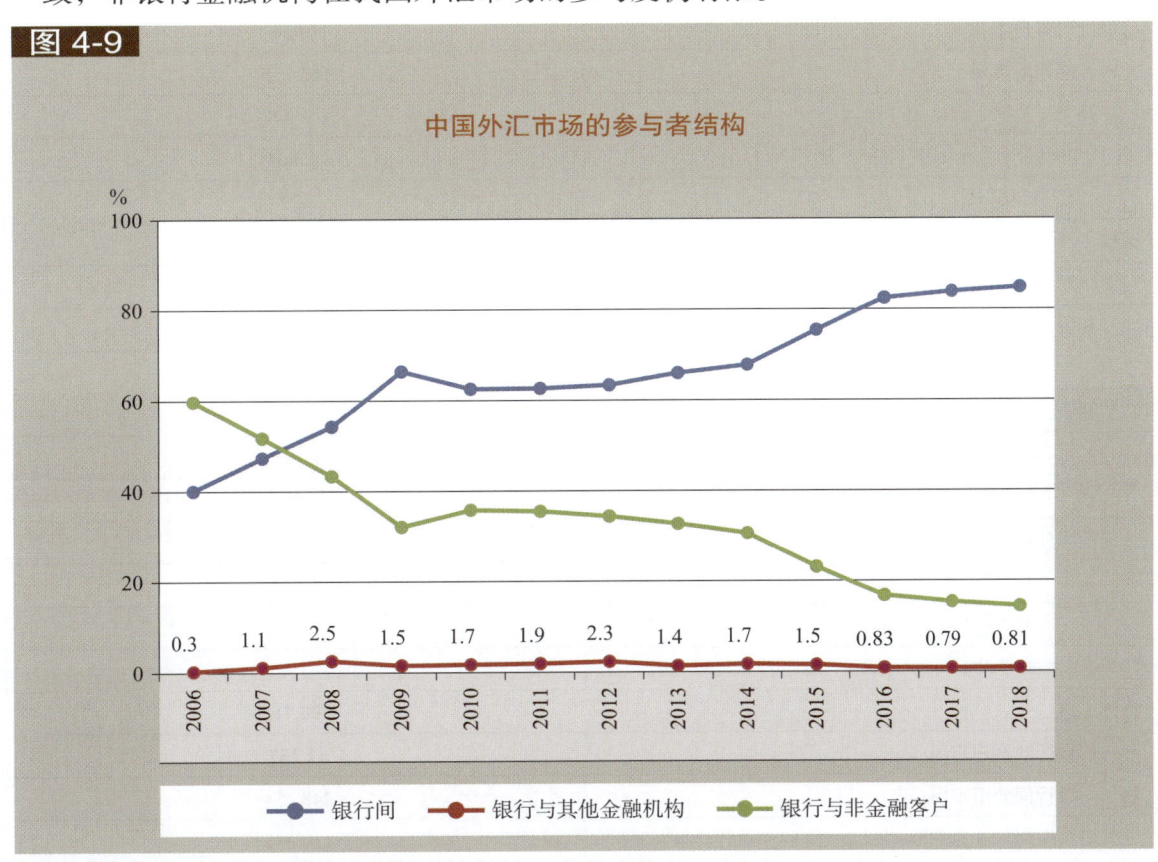

中国外汇市场的参与者结构

数据来源：国家外汇管理局、中国外汇交易中心。

表 4-1　2018 年人民币外汇市场交易概况

交易品种	交易量（亿美元）
即期	110 647
银行对客户市场	34 315
银行间外汇市场	76 332
远期	5 419
银行对客户市场	4 543
其中：3 个月（含）以下	2 048
3 个月至 1 年（含）	2 144
1 年以上	352

交易品种	交易量（亿美元）
银行间外汇市场	**875**
其中：3 个月（含）以下	552
3 个月至 1 年（含）	293
1 年以上	31
外汇和货币掉期	**166 171**
银行对客户市场	**1 036**
银行间外汇市场	**165 135**
其中：3 个月（含）以下	141 448
3 个月至 1 年（含）	22 864
1 年以上	823
期权	**8 474**
银行对客户市场	**2 363**
其中：买入期权	1 146
卖出期权	1 217
其中：3 个月（含）以下	980
3 个月至 1 年（含）	1 187
1 年以上	196
银行间外汇市场	**6 111**
其中：3 个月（含）以下	4 359
3 个月至 1 年（含）	1 735
1 年以上	17
合计	**290 711**
银行对客户市场	**42 257**
银行间外汇市场	**248 454**
其中：即期	110 647
远期	5 419
外汇和货币掉期	166 171
期权	8 474

注：数据均为单边交易额，采用四舍五入原则。

数据来源：国家外汇管理局、中国外汇交易中心。

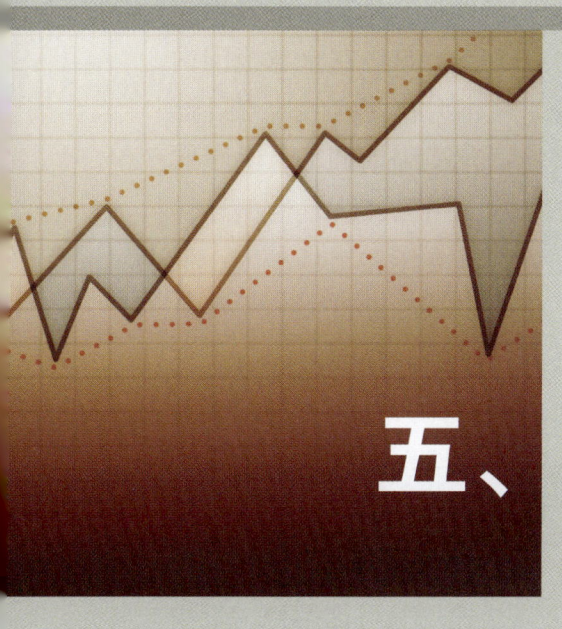

五、国际收支形势展望

2019 年，国际环境依然复杂多变，存在一些不确定因素，包括全球经济增长放缓，贸易保护主义影响国际贸易发展和市场信心，国际政治不稳定可能推升市场避险情绪等。但经济、政策、市场等国内基本面还会发挥根本性的作用，预计我国将继续呈现经常账户基本平衡、跨境资本流动总体稳定、国际收支自主平衡的发展格局。

我国国际收支平稳运行的内部基础依然稳固。第一，我国经济长期向好的发展态势不会变。我国经济依然具有足够的韧性和巨大的潜力，经济增速将在全球范围内保持较高水平，而且是在更大经济总量的基数上实现的，这将为我国有效应对外部环境变化提供牢固的经济基础。2019 年，我国宏观政策将强化逆周期调节，继续实施积极的财政政策和稳健的货币政策，宏观杠杆率趋于稳定，国民经济良性循环将逐步形成。第二，我国推动全方位对外开放的进程不会变。2019 年在市场准入、保护知识产权、贸易投资便利化、资本市场开放等方面，我国还会提供更大的支持与便利，这将为境外资本投资国内市场提供坚实的政策基础。第三，我国国际收支运行机制日臻完善的趋势不会变。当前，人民币汇率双向浮动增强，有利于巩固更加多元、理性的市场预期；跨境资本流动宏观审慎和微观监管相结合，有利于维护外汇市场健康秩序，这将为促进跨境资本流动平稳运行、国际收支自主平衡提供良好的市场基础。

经常账户将保持基本平衡。首先，货物贸易出口和进口增速均有可能回稳，货物贸易仍将维持一定规模顺差。一方面，我国出口需有所回落但出口竞争力依然较强。根据国际货币基金组织最新预测，2019 年全球经济增长 3.5%，较 2018 年放缓 0.2 个百分点。同时，我国制造业具有成熟的基础设施、完备的产业链条、大量的技术工人，再加上持续推动的转型升级，有助于相关产品维持较强的国际竞争力，在国内外均拥有较大市场。另一方面，在我国注重经济高质量发展、内部需求相对稳定的背景下，进口增长也会更加平稳。其次，服务贸易逆差变动将逐步趋稳。旅行项目逆差仍是服务贸易逆差的主要来源，当前我国居民境外旅游、留学需求已经有所回稳，如近几年旅游逆差增幅均回落至个位数，说明相关需求在达到历史高位后，进一步增长的空间开始收窄，这是一个自然的规律和过程。此外，随着国内服务业质量的提升，以及生态环境、制度等软实力的增强，国内居民跨境消费将更加理性和平稳。

资本项下以中长期投资为目的的资本流入具有较大提升空间。直接投资方面，我国实际利用外资仍保持较大规模，未来随着开放领域的进一步拓宽以及国内市场重要性的不断提升，我国在吸引直接投资方面仍有较大潜力。据联合国贸发会议统计，2017 年末我国外商直接投资存量与 GDP 之比为 12%，同期全球平均水平为 39%，发展中国家平均水平为 33%。证券投资方面，2018 年，境外央行等机构以中长期资产配置为目的的资金流入较多。目前，国内资本市场中的境外投资者比重依然偏低。未来，随着我国股市、债市更加深度地纳入国际主要指数，在进一步开放和便利化政策下，我国将成为国际资本多元化配置资产的重要目的地。

专栏5

证券市场成为境外投资者投资我国的重要渠道

近年来，我国银行间债券市场开放步伐加快，合格境外机构投资者制度改革不断深化，沪港通、深港通和债券通相继实施，境外投资者投资我国证券市场更加便利。同时，随着我国债券、股票逐步纳入国际主流指数，境外投资者配置我国债券和股票的需求上升。据外汇局统计，近年来境外机构不断增持我国债券和上市股票（含基金，下同），持有的合计规模从2014年末的2 192亿美元上升到2018年末的4 448亿美元，增长103%。其中，持有的债券规模从1 085亿美元上升到2 638亿美元，增长143%；持有的股票规模从1 107亿美元上升到1 810亿美元，增长64%。未来，我国证券市场在吸引境外投资者方面仍具有较大潜力。

从市场规模看，我国债市和股市在全球排名均位列前三，市场容量较大。根据国际清算银行统计，2018年第三季度末，全球债券市场市值排名前五位国家分别是美国（41万亿美元）、日本（12.6万亿美元）、中国（12.4万亿美元）、英国（5.8万亿美元）和法国（4.6万亿美元）。我国债市与排名第二的日本债市市值仅相差0.2万亿美元（见图C5-1）。根据彭博统计，2019年2月末，美国股市市值以30万亿美元排在世界第一位，我国（6.7万亿美元）排在第二位，日本（5.73万亿美元）排在第三位（见图C5-2）。

图 C5-1

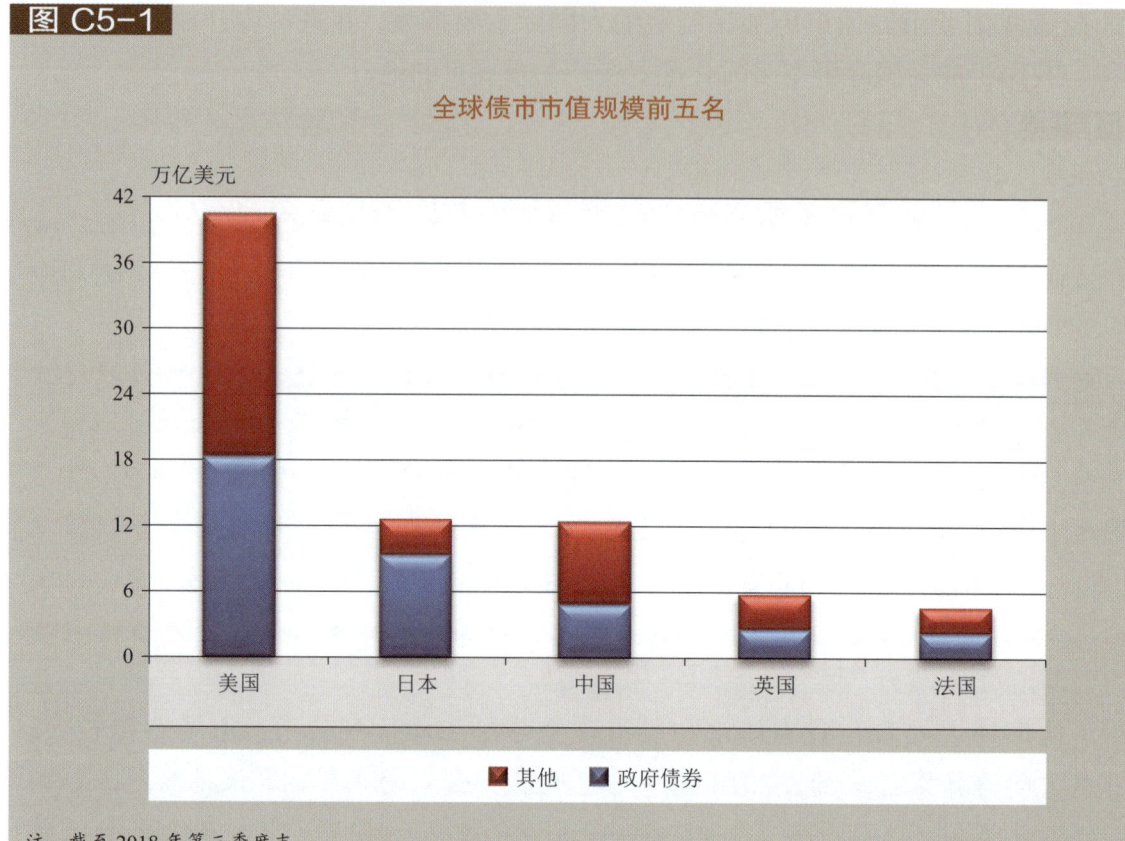

全球债市市值规模前五名

万亿美元

注：截至 2018 年第三季度末。
数据来源：国际清算银行。

图 C5-2

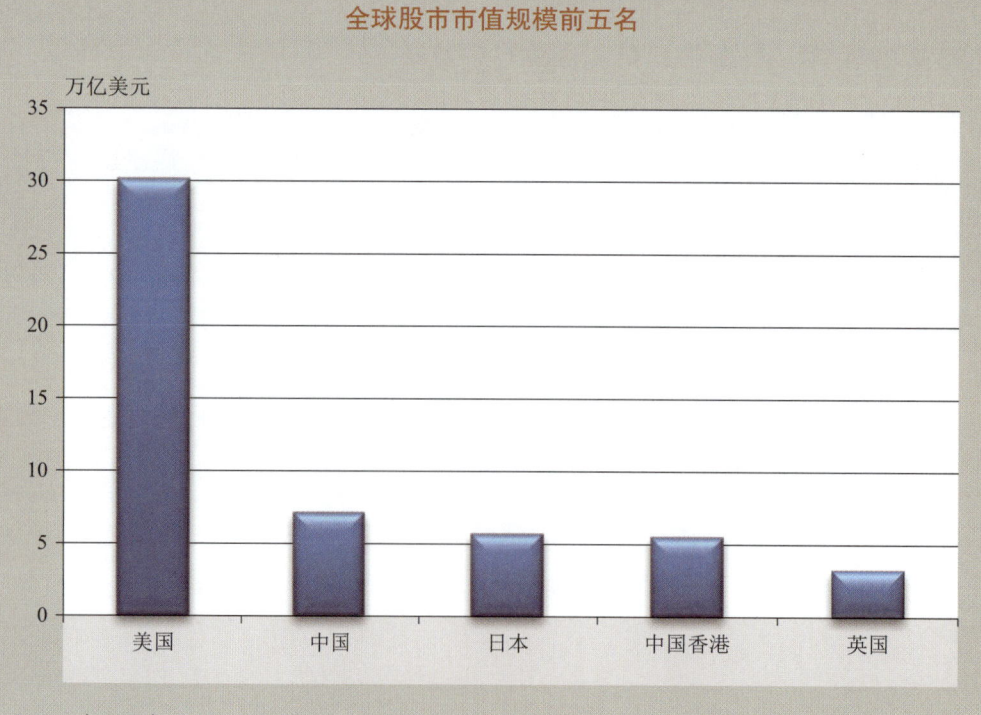

全球股市市值规模前五名

万亿美元

注：截至 2019 年 2 月末。
数据来源：彭博资讯。

与其他主要国家的证券市场相比，我国外资占比仍然较低，未来具有较大的提升空间。从2018年末的债市数据（含银行间和交易所市场）看，外资在我国债券市场上的投资金额占比为2.1%，低于美国（25%）、日本（12%）、韩国（6%）和巴西（5%）（见图C5-3）。从2018年末的股市数据看，美国外资持股占美国股市总份额的15%，日本占比为30%，巴西占比为21%，韩国为33%，而我国的外资持股占境内流通股票市值的比例为3.5%，不仅远低于日本和美国等发达国家，还低于韩国和巴西等新兴市场国家。

当前，我国证券市场发展与开放的经济环境持续稳健、制度环境日臻完善。一方面，国内经济保持总体平稳、稳中向好的运行态势，经济增速在世界范围内相对较快，主权信用良好，汇率相对稳定，为证券市场良性发展奠定了基础。而且，我国债券市场的整体收益水平依然高于主要发达市场，股票市场也具有发展潜力。另一方面，我国证券市场的金融服务更加完备，境外投资者投资的自由度和便利化程度不断提高。如2018年境外投资者净买入境内债券和股票合计1 392亿美元，较2017年增长73%。其中，买入8 977亿美元，增长51%；卖出7 585亿美元，增长48%，说明境外投资者投资境内的资金汇出入都十分通畅。

2019年，外汇管理部门将认真贯彻落实党中央、国务院决策部署，坚持稳中求进的工作总基调，坚持以供给侧结构性改革为主线，坚持深化市场化改革，扩大高水平开放，深化"放管服"改革，落实好"六个稳"要求，深入推进外汇领域改革开放，继续打好三大攻坚战，积极服务实体经济持续健康发展。

一方面，深化外汇管理改革，推动金融市场双向开放，服务国家全面开放新格局。促进跨境贸易和投资便利化，适应我国经济和金融市场对外开放需要，进一步优化支持贸易方式创新的外汇管理政策；优化金融服务和营商环境，促进外商来华直接投资稳定增长，积极支持国内有能力、有条件的企业开展真实合规的对外投资；稳妥有序推进资本项目可兑换，推进境内股票、债券市场开放；建立健全开放的、有竞争力的外汇市场，增加外汇市场深度，扩大交易主体，丰富交易工具，拓展交易范围，推动市场开放，满足不同主体的避险需求；积极支持自贸试验区、粤港澳大湾区、雄安新区在外汇管理改革方面先行先试，支持海南全面深化改革开放。

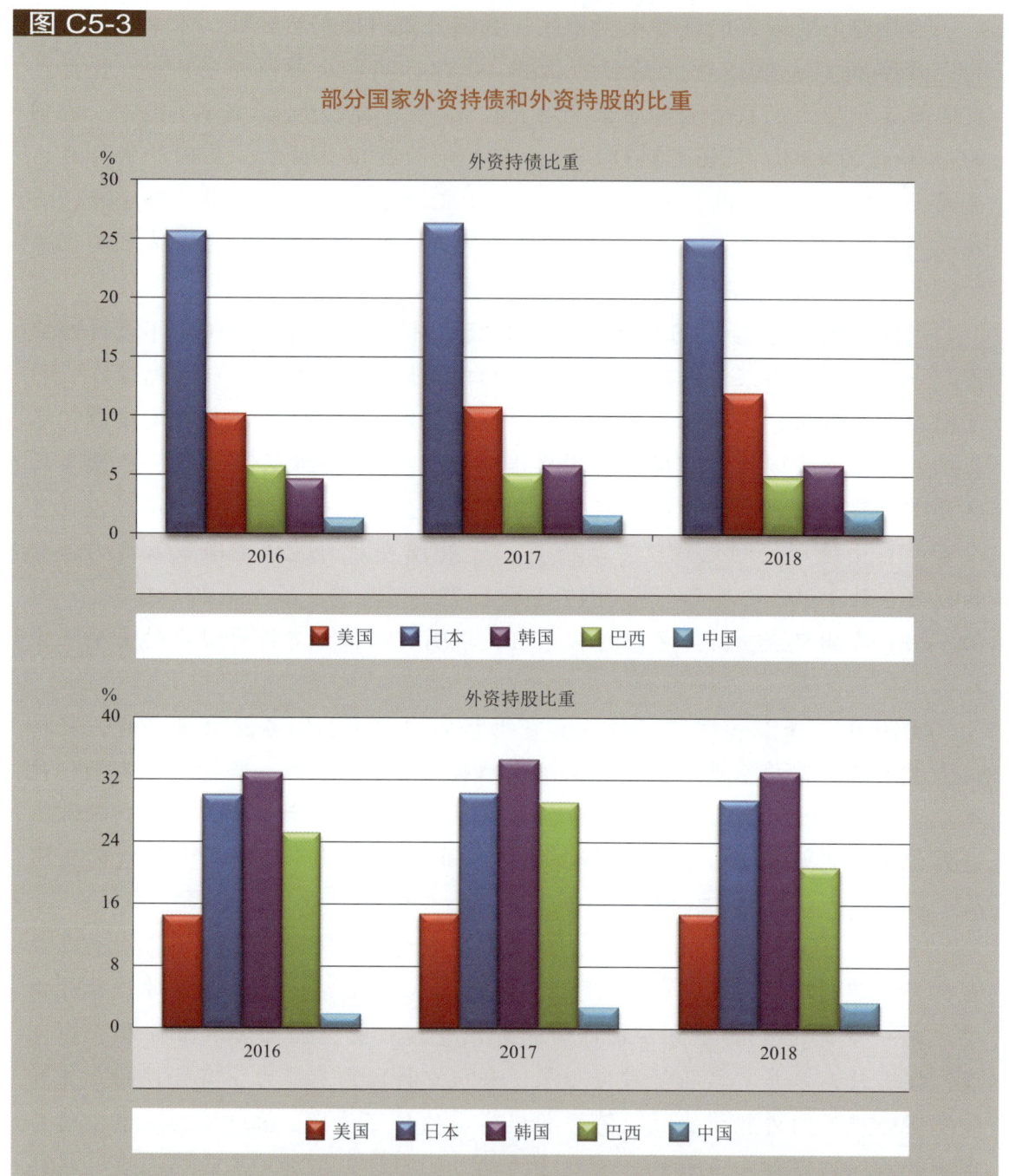

图 C5-3

部分国家外资持债和外资持股的比重

外资持债比重

外资持股比重

数据来源：彭博资讯、环亚数据库、国际清算银行、美国财政部、美联储、日本财务省、日本央行、东京证券交易所、中国人民银行、国家外汇管理局、上海证券交易所、深圳证券交易所、外汇局工作人员计算。

注：日本的2018年末外资持股金额使用2018年末IIP的负债方的股权证券项目；日本、韩国、巴西的2018年末外资持债比重采用第三季度末的数据代替，其中，日本外资持债金额为IIP的负债方的债务证券项目。

     另一方面，坚持底线思维，维护外汇市场稳定，防范跨境资本流动风险，保障外汇储备安全、流动、保值增值，维护国家经济金融安全。继续完善汇率

形成机制，保持人民币汇率在合理均衡水平上的基本稳定。健全跨境资本流动
"宏观审慎＋微观监管"两位一体的管理框架，完善跨境资本流动宏观审慎管
理的监测、预警和响应机制，丰富跨境资本流动宏观审慎管理的政策工具，以
市场化方式逆周期调节跨境资金流动；保持外汇微观监管跨周期的稳定性、一
致性和可预期性，严厉打击外汇违法违规活动。

I. Overview of the Balance of Payments

(Ⅰ) The Balance of Payments Environment

During 2018, China's balance of payments experienced more complicated and changing internal and external environments. There was a continuous decline in the growth of the global economy but were more uncertain factors, and the growth rate has slowed down. In general, the domestic economy progressed steadily, forming a solid foundation for the balance of payments.

Recovery of the global economy slowed down somewhat. In 2018 disparities emerged between the advanced and the developing economies. We have already witnessed a slowdown of U. S. growth in Q3 and Q4, with a drop in the unemployment rate. Growth also apparently dropped in the Euro zone, where Germany's GDP during Q3 declined by 0.2 percent— the first contraction since 2015. Inflation remained mild. As for Japan, economic growth continued to decline, and negative GDP growth occurred in both Q1 and Q3, with a modest inflation rate. Due to the influence of the Brexit, economic development in the UK also moved slowly. GDP growth in Q1 reached its lowest point in six years. Performance in the emerging markets continued to vary, but in general it was stable as the markets were recovering from the financial crisis. Some of the developing countries, however, were dragged down by the turbulence in the financial markets and by high unemployment. (See Chart 1−1)

Global monetary policies continued to diverge. The Federal Reserve raised its interest rates on four occasions, from 1.25 percent–1.50 percent to 2.25 percent–2.50 percent. In the meantime, the Federal Reserve continued with its plans to shrink the size of the balance sheet. The European Central Bank maintained its interest rates and announced that interest rates would remain unchanged until the summer of 2019. The European Central Bank also gradually cut monthly purchases of assets and it decided to end all such purchases by the end of 2018. The Bank of Japan continued with its extremely low interest rate and maintained the same size of its asset purchases. At its meeting on August 2, 2018, the Bank of England raised the Basic Rates by 25 basis points, and continued with this rate and with the size of its assets purchases. However, monetary policies in the emerging market economics diverged, as many turned to rising rates or more neutral policies against the backdrop of a tightening financial environment and depreciating pressures. The central banks of Russia, India, Turkey, Argentina, Mexico, and so forth all implemented hawkish monetary policies in order to counteract problems such as depreciation, capital outflows, and inflation. In contrast, central banks, in Korea and Brazil for example, maintained relatively loose monetary policies.

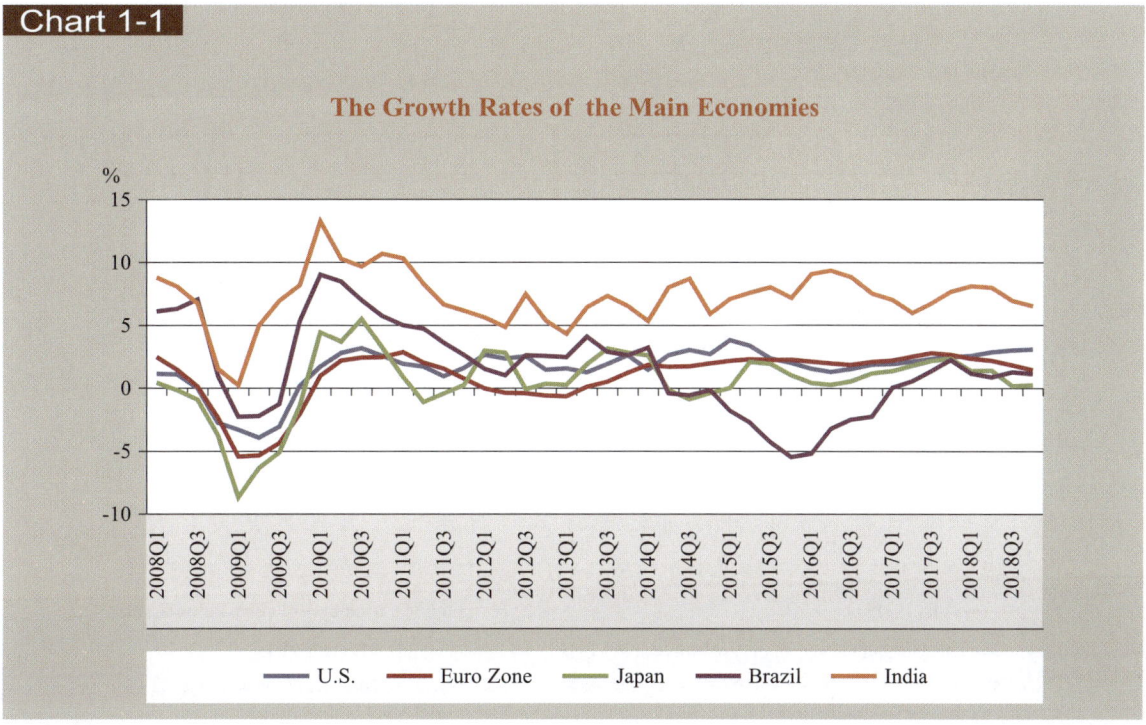

Chart 1-1

The Growth Rates of the Main Economies

Note: The U. S. growth rate is the annualized quarterly growth, whereas the rates of the other economies are the quarterly growth rates year on year.
Source: CEIC.

Volatility in global financial markets increased. In 2018, affected by trade frictions, Fed rate hiking and possible slowdown in global economic growth, there were increased disturbances in the international financial market. The DXY Index surged by 4.4 percent since the end of 2017, while both the Euro and the British Pound depreciated. The stock markets of the main economies dropped, with the Dow Jones Index and the STOXX 50 decreasing by 6.0 percent and 14.0 percent respectively. Financial markets in the emerging markets suffered from serious turbulence due to internal and external factors. Some currencies depreciated greatly, leading to simultaneous falls in the foreign−exchange market, the debt market, and the stock market. The Emerging Markets Currency Index collected by JP Morgan and the MSCI Index fell by more than 10 percent and 16 percent respectively in 2018. As for commodities, the international commodity market remained weak during 2018, indicated by a 15.4 percent drop in the S&P GSCI Commodity Price Index（See Charts 1−2, 1−3）.

Chart 1-2

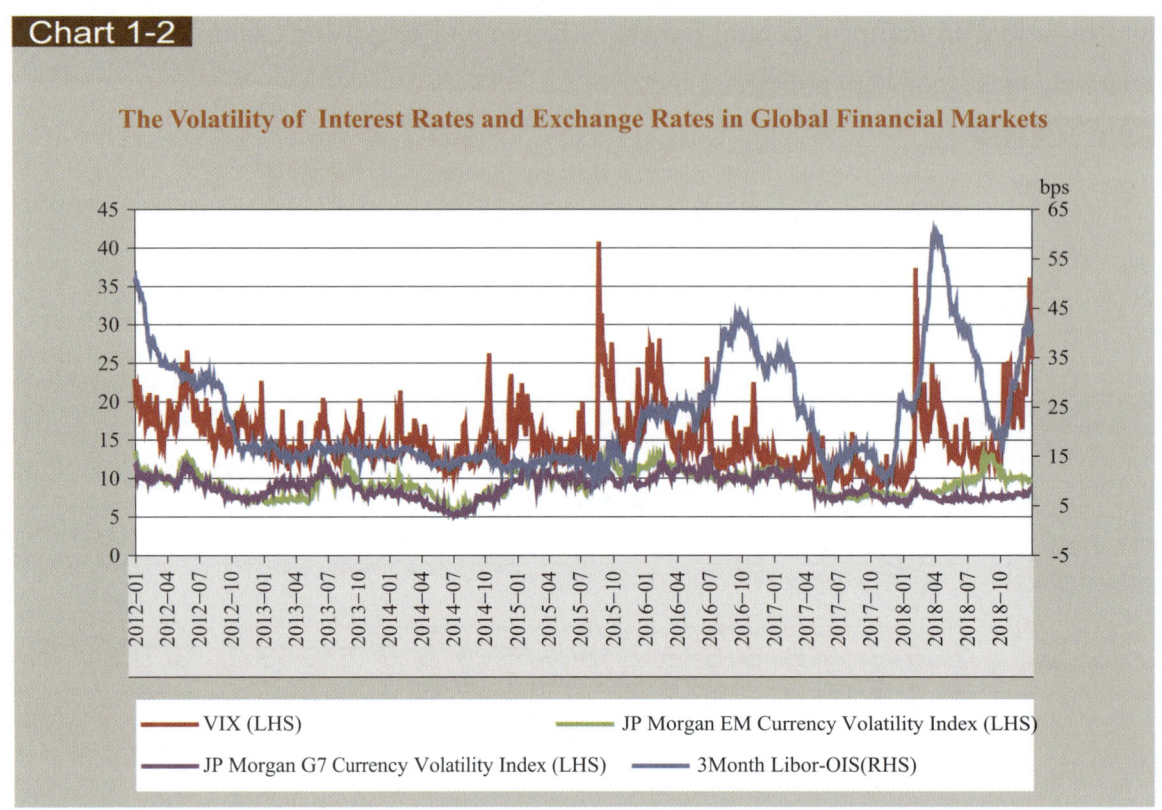

The Volatility of Interest Rates and Exchange Rates in Global Financial Markets

VIX (LHS)   JP Morgan EM Currency Volatility Index (LHS)

JP Morgan G7 Currency Volatility Index (LHS)   3Month Libor-OIS(RHS)

Source: Bloomberg.

The domestic economy remained stable. In 2018 the Chinese economy remained generally stable, but with a continuing amelioration in the economic structure. Chinaʼs GDP reached 90 trillion RMB, an increase of 6.6 percent compared to the last year. The CPI increased by 2.1 percent (See Chart 1-4). Industrial and services production remained stable. The economic structures were constantly being enhanced. Consumption contributed more to economic growth, with particularly strong growth of online retail businesses. However, although the economy was generally stabilized, there were certain concerns worth noting: the internal motivation for economic growth remained relatively weak and the structural conflicts in the economy were still quite prominent and the task of economic restructuring and reform still has a long way to go.

Chart 1-3

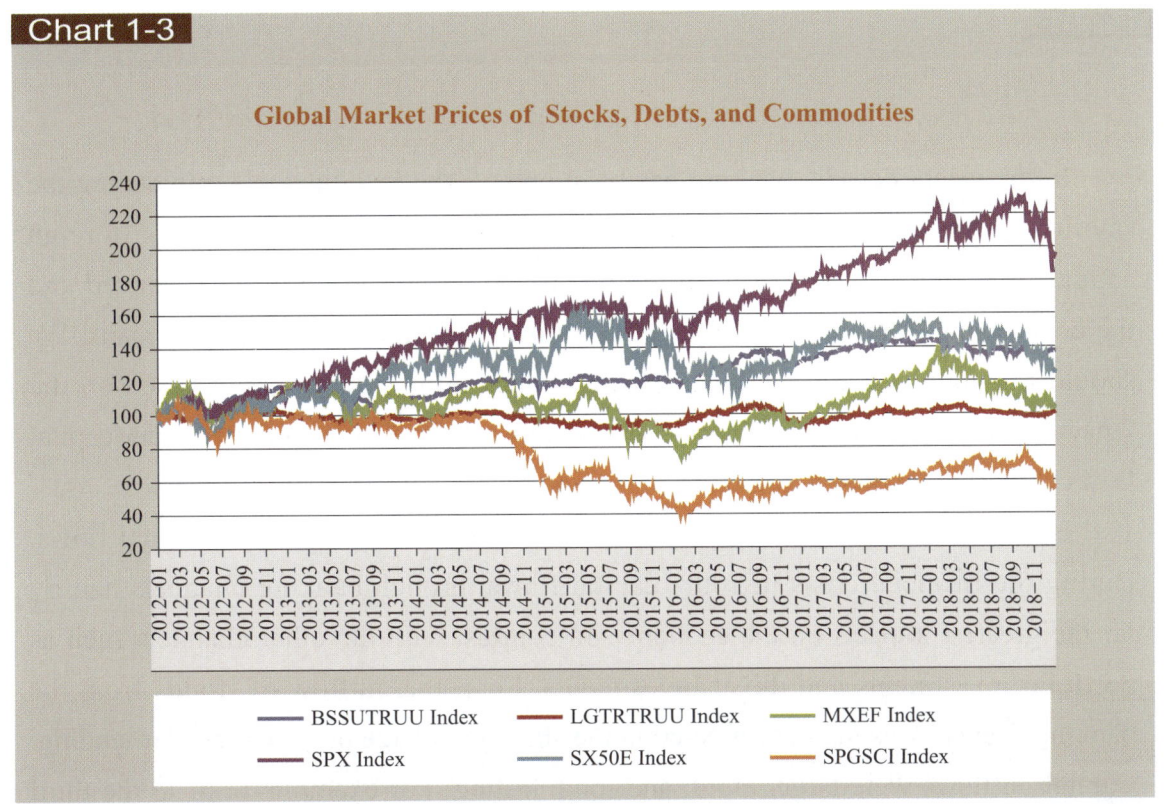

Global Market Prices of Stocks, Debts, and Commodities

Note: The BSSUTRUU and LGTRTRUU are the Bloomberg Barclays Global Aggregate Bond Index, the Bloomberg Barclay Emerging Market Index, and the developed countries' Sovereign Securities Index respectively. The MXEF and MSCI are equity indexes for the emerging markets. The SPX is the U. S. S&P 500 Stock Index. The SX50E is the Euro zone STOXX 50 Stock Index. The SPGSCI is the S&P GSCI Commodity Price Index. All use (2012=100) as a benchmark.

Source: Bloomberg.

Chart 1-4

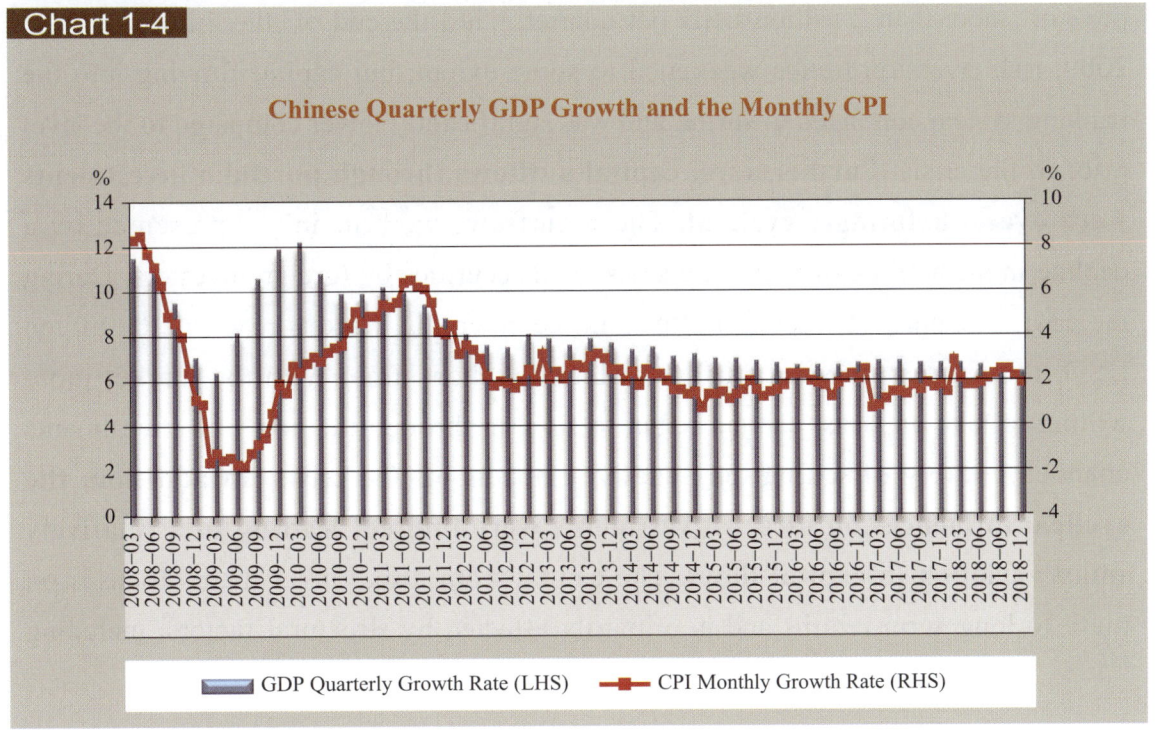

Chinese Quarterly GDP Growth and the Monthly CPI

Source: National Bureau of Statistics.

Box 1

Features and Implications of Cross-border Capital Flows

In the recent decade, banking has been one of the key channels influencing the stability of cross-border capital flows. When there were external shocks, foreign capital flew outwards primarily through banking system in both the advanced and the developing economies, mainly in the form of shrinking cross-border loans. We should maintain a stable banking system and monitor external risks based on the "macro-prudential + micro-supervision" framework for China's cross-border capital flows. This will be helpful to secure our economy and our financial markets.

Banking is of great importance for the stability of cross-border capital flows. During the financial crisis in 2008, capital flows through banking channels had by far the greatest impacts on the economy. In contrast with the other channels such as portfolio investments and direct investments. First, the outflow of funds from the banking channel was mainly reflected in the sharp shrinkage of cross-border lending. Capital outflows were large, rapid, and long-lasting. For example, prior to the third quarter of 2008, inflows through banking channels in the advanced countries were always more than 1 trillion USD every quarter. After the bank ruptcy of Lehman Brothers, there was a sharp outflow of capital through the banking system, with a peak of more than 2 trillion USD per quarter. Until the end of the third quarter of 2009, risk-aversion trends weakened to some extent, but capital flowing into the banking system continued to shrink and was significantly lower compared to the level prior to the crisis. **Furthermore, capital outflows through portfolio investments were over whelmingly cyclical.** These outflows were mainly represented by a decline in the holding of domestic stocks and securities by foreign investors. During the crisis, the peak of capital outflows in the emerging markets reached 100 billion USD, though this only lasted for a relatively short time. With the market more willing to take on risks, capital began to flow in through the portfolio investments channel, entirely offsetting the negative impacts of the crisis. **In addition, the cyclical influences on direct investments were limited, leading to a relatively small variation in capital flows.** The capital from direct investments focuses on mid- to long-term returns and is primarily affected by structural factors, including competitiveness, industrial chains, the taxation system, and the geographical location. In generally, cyclicality has little impact on these factors (See Chart C1-1, C1-2).

Chart C1-1

Capital Inflows in the Advanced Countries

Chart C1-2

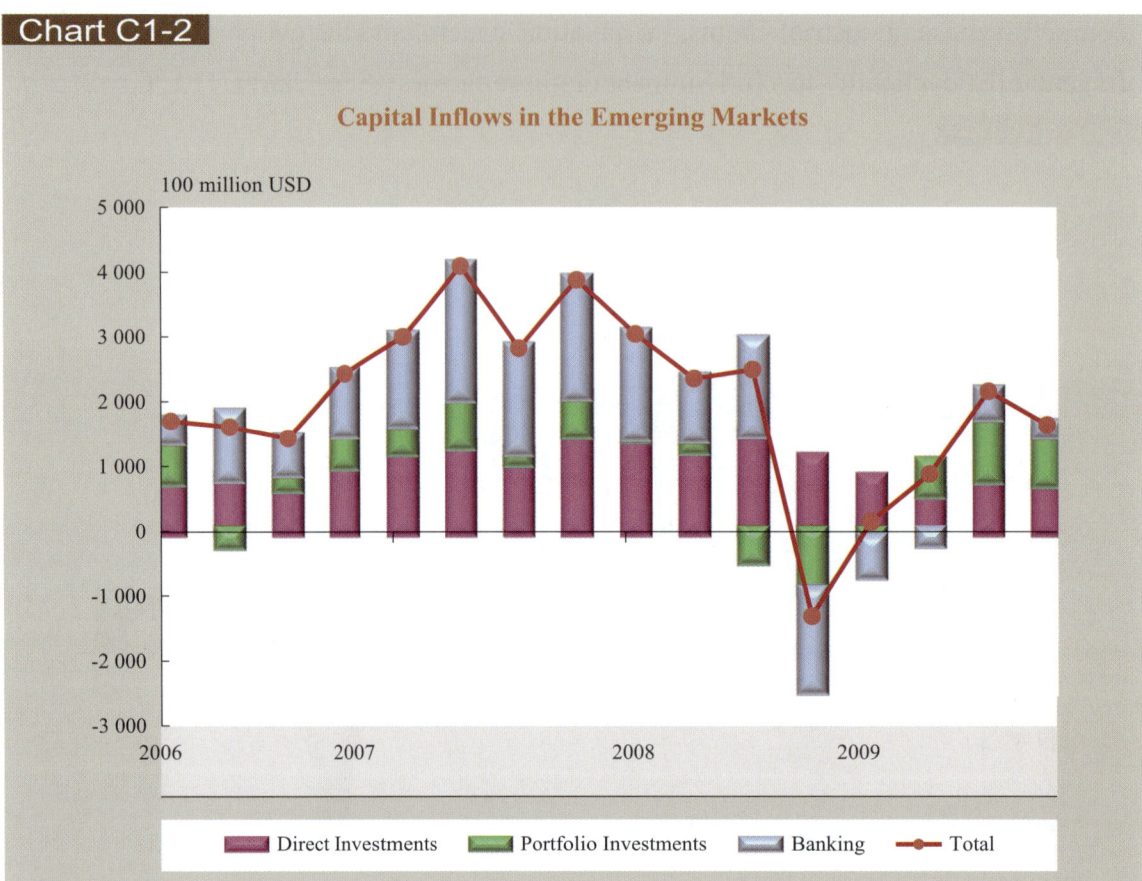

Capital Inflows in the Emerging Markets

Note: Organized according to each country's quarterly balance of payments.(1) China is not included in the data for the emerging markets.
Source: IMF.

As capital continued to flow out through the banking channel, the effects of portfolio investments and direct investments differed between the advanced countries and the emerging markets. Capital inflows in portfolio investments recovered faster in the developed countries, partly offsetting outflows in the banking sector. However, in the emerging markets, quarterly inflows of capital from direct investments averaged 100 billion USD, constituting a more important buffer for cross-border capital flows.

In the emerging markets, the self-reinforcing behavior by banks and enterprises intensified the shortage of USD, leading to a chain reaction. Take

---

① The data on the chart only consider capital inflows from foreign entities and not domestic investors' overseas investments. Negative numbers represent the withdrawal of funds from foreign markets. The funds for the advanced countries and the emerging markets are the sums of the individual countries without offsetting. Portfolio investments do not include derivatives investments or bank-related investments. The banking channel is marked as other investments, subtracting trade loans and changes in government funds while adding changes in the banks' investments in stocks and securities.

Korea as an example; before the financial crisis of 2008, dollar debt of domestic debts far exceeded the dollar assets necessitating the borrowing of dollars when the debts matured. However, import and export enterprises were unilaterally bullish regarding the Korean Won while holding a lot of US dollar loans. It was common for mid and small−sized corporations to generally use foreign−exchange derivatives to bet on the appreciation of the Korean Won against the US dollar and also to accumulate a large amount of US dollar debt. During the crisis, global risk aversion intensified, dollar financing costs surged, cross−border lending shrunk, and domestic inter−bank markets were extremely short of dollars. Banks ended loans to corporations, so corporations could only get dollars from selling assets, intensifying the drop in domestic assets and in the exchange rates. This in turn led to a further sell out of Korean stocks and securities by foreign investors. As a result, the real effective exchange rate of the Korean Won once dropped by nearly 40 percent.

Ever since 2010 the banking system has been the most essential channel for cross-border capital flows. In 2015, when there were enormous pressures on capital outflows in the emerging markets, there was an outflow of funds through the banking and securities channels. During this period, outflows through the banking channel were the most obvious, peaking at 80 billion USD per quarter. In the meantime, capital inflows via direct investments remained stable, buffering the capital outflows.

At present, Chinese cross-border capital flows exist under a "macro-prudential + micro-supervision" framework, with the banking channels playing an important role inmacro-prudential management. As revealed through historical experience, it is beneficial to maintain a secure financial and economic system by strengthening the banking system and monitoring external risks. On the one hand, maintaining a steady banking system and safeguarding the liquidity of foreign currencies in the banking sectors establish a buffer for exterior shocks and secure stable capital flows. On the other hand, when applying for a counter−cyclical adjustment of cross−border capital flows, we should pay more attention to external risks, such as the ratio of exchange−rate hedging and the leveraging of foreign exchange, so as to prevent the expansion of foreign−exchange holdings by banks and corporations and the intensification of external shocks. Meanwhile, we should also guide corporations to utilize foreign−exchange derivatives and prevent a hike in recessive leveraging and abnormal cross−border capital flows.

(II) The Main Characteristics of the Balance of Payments

The current account maintained a basic balance and the non-reserve financial account retained a surplus. In 2018 the current account recorded a surplus of USD 49.1 billion, and the non−reserve financial account posted a surplus of USD 130.6 billion (see Table 1−1).

Table 1−1   Structure of the BOP Surplus   Unit: 100 million USD

Item	2013	2014	2015	2016	2017	2018
Current Account Balance	1 482	2 360	3 042	2 022	1 951	491
As a % of GDP	1.5%	2.3%	2.7%	1.8%	1.6%	0.4%
Capital and financial account balance	3 430	−514	−4 345	−4 161	1 095	1 306
As a % of GDP	3.6%	−0.5%	−3.9%	−3.7%	0.9%	1.0%

Sources: SAFE, NBS.

The balance for trade in goods improved. Based on balance−of−payments statistics,[①] in 2018 exports and imports of trade in goods totaled USD 2 417.4 billion and USD 2 022.3 billion respectively, up 9 percent and 16 percent, and achieving a surplus of USD 395.2 billion, down 17 percent (see Chart 1−5).

The deficit in trade in services grew steadily. In 2018 revenue from trade in services totaled USD 233.6 billion, up 10 percent, and expenditures totaled USD 525.8 billion, up 11 percent. Trade in services thus recorded a deficit of USD 292.2 billion, up13 percent (see Chart 1−5). In particular, the transportation deficit totaled USD 66.9 billion, up 20 percent, and the travel deficit totaled USD 237 billion, up 8 percent.

---

①   The BOP statistics and the statistics of the General Administration of Customs with respect to trade in goods can be reconciled by the following: First, imports based on the BOP statistics only record goods with ownership transferred (such as general trade and feeding process trade). Goods that don't change ownership (including trade of processing with customers' or domestic materials) will be noted in trade in services. Second, the BOP statistics use offshore prices for both exports and imports, while the custom uses offshore prices for exports but onshore prices for imports. Therefore, BOP statistics extracts fees of transports and insurances from the custom's imports and relocates them under trade in services. Third, BOP adds part of exports and imports shipment returns. Fourth, BOP also adds net exports of goods from regrating missed by the custom.

Chart 1-5

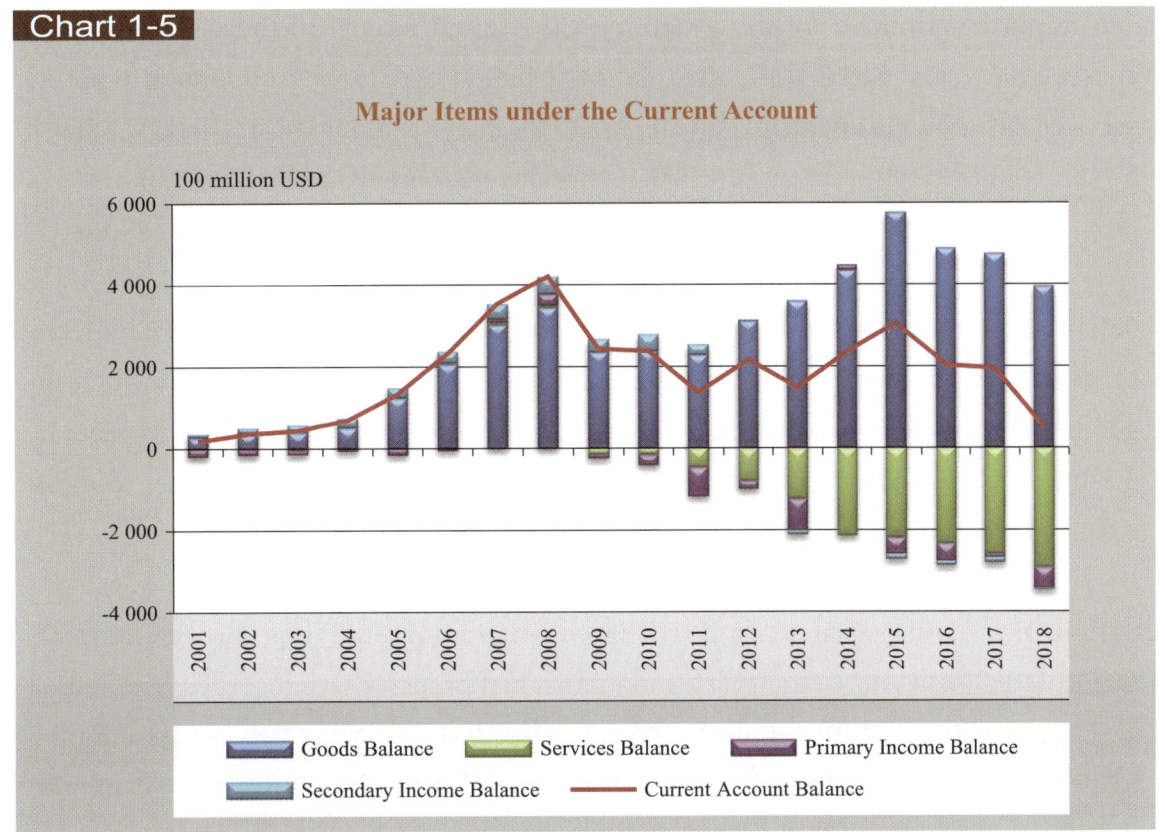

Major Items under the Current Account

100 million USD

Legend: Goods Balance Services Balance Primary Income Balance Secondary Income Balance Current Account Balance

Source: SAFE.

Box 2

Improving the Competitiveness of China's Services Industry and Optimizing the Revenue and Expenditure Structure for Trade in Services

In the year 2000, China's trade in services began to develop rapidly. For five consecutive years, exports and imports of China's trade in services were ranked as the world's second largest. As national income increased, travel spending rose sharply, yet domestic high value–added services still had to be developed. The deficit in trade in services has exceeded USD 200 billion since 2014, and it reached USD 292.2 billion in 2018. Currently, as trade in services has become more important in the global trade system, it will be important to maintain a balanced BOP situation by enhancing the competitiveness of China's services industries and optimizing the structure of trade in services.

I. Current developments in China's trade in services

China's trade in services to GDP continued to increase. The total of exports and imports continued to grow, ranking the second largest in the world for five consecutive years. Since 2001, the total of China's exports and imports in trade in services has grown 14 percent annually. In 2018, the total amount came to USD 759.4 billion, up 11 percent year on year. The imports were more than twice the exports.

Trade in services plays an important role in China's balance of payments. According to the statistics of the International Monetary Fund in 2017, China's deficit in trade in services ranked the largest in the world, accounting for 38 percent of the overall deficit of all economies. In recent years, China's surplus in trade in goods has narrowed, and the deficit in trade in services grown at a declining pace. In the future, if the deficit in trade in services remains stable or even declines, a more balanced BOP situation will be achieved.

Travel, transport, and intellectual property fees were the main sources of the deficit in trade in services. In 2018, travel (including studying abroad, tourism, medical treatment, etc.) , transport, and intellectual property fees recorded a deficit of USD 237 billion, USD 66.9 billion, and USD 30.2 billion respectively, accounting for 81 percent, 23 percent, and 10 percent of the total deficit. Take travel as an example; As the economy developed and national income increased, travel expenditures grew rapidly and at a pace significantly higher than that of travel revenue. As a result, China's travel expenditures reached USD 277.3 billion in 2018. The ratio of the expenditures to GDP increased from 1.3 percent in 2013 to 2 percent in 2018. This growth pattern was similar to that in Japan in the 1990s, when demand for a better life as well as an essential stage for an economic opening drove up travel expenditures. Currently, the growth rates for travel revenue, expenditures, and deficit have slowed down. For instance, in 2018 the deficit grew at 8 percent, whereas it grew at 12 percent in 2015. The proportion of travel revenue and expenditures for trade in services tends to be stable, a phenomenon similar to that in Japan, when Japanese's travel expenditures remained stable after a period of a sharp increase driven by the rapid development of the service industry.

II. Key areas to enhance the competitiveness of China's services industries

There is a great potential to develop high value–added services such as tourism and education. In 2017, the top five largest trade–in–services surplus economies held advantages mainly in the field of high value—added industries, such as tourism, education, and financial services. Due to upgrades in domestic consumption, Chinese demands for outbound travel, studying abroad, and medical treatment have increased significantly. In 2018, there were 150 million outbound tourists and 140 million inbound tourists.[①] Despite the small difference between the number of outbound and inbound tourists, the difference between the consumption of outbound travel and that of inbound travel was quite large. This indicates that high value—added industries, such as inbound tours, have a great potential and China needs to export more high value—added services instead of low value—added services. To achieve more balanced travel, China should optimize the structure of tourism products and enhance the quality of domestic tourism products.

The potential to upgrades traditional services such as transport is enormous. Competition in the international transportation industry is fierce and market concentration is high. Among the top five largest shipping companies. Which account for approximately 70 percent of market shares, there is only one Chinese shipping company, which holds about 10 percent of global market shares. Due to the relatively rapid growth in import goods, China's transport imports have continued to grow. In 2018, imports reached USD 109.2 billion and exports totaled USD 42.3 billion. The large imports were mainly because the carriers were usually foreign shipping companies and China's transport companies held limited shares. As China's trade in goods totaled approximately USD 4 trillion in 2017, accounting for more than 20 percent of global trade, China has to make full use of its advantage as a large foreign—trade economy by enhancing the complementary relationship between transport and trade, strengthening the close cooperation between shipping companies and cargo owners, expanding the transport—services network, and making greater contribution to Chinese foreign trade.

There is still more room for the export of technology products. In 2018 exports and imports of the fees for the use of intellectual property were USD 5.6 billion and USD 35.8 billion respectively, a year—on—year increase of USD 800 million and USD 7 billion, respectively Combined with China's division of labor in the global industrial chain, China's technology imports are mainly concentrated in the communications and automobile industries. China had a late start in developing

---

① Source: Official website of the Ministry of Culture and Tourism of the People's Republic of China.

its technology products. At the early stage, the introduction of high-tech products helped to promote production and management, but more time was needed to develop dividends from technology exports. Overtime, the overall technical level of Chinese enterprises has been constantly improving. In 2018 the ratio of China's R&D spending to GDP reached 2.18 percent. Relying on big data, the Internet of things, cloud computing, and other new technologies, Chinese enterprises can boost their core competitiveness by establishing an independent technology-cultivation system, strength eningin dependent innovative technology products, and reducing its external dependence. To promote the trade industry, science and technology will be an important factor to implement supply-side structural reforms and to promote high-quality development of the economy.

Trade in services plays an increasingly prominent role in the global economy and occupies an important position in the global value chain system. Further promoting the opening and development of China's services industries, optimizing the allocation of resources, improving the operating efficiency as well as the quality of services, and enhancing international competitiveness will not only help China adapt to the new pattern of opening up to the outside world but will also reinforce the goal of implementing supply-side structural reforms.

Primary income recorded a deficit.[①] In 2018 revenue from primary income totaled USD 234.8 billion, down 18 percent, and expenditures totaled USD 286.2 billion, down 4 percent. The deficit in primary income totaled USD 51.4 billion. In particular, the surplus in employee compensation was USD 8.2 billion, while investment income recorded a deficit of USD 61.4 billion (see Chart 1-5). Revenue from outward investments totaled USD 214.6 billion, and expenditures for inward investments, including the profits and dividends of foreign-funded enterprises, totaled USD 276 billion.

The deficit in secondary income narrowed. In 2018 the revenue and expenditures of secondary income totaled USD 27.8 billion and USD 30.2 billion respectively, down 1 percent and 25 percent. The deficit in secondary income amounted to USD 2.4 billion, down 80 percent (see Chart 1-5).

The surplus in direct investments increased. Based on balance-of-payments

---

① The IMF's *Balance of Payments and International Investment Manual* (6th edition) renamed the income item under the current account as primary income and renamed current transfers as secondary income.

statistics,①in 2018 direct investments posted a surplus of USD 107 billion, up 2.9 times (see Chart 1-6).In particular, net outflows of outward direct investments (the net increase indirect-investment assets) amounted to USD 96.5 billion, down 30 percent. Net inflows of foreign direct investments (the net increase in direct-investment liabilities) totaled USD 203.5 billion, up 23 percent.

The surplus in portfolio investments rose significantly. In 2018 portfolio investments recorded a surplus of USD 106.7 billion, up 2.6 times (see Chart 1-6).In particular, net outflows of outward portfolio investments (the net increase in assets) totaled USD 53.5 billion, down 44 percent, and net inflows of inward portfolio investments (the net increase in liabilities) totaled USD 160.2 billion, up 29 percent.

There was a deficit in other investments. In 2018 other investments, including loans, trade credits, and deposits, posted a deficit of USD 77 billion, whereas in 2017 they had recorded a surplus of USD 51.9 billion (see Chart 1-6).In particular, net outflows of outward other investments (the net increase in assets) totaled USD 198.4 billion, up 97 percent, and the net inflows of inward other investments (the net increase in liabilities) totaled USD 121.4 billion, down 21 percent.

---

① The BOP compiles and reports direct investments following balance-sheet rules, whereas the Ministry of Commerce compiles and reports direct investments by direction, and there are differences between the principles for reverse investments and investments among affiliates. In addition, direct investments based on BOP statistics also include unpaid and unremitted profits, retained earnings, shareholder loans, foreign capital utilized by financial institutions, and real-estate purchases by non-residents.

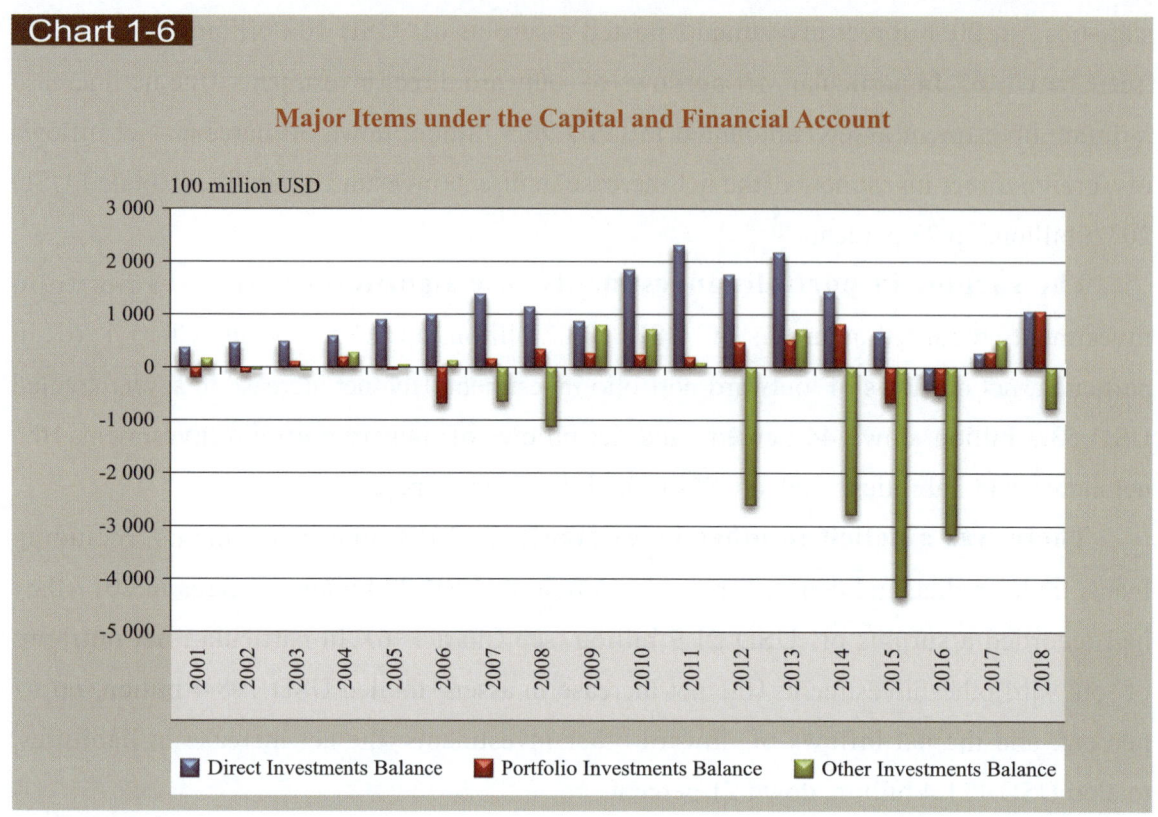

Chart 1-6

Major Items under the Capital and Financial Account

Source: SAFE.

Reserve assets remained basically stable. In 2018 reserve assets involving transactions (excluding the effects of non-transactional values, such as the exchange rates and prices) increased by USD 18.9 billion. In particular, foreign currency reserves involving transactions increased by USD 18.2 billion (see Chart 1-7). By the end of 2018, China's foreign currency reserves totaled USD 3 072.7 billion, down USD 67.2 billion since the end of 2017, mainly affected by the changes in non-transactional values such as the exchange rates and prices.

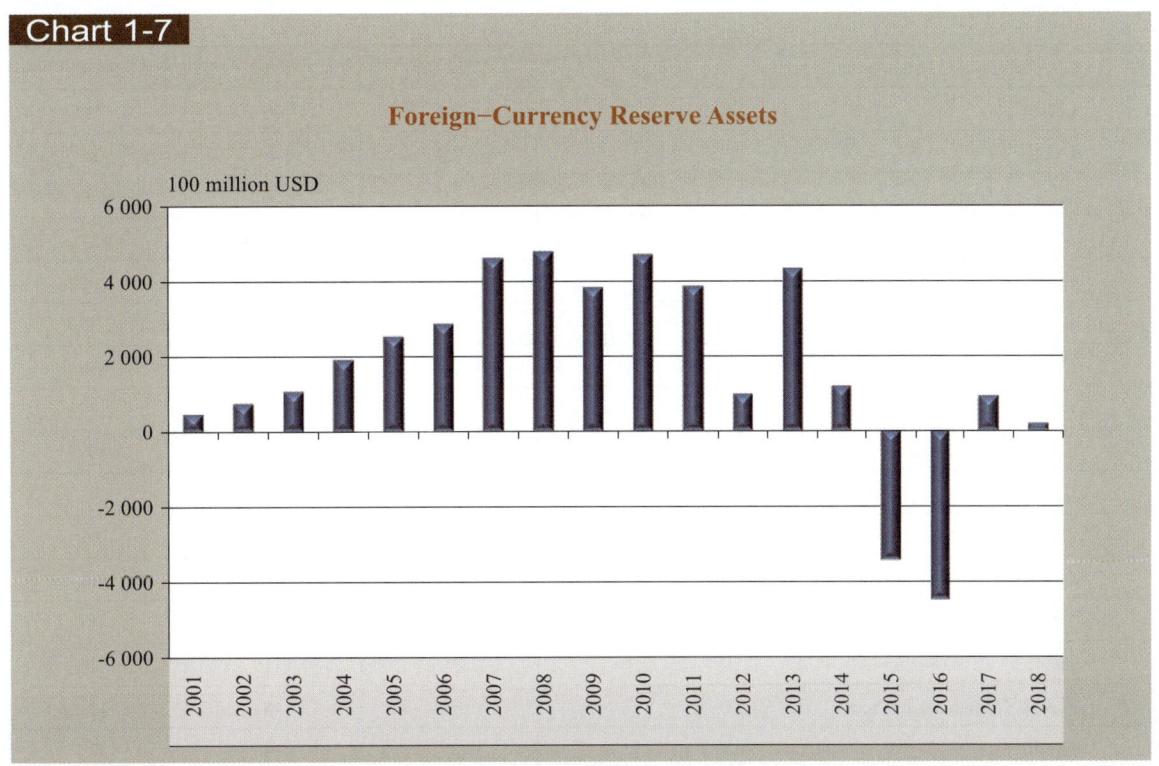

Chart 1-7

Foreign–Currency Reserve Assets

100 million USD

Source: SAFE.

Table 1-2   Balance of Payments in 2018

100 million USD

Item	Line No.	2017	2018
1. Current account	1	**1 951**	**491**
Credit	2	27 450	29 136
Debit	3	−25 499	−28 645
1. A Goods and services	4	**2 170**	**1 029**
Credit	5	24 293	26 510
Debit	6	−22 123	−25 481
1. A. a Goods	7	**4 759**	**3 952**
Credit	8	22 162	24 174
Debit	9	−17 403	−20 223
1. A. b Services	10	**−2 589**	**−2 922**
Credit	11	2 131	2 336
Debit	12	−4 720	−5 258
1. A. b.1 Manufacturing services on physical inputs owned by others	13	**179**	**172**
Credit	14	181	174
Debit	15	−2	−3
1. A. b.2 Maintenance and repair services n. i. e	16	**37**	**46**

(Continue)

Item	Line No.	2017	2018
Credit	17	60	72
Debit	18	−23	−25
1. A. b.3 Transport	19	**−560**	**−669**
Credit	20	373	423
Debit	21	−933	−1 092
1. A. b.4 Travel	22	**−2 193**	**−2 370**
Credit	23	386	404
Debit	24	−2 579	−2 773
1. A. b.5 Construction	25	**36**	**49**
Credit	26	123	136
Debit	27	−86	−86
1. A. b.6 Insurance and pension services	28	**−74**	**−66**
Credit	29	41	49
Debit	30	−115	−116
1. A. b.7 Financial services	31	**18**	**12**
Credit	32	34	33
Debit	33	−16	−21
1. A. b.8 Charges for the use of intellectual property	34	**−239**	**−302**
Credit	35	48	56
Debit	36	−287	−358
1. A. b.9 Telecommunications, computer, and information services	37	**75**	**65**
Credit	38	269	300
Debit	39	−194	−235
1. A. b.10 Other business services	40	**169**	**191**
Credit	41	593	662
Debit	42	−424	−470
1. A. b.11 Personal, cultural, and recreational services	43	**−20**	**−24**
Credit	44	8	10
Debit	45	−27	−34
1. A. b.12 Government goods and services n. i. e	46	**−18**	**−27**
Credit	47	17	18
Debit	48	−35	−45
1. B Primary income	49	**−100**	**−514**
Credit	50	2 876	2 348
Debit	51	−2 976	−2 862
1. B.1 Compensation of employees	52	**149**	**82**

(Continue)

Item	Line No.	2017	2018
Credit	53	217	181
Debit	54	−68	−99
1. B.2 Investment income	55	**−254**	**−614**
Credit	56	2 652	2 146
Debit	57	−2 906	−2 760
1. B.3 Other primary income	58	**4**	**18**
Credit	59	7	21
Debit	60	−3	−3
1. C Secondary income	61	**−119**	**−24**
Credit	62	282	278
Debit	63	−400	−302
1. C.1 Personal transfers	64	−25	−4
Credit	65	70	62
Debit	66	−95	−66
1. C.2 Other secondary income	67	−93	−20
Credit	68	212	216
Debit	69	−305	−236
2. Capital and financial account	70	**179**	**1 111**
2.1 Capital account	71	**−1**	**−6**
Credit	72	2	3
Debit	73	−3	−9
2.2 Financial account	74	**180**	**1 117**
Assets	75	−4 239	−3 721
Liabilities	76	4 419	4 838
2.2.1 Financial account excluding reserve assets	77	**1 095**	**1 306**
Financial assets excluding reserve assets	78	−3 324	−3 532
Liabilities	79	4 419	4 838
2.2.1.1 Direct investment	80	**278**	**1 070**
2.2.1.1.1 Assets	81	**−1 383**	**−965**
2.2.1.1.1.1 Equity and investment fund shares	82	−1 363	−790
2.2.1.1.1.2 Debt instruments	83	−20	−175
2.2.1.1.1. a Financial sector	84	−178	−208
2.2.1.1.1.1. a Equity and investment fund shares	85	−176	−200
2.2.1.1.1.2. a Debt instruments	86	−2	−8
2.2.1.1.1. b Non−financial sector	87	−1 205	−757
2.2.1.1.1.1. b Equity and investment fund shares	88	−1 186	−590

(Continue)

Item	Line No.	2017	2018
2.2.1.1.1.2. b Debt instruments	89	−18	−167
2.2.1.1.2 Liabilities	90	**1 661**	**2 035**
2.2.1.1.2.1 Equity and investment fund shares	91	1 406	1 544
2.2.1.1.2.2 Debt instruments	92	255	491
2.2.1.1.2. a Financial sector	93	121	176
2.2.1.1.2.1. a Equity and investment fund shares	94	90	149
2.2.1.1.2.2. a Debt instruments	95	32	26
2.2.1.1.2. b Non−financial sector	96	1 539	1 859
2.2.1.1.2.1. b Equity and investment fund shares	97	1 316	1 395
2.2.1.1.2.2. b Debt instruments	98	223	465
2.2.1.2 Portfolio investment	99	**295**	**1 067**
2.2.1.2.1 Assets	100	**−948**	**−535**
2.2.1.2.1.1 Equity and investment fund shares	101	−328	−177
2.2.1.2.1.2 Debt securities	102	−620	−358
2.2.1.2.2 Liabilities	103	**1 243**	**1 602**
2.2.1.2.2.1 Equity and investment fund shares	104	362	607
2.2.1.2.2.2 Debt securities	105	881	995
2.2.1.3 Financial derivatives (other than reserves) and employee stock options	106	**4**	**−62**
2.2.1.3.1 Assets	107	15	−48
2.2.1.3.2 Liabilities	108	−12	−13
2.2.1.4 Other investment	109	**519**	**−770**
2.2.1.4.1 Assets	110	**−1 008**	**−1 984**
2.2.1.4.1.1 Other equity	111	0	0
2.2.1.4.1.2 Currency and deposits	112	−571	−731
2.2.1.4.1.3 Loans	113	−435	−818
2.2.1.4.1.4 Insurance, pension, and standardized guarantee schemes	114	0	−6
2.2.1.4.1.5 Trade credit and advances	115	−194	−653
2.2.1.4.1.6 Other accounts receivable	116	191	224
2.2.1.4.2 Liabilities	117	**1 527**	**1 214**
2.2.1.4.2.1 Other equity	118	0	0
2.2.1.4.2.2 Currency and deposits	119	1 079	514
2.2.1.4.2.3 Loans	120	501	321
2.2.1.4.2.4 Insurance, pension, and standardized guarantee schemes	121	7	2
2.2.1.4.2.5 Trade credit and advances	122	−12	408

(Continue)

Item	Line No.	2017	2018
2.2.1.4.2.6 Other accounts payable	123	−47	−31
2.2.1.4.2.7 Special drawing rights	124	0	0
2.2.2 Reserve assets	125	**−915**	**−189**
2.2.2.1 Monetary gold	126	0	0
2.2.2.2 Special drawing rights	127	−7	0
2.2.2.3 Reserve position in the IMF	128	22	−7
2.2.2.4 Foreign exchange reserves	129	−930	−182
2.2.2.5 Other reserve assets	130	0	0
3. Net errors and omissions	131	**−2 130**	**−1 602**

Notes:

1. This table was compiled according to the *Balance of Payments and International Investment Manual* (6th edition) .

2. In the financial account, a positive value for assets indicates a net decrease, whereas a negative value indicates a net increase. A positive value for liabilities indicates a net increase, whereas a negative value indicates a net decrease.

3. The chart is based on rounding principles.

Source: SAFE.

(III) Evaluation of the Balance of Payments

China's balance of payments maintained a basic balance. The current account continued to be within a reasonable surplus range, with a surplus of USD 49.1 billion in 2018, which was 0.4 percent of GDP. The more balanced current account mainly reflects the transformation of the domestic manufacturing industry and the increase and upgrading of consumer demand, which also contribute significantly to rebalancing in the global economy. Against the background of a sharp depreciation in local currency and capital outflows in some emerging economies, China's non−reserve financial account recorded a surplus of USD 130.6 billion in 2018, showing a net inflow for the second consecutive year. Overall, although the external environment is complex and serious, the flexibility of the RMB exchange rate has increased, the ability of the BOP to self−balance has been further enhanced, and foreign−exchange reserve assets involving transactions have remained basically stable (see Chart 1−8) .

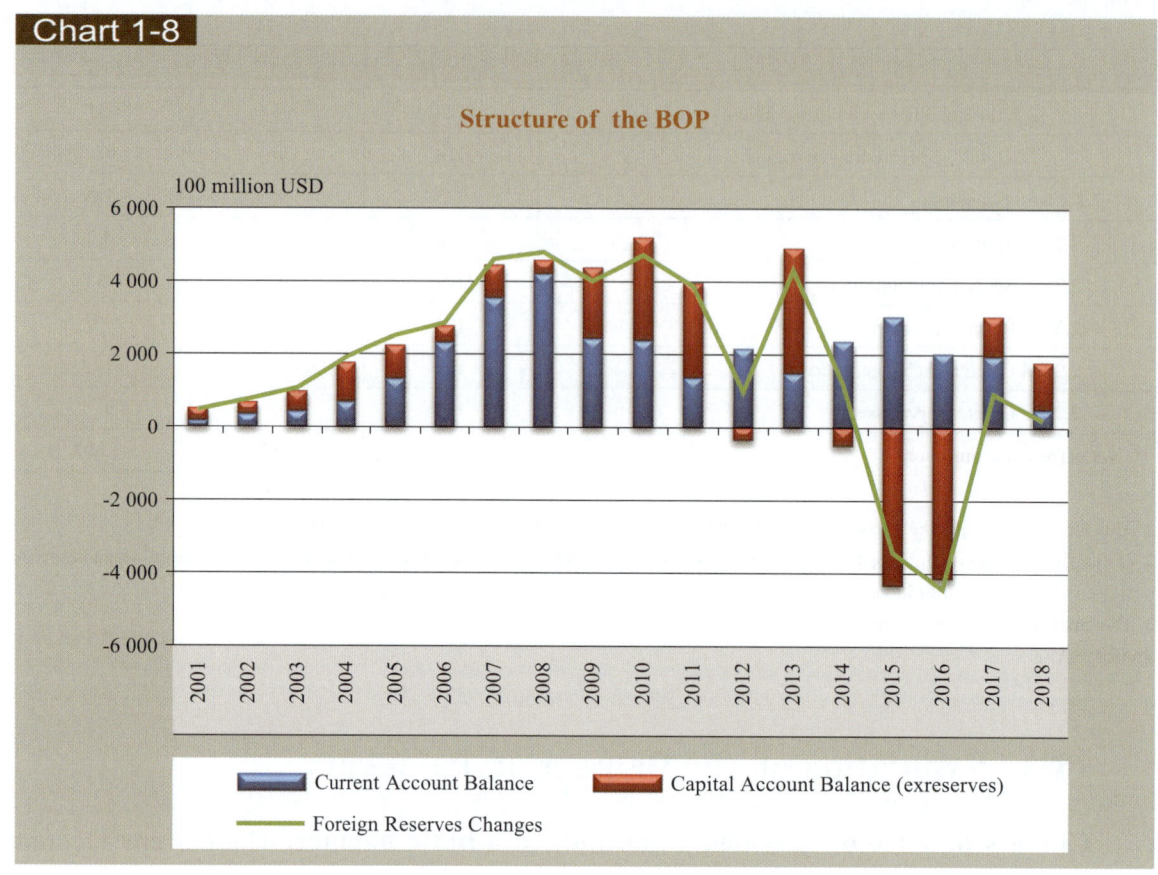

Chart 1-8

Structure of the BOP

Source: SAFE.

The current account was reasonable and stable. First, the structure of the main items under the current account was reasonable. The surplus of trade in goods and trade in services totaled USD 102.9 billion, and the ratio to GDP was 0.8 percent—the lowest level since 1994—showing that goods and services had reached a better balance. The deficit in primary income totaled USD 51.4 billion, and its ratio to GDP was –0.4 percent, which was the average level in the recent 10 years (see Chart 1–9). Second, the current account balance improved quarter by quarter. During the first quarter of 2018, the current account recorded a deficit of USD 34.1 billion, and the ratio to GDP was –1.1 percent. From the second to the fourth quarter, the current account turned to surpluses of USD 5.3billion, USD 23.3 billion, and USD 54.6 billion respectively, and the ratio to GDP rose to 0.2 percent, 0.7 percent, and 1.5 percent. At present, China's current account is in a relatively balanced range. Small surpluses or deficits during different periods fall well within the category of a basic balance.

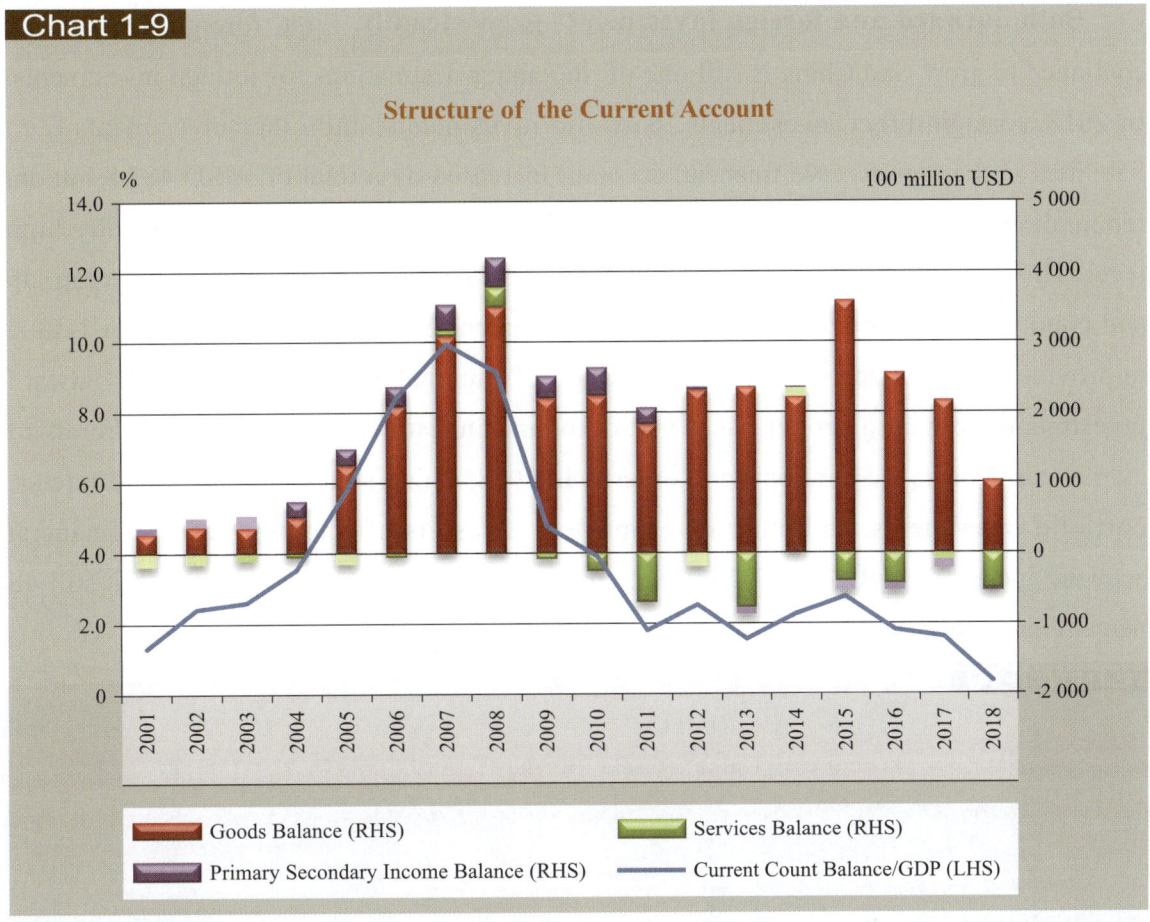

Chart 1-9

Structure of the Current Account

Goods Balance (RHS)
Services Balance (RHS)
Primary Secondary Income Balance (RHS)
Current Count Balance/GDP (LHS)

Sources: SAFE, NBS.

The structure of non-reserve financial accounts was further optimized. First, direct investments with mid and long−term characteristics are still relatively stable sources of a surplus. In 2018 the net inflow of direct investments based on the balance−of− payments statistics was USD 107 billion. Direct investments maintained surpluses for two consecutive years after the short deficit in 2016. Second, the effect of the opening up of the capital market was remarkable. In 2018 the net inflow of portfolio investments reached an all−time high of USD 106.7 billion, a large part of which came from investments by foreign central banks, and the demand for mid and long−term asset allocations was high. Third, other investments were more stable. In 2018, despite the complicated and serious external environment, other investments posted a deficit of only USD 77 billion, much lower than the annual level of USD 300 billion or USD 400 billion in 2015 and 2016, which showed that market players were becoming more rational in their cross−border financing.

Both outward and foreign investments grew steadily. First, foreign investments continued to grow, and China is still one of the major destinations for foreign investments. In 2018, foreign direct investments, portfolio investments, and other investments (i.e., liabilities in the non–reserve financial account) increased by a total of USD 483.8 billion, rebounding for the third consecutive year and the scale returning to a historically high level. This not only reflects the policy effects of promoting a high level of opening–up and continuously improving the business environment but also shows that China is able to provide sufficient space for fair competition of international capital. Second, outward investments grew at a proper pace, and outbound investments and asset allocations of market participants were rational and orderly. In 2018, China's outward direct investments, portfolio investments, and other investments (i.e., assets of the non–reserve financial account) increased by USD 353.2 billion, an increase of 6 percent over 2017, but still 48 percent lower than that in 2016 (see Chart 1–10).

Chart 1-10

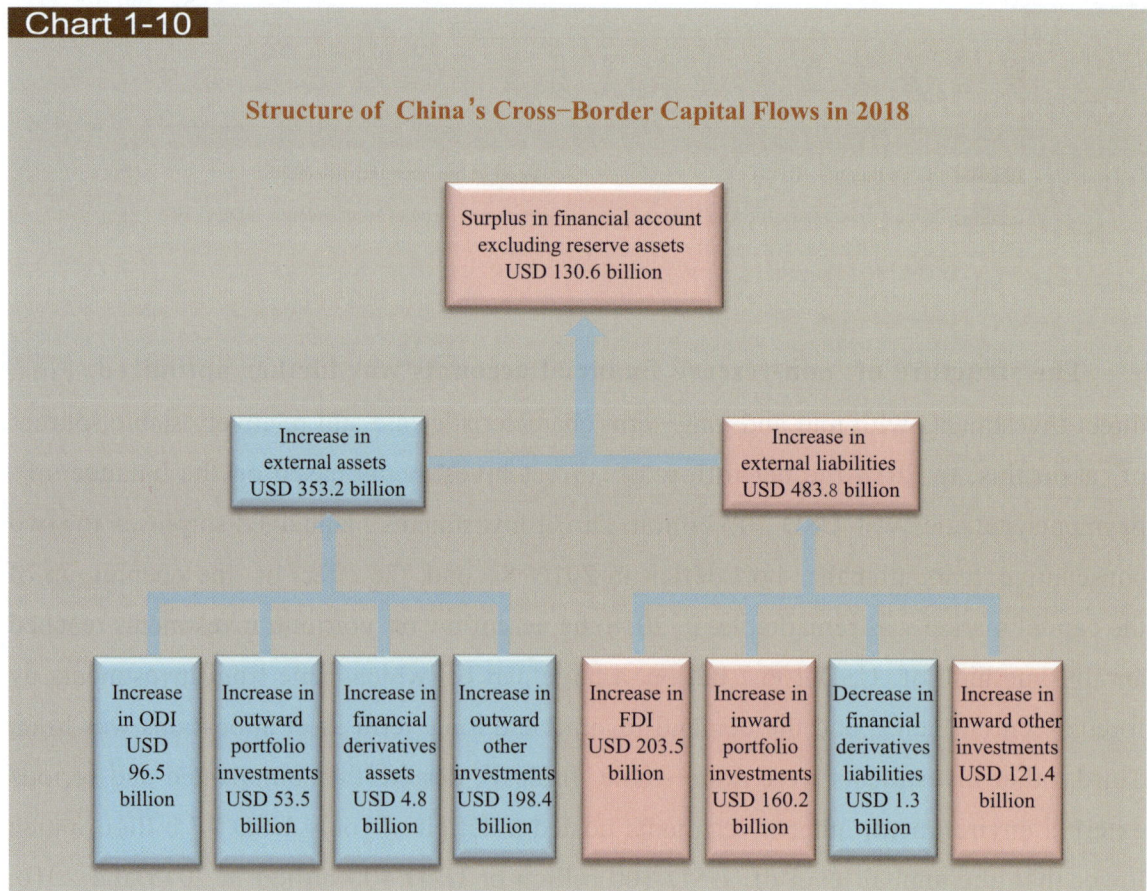

Structure of China's Cross–Border Capital Flows in 2018

Source: SAFE.

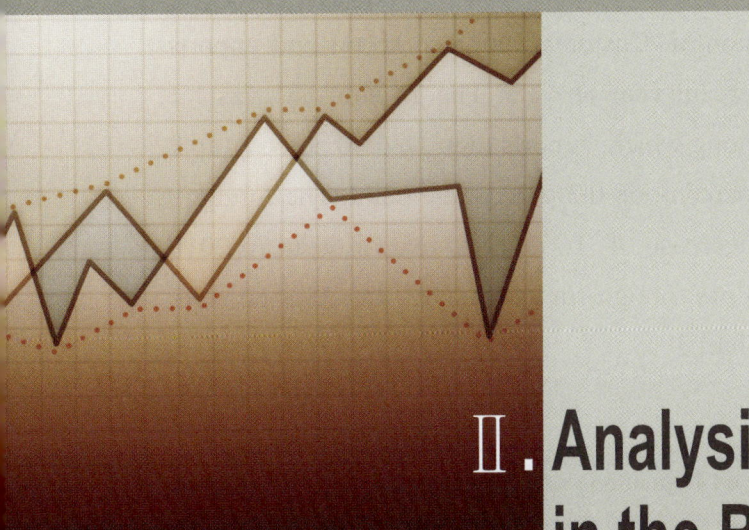

II. Analysis of the Major Items in the Balance of Payments

（I）Trade in goods

Exports and imports of trade in goods became more balanced and dependence on foreign trade remained stable. In the context of a more complex global trade environment, China's foreign trade has remained generally stable and steady. According to 2018 statistics of the General Administration of Customs, China's exports and imports of goods totaled USD 4.6 trillion, up 13 percent year on year. The growth rate was 1.1 percentage points higher than that in 2017, among which, exports increased 10 percent, up 2 percentage points, and imports increased 16 percent, up 0.3 percentage point. The foreign-trade surplus reached USD 351.5 billion, a decrease of 16 percent year on year. In 2018 China's foreign-trade dependence (the ratio of foreign trade to GDP) was 33.9 percent, approximately the same as that in 2017 (see Chart 2-1) .

Chart 2-1

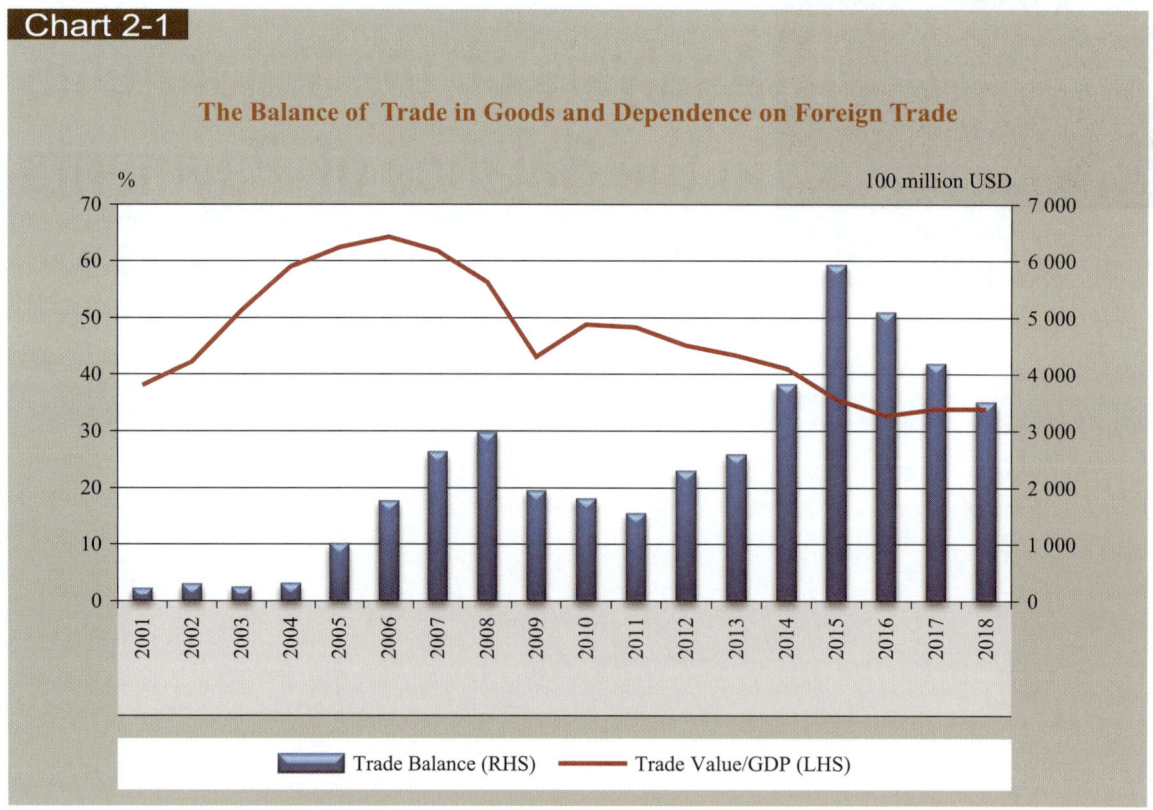

The Balance of Trade in Goods and Dependence on Foreign Trade

Trade Balance (RHS) —— Trade Value/GDP (LHS)

Sources: General Administration of Customs, National Bureau of Statistics.

The structure of export commodities improved, and both the volume and the prices of imports increased. In 2018 exports of high-tech products reached USD 746.9 billion, up 12 percent year on year, accounting for 30 percent of China's total exports, up

1 percentage points. Exports of typical labor-intensive products. Such as textile yarns, clothing, toys, shoes, and hats, totaled USD 322.7 billion, accounting for 13 percent of total exports, down 1 percentage points (see Chart 2-2) .According to customs statistics (in RMB) in 2018, the import volume index and the price index recorded growth of 6.4 percent and 6.1 percent respectively. Based on preliminary calculations, the increase in the volume of imports contributed 51 percent to the growth in imports, and the price change contributed 49 percent. Among the imports, crude oil contributed 26 percent to the growth in imports, by up10 percent in volume and up by 47 percent in price.

Chart 2-2

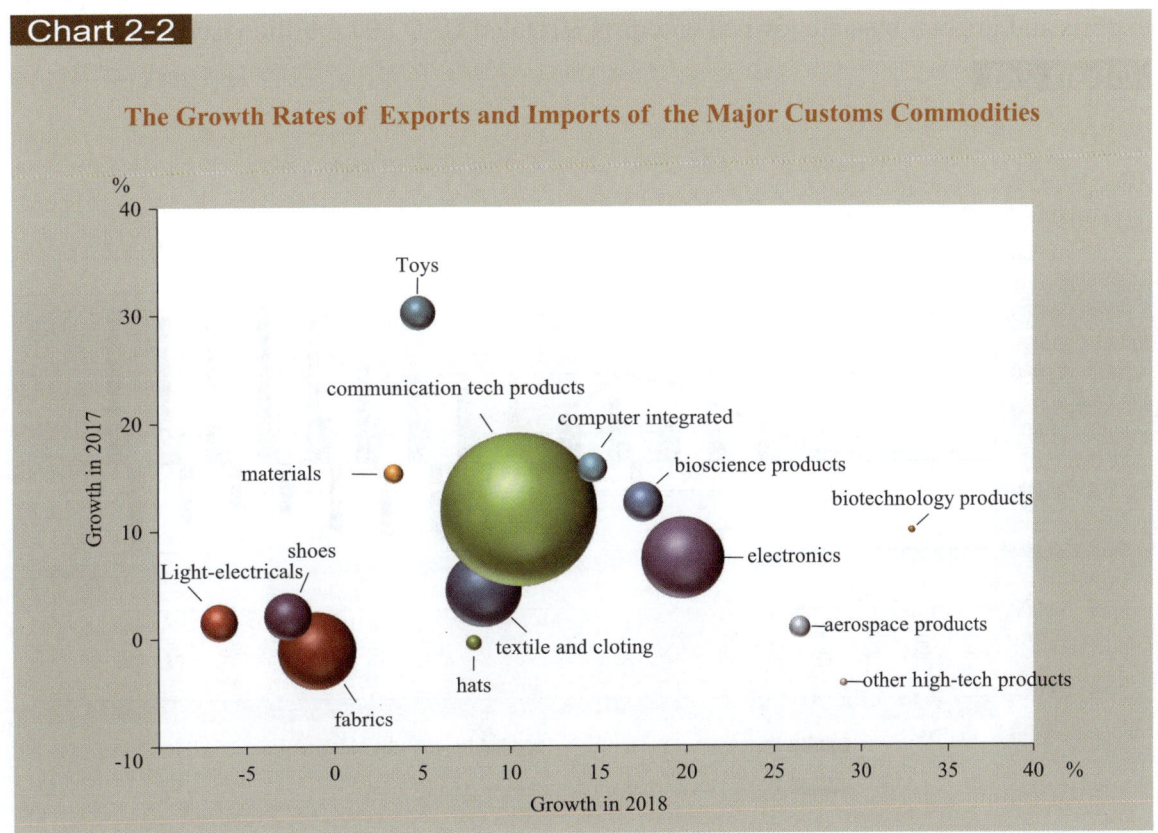

The Growth Rates of Exports and Imports of the Major Customs Commodities

Note: 1. In this chart, labor-intensive commodities include five categories of products, e. g., textile yarn, clothing, toys, shoes, and hats. High-tech commodities include nine categories of products, e. g., life science and technology commodities, electronic technology commodities, biotechnology commodities, computers, and communications technology products.
2. In the bubble chart, the x-axis stands for the growth rates of exports of a given category of commodities in 2018, and the y-axis stands for the growth rates of exports of a given category of commodities in 2017. The bubble size stands for the absolute amount of exports of given goods in 2018.
Source: General Administration of Customs.

There was strong momentum for growth of foreign trade by private enterprises. Foreign-funded enterprises recorded a slight decline in the surplus. In 2018, exports and imports of trade in goods by private enterprises totaled USD1.8 trillion, up 16 percent year on year, accounting for 38 percent of Chinaʼs total foreign trade. The ratio was 1.2 percentage points higher than that in 2017. The growth contributed approximately 50 percent to the overall growth in 2018. The surplus in foreign trade by private enterprises reached USD 528.8 billion, up 5 percent year on year. Exports and imports of trade in goods by foreign−invested enterprises totaled USD 1.97 trillion, up 7 percent year on year, accounting for 43 percent of total foreign trade. Among this, exports came to USD 1.036 trillion, up 6 percent year on year, and imports came to USD 932.1 billion, up 8 percent year on year. The surplus reached USD 104 billion, down 10 percent year on year. In 2018 exports and imports by state−owned enterprises totaled USD 804.6 billion（see Chart 2−3）.

Chart 2-3

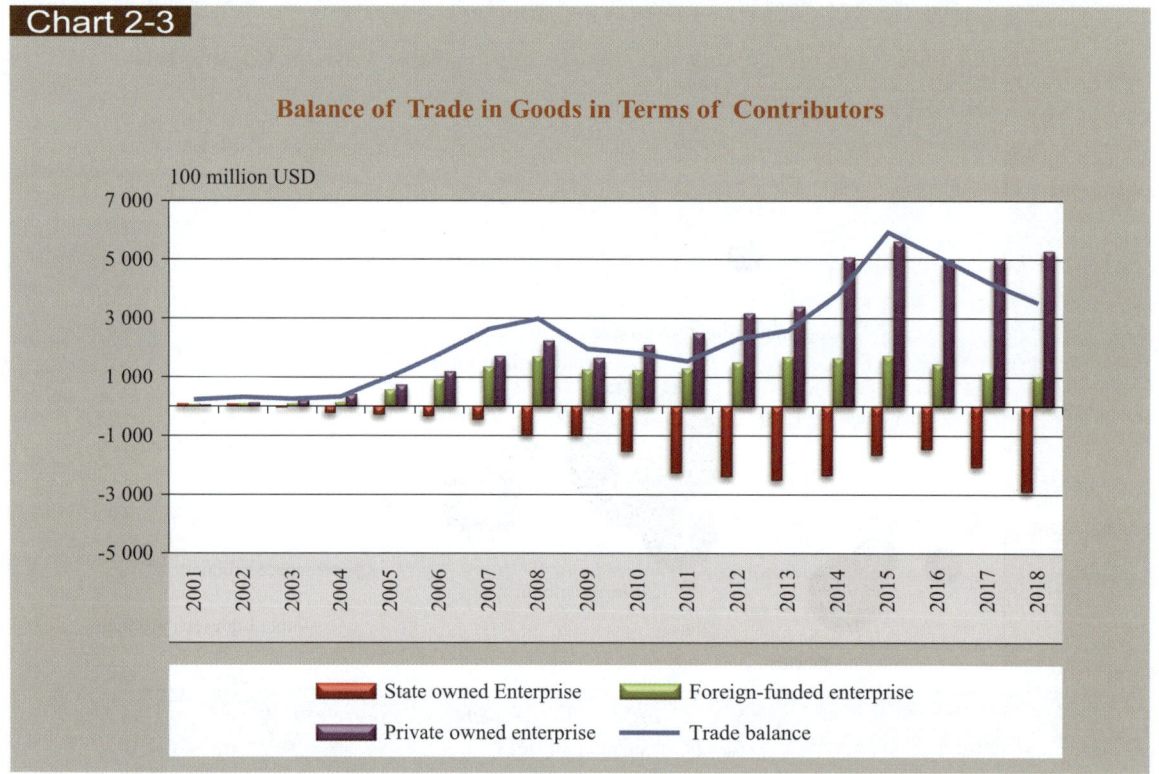

Balance of Trade in Goods in Terms of Contributors

Source: General Administration of Customs.

Exports and imports with major trade partners increased. The "Belt and Road" economies have become anew driving force in Chinaʼs foreign trade. In 2018, Chinaʼs exports and imports to the United States, the European Union, and Japan increased 9 percent, 11 percent, and 8 percent respectively, accounting for 36 percent of overall exports and imports. The growth rate of exports and imports to the ASEAN and African countries was 14 percent and 20 percent respectively, up 1.2 percentage points and 7.3 percentage points. Exports and imports to the ASEAN and African countries accounted for 17 percent of China's foreign trade, up 0.4 percentage point from that in 2017. During the same period, China's import and export growth rate along the "Belt and Road" countries was 16 percent, which was 3.7 percentage points higher than China's global import and export growth rate. (see Chart 2-4).

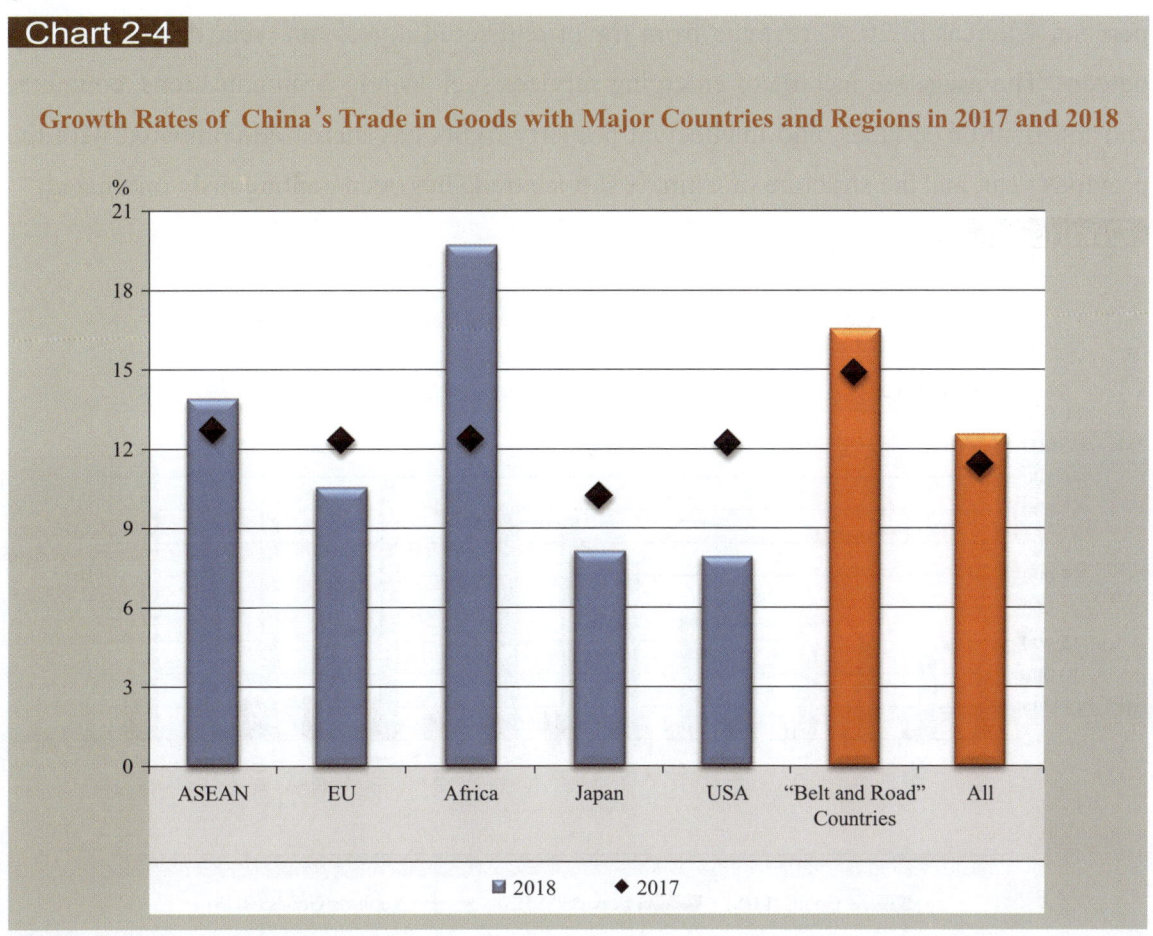

Chart 2-4

Growth Rates of China's Trade in Goods with Major Countries and Regions in 2017 and 2018

Source: General Administration of Customs.

(II) Trade in Services

Trade in services continued to grow. In 2018, China's trade in services totaled USD 759.4 billion, up 11 percent year on year. The ratio of trade in services to trade in goods was 17 percent (see Chart 2-5). In particular, the highest revenue item was the export of other business services, amounting to USD 66.2 billion, and the highest expenditure item was the import of travel services, amounting to USD 277.3 billion.

Revenue from trade in services increased. In 2018, revenue from trade in services totaled USD 233.6 billion, a year-on-year increase of 10 percent (see Chart 2-6). Among the major items, revenue from other business services, referring to consulting, professional, and other services, accounted for 28 percent, a year-on-year increase of 12 percent. Revenue from transport services accounted for 18 percent, a year-on-year increase of 13 percent. Revenue from travel accounted for 17 percent, a year-on-year increase of 5 percent, whereas in 2017, revenue from travel registered a year-on-year decrease of 13 percent. The usage fee income of emerging services such as telecommunications, computer and information services, and intellectual property rights has increased compared with the previous year, and the structure of Chinaʼs service trade has been continuously optimized.

Chart 2-5

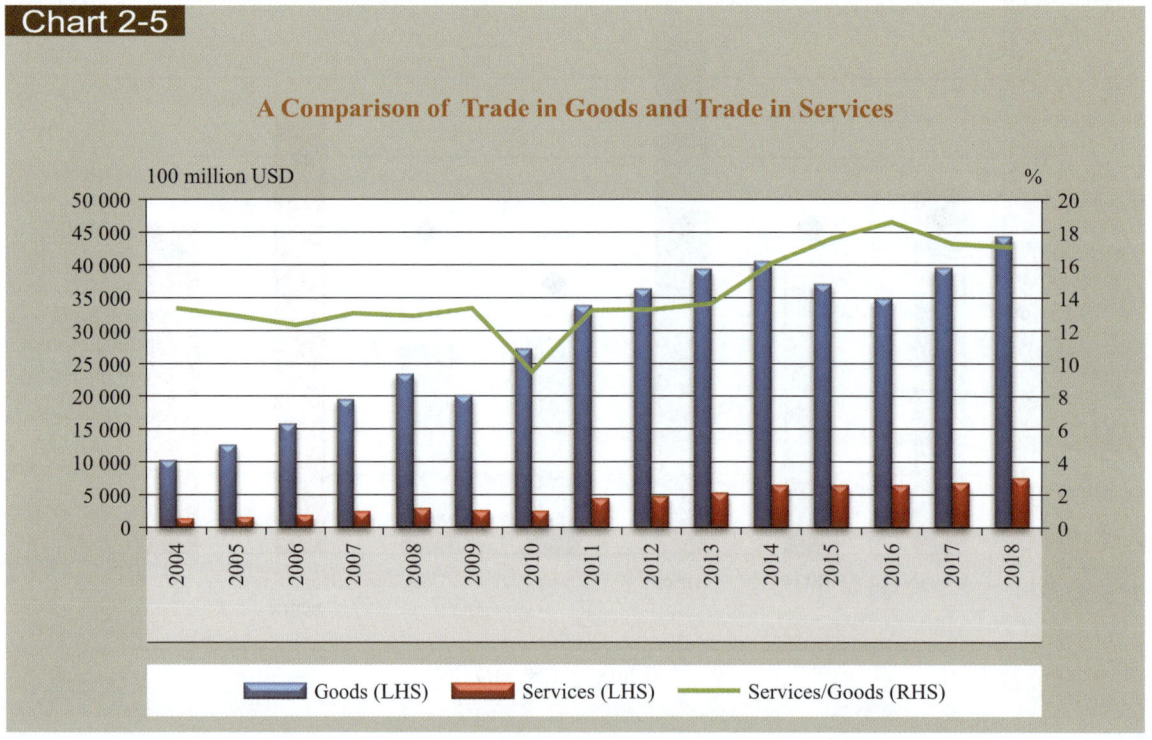

A Comparison of Trade in Goods and Trade in Services

Goods (LHS)   Services (LHS)   Services/Goods (RHS)

Source: SAFE.

Expenditures for trade in services continued to grow. In 2018, expenditures for trade in services reached USD 525.8 billion, a year-on-year increase of 11 percent. Among the major items, travel accounted for 53 percent of total expenditures, a year-on-year increase of 8 percent. Transport accounted for 21 percent, a year-on-year increase of 17 percent. Fees for the use of intellectual property registered a rapid increase, amounting to USD 35.8 billion, or a year-on-year increase of 24 percent.

Chart 2-6

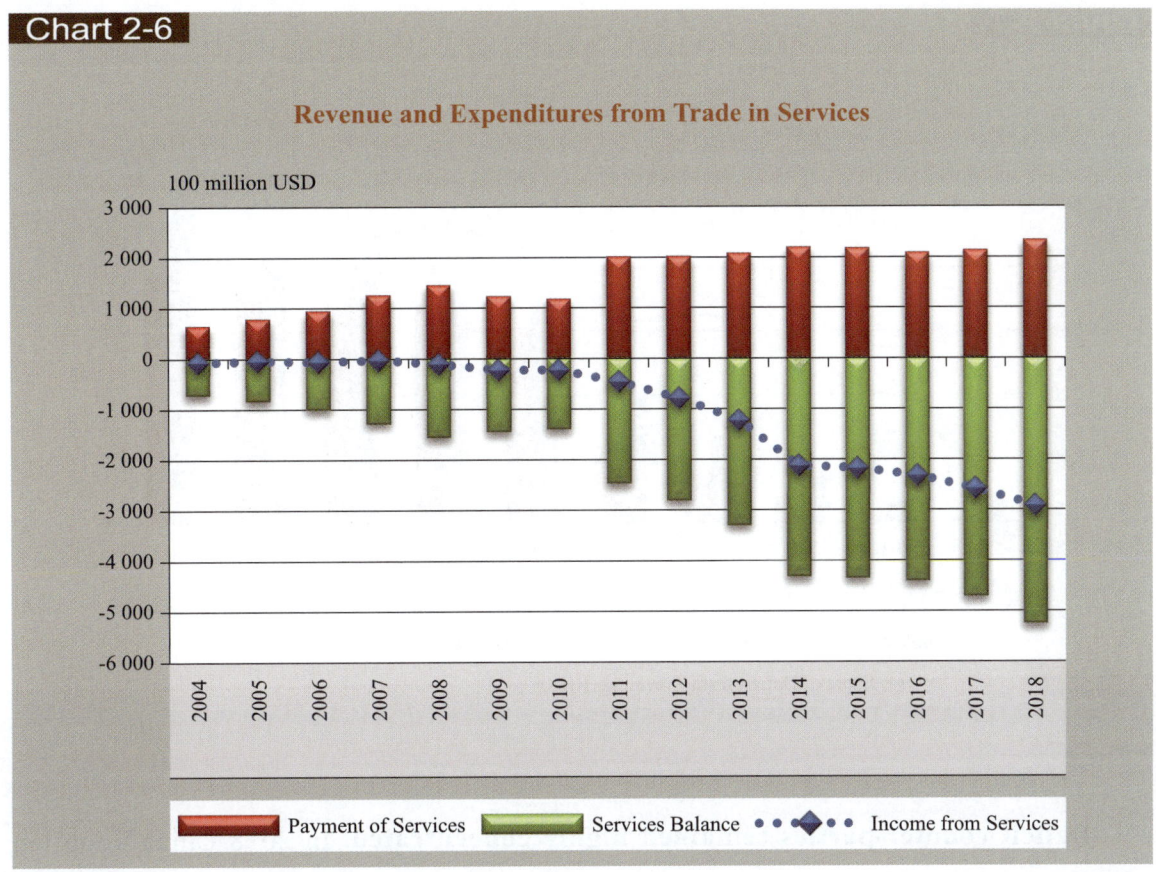

Revenue and Expenditures from Trade in Services

100 million USD

Legend: Payment of Services   Services Balance   ●●●◆●● Income from Services

Source: SAFE.

The trade in services deficit continued to expand. In 2018, trade in services recorded a deficit of USD 292.2 billion, a year-on-year increase of 13 percent. The remaining main source of the deficit in trade in services was the travel deficit, which recorded USD 237.0 billion, a year-on-year increase of 8 percent (see Chart 2-7). As China's opening up expanded, the demand from residents for overseas tourism and education stabilized and the travel deficit remained steady. The second largest deficit item was transport, which recorded a deficit of USD 66.9 billion, an increase of 20 percent year on year. The third largest deficit item was charges for the use of intellectual property, which recorded a deficit of USD 30.2 billion, an increase of 26 percent year on year.

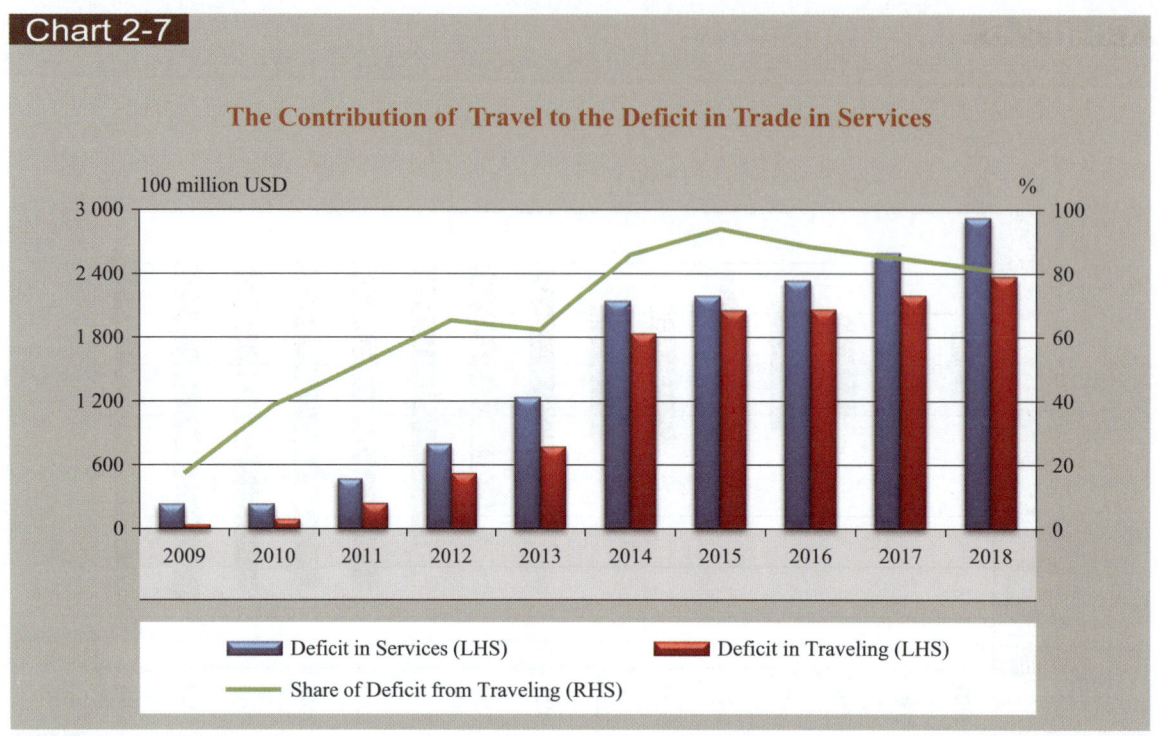

Chart 2-7

The Contribution of Travel to the Deficit in Trade in Services

Deficit in Services (LHS)   Deficit in Traveling (LHS)
Share of Deficit from Traveling (RHS)

Source: SAFE.

Deficit counter-parties remained highly concentrated. In 2018 China's top ten partners in terms of trade in services were the Hong Kong SAR, the United States, Japan, Germany, the United Kingdom, Singapore, Korea, Australia, Canada, and Russia. Trade in services with these economies amounted to USD 528.6 billion, accounting for 70 percent of the total. With the exception of Singapore, China posted deficits with its nine other partners. The United States, the Hong Kong SAR, Japan, Australia, Canada, Germany, the United Kingdom, and Russia were the economies with which China posted deficits of over 10 billion US dollars respectively (see Chart 2−8) .

Chart 2-8

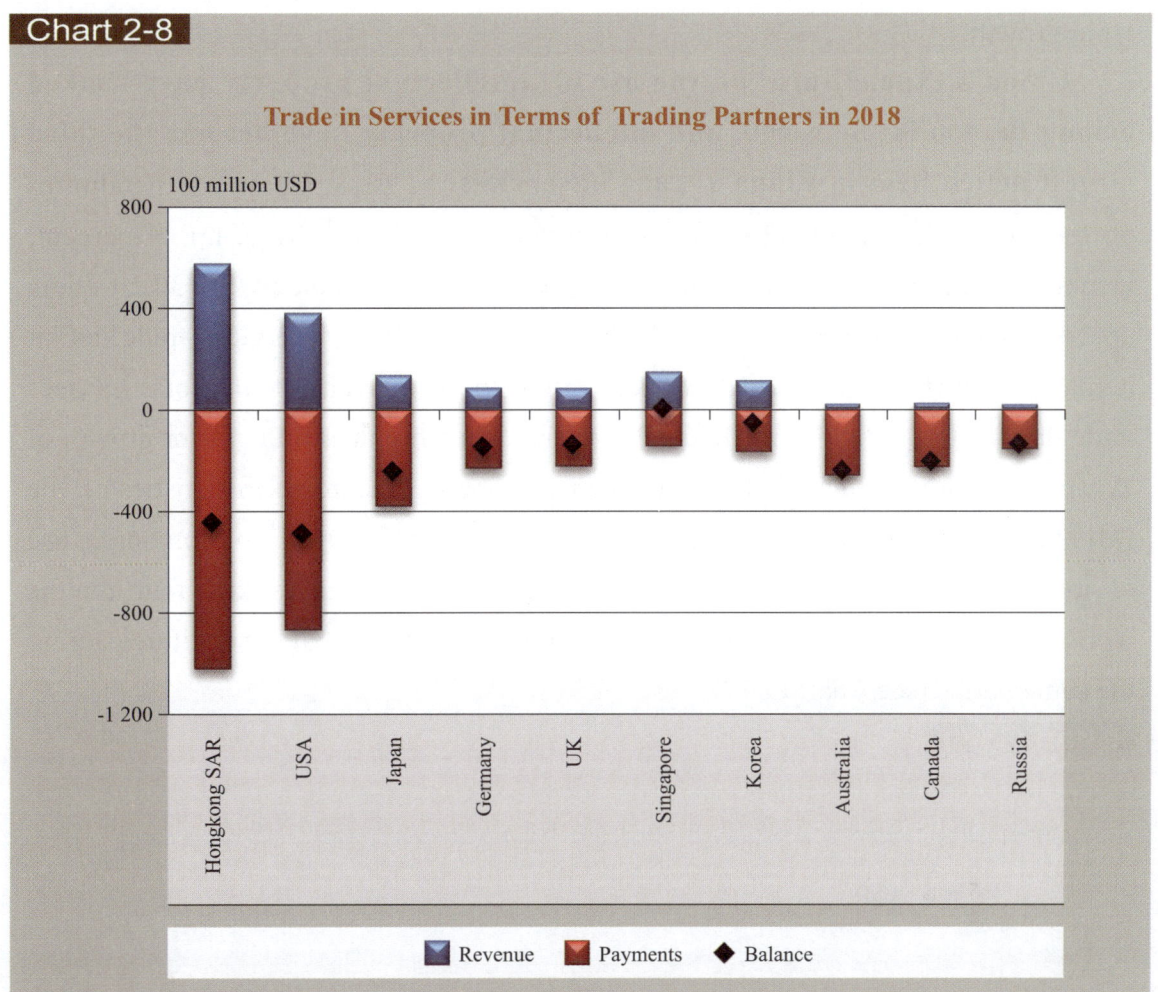

Trade in Services in Terms of Trading Partners in 2018

100 million USD

Legend: ■ Revenue ■ Payments ◆ Balance

Box 3

China's Expenditures on the Use of Intellectual Property Rank Among the Top in the World

The balance-of-payments statistics show that since 1997,[①] China's expenditures on the use of intellectual property increased year by year, reaching USD 35.8 billion in 2018, with an average annual growth rate of 22 percent. This reflects that, on the one hand, the objective demand for China's economic development and industrial upgrading of advanced technology is increasing; on the other hand, China pays great attention to intellectual property protection and respects the market value of "innovation." In addition, China's R&Don intellectual property has made considerable progress, with the income of intellectual property royalties showing

① In 1997, expenditures on intellectual property in China's balance of payments began from zero.

rapid growth.

China's expenditures on the use of intellectual property have ranked among the top in the world, and intellectual property have become the third largest deficit item in China's trade in services. In 2018, China's expenditures on fees for the use intellectual property totaled USD 35.8 billion, up 24 percent; income totaled USD 5.6 billion, up 16 percent; the deficit totaled USD 30.2 billion, up 26 percent（see Chart C3–1）, which was the third largest services trade deficit item after travel and transportation, accounting for 10 percent of the total services trade deficit. The deficit in intellectual property is mainly due to the faster growth of expenditures than of income from intellectual property. According to statistics of the IMF, during the first three quarters of 2018, China spent USD 27.7 billion on the use of intellectual property, far higher than Japan and Germany and ranking fourth in the world; expenditures accounted for about 7 percent of total global expenditures during the same period（see Chart C3–2）.

Chart C3–1

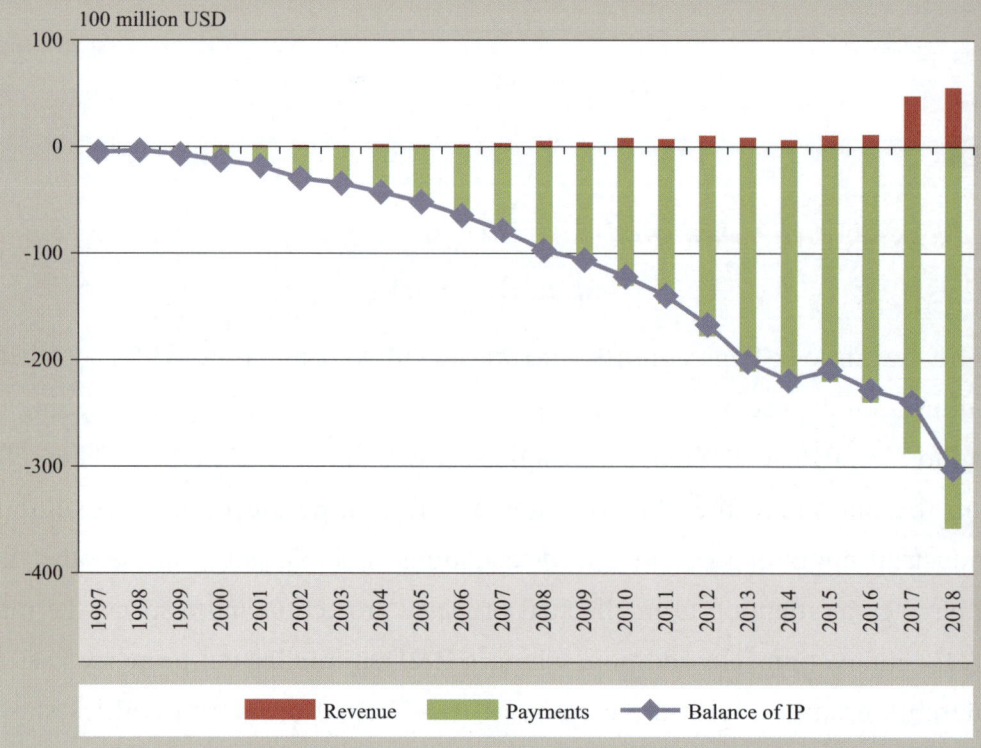

Changes in the Income, Expenditures, and Balance from Intellectual Property in China

Source: SAFE.

Chart C3-2

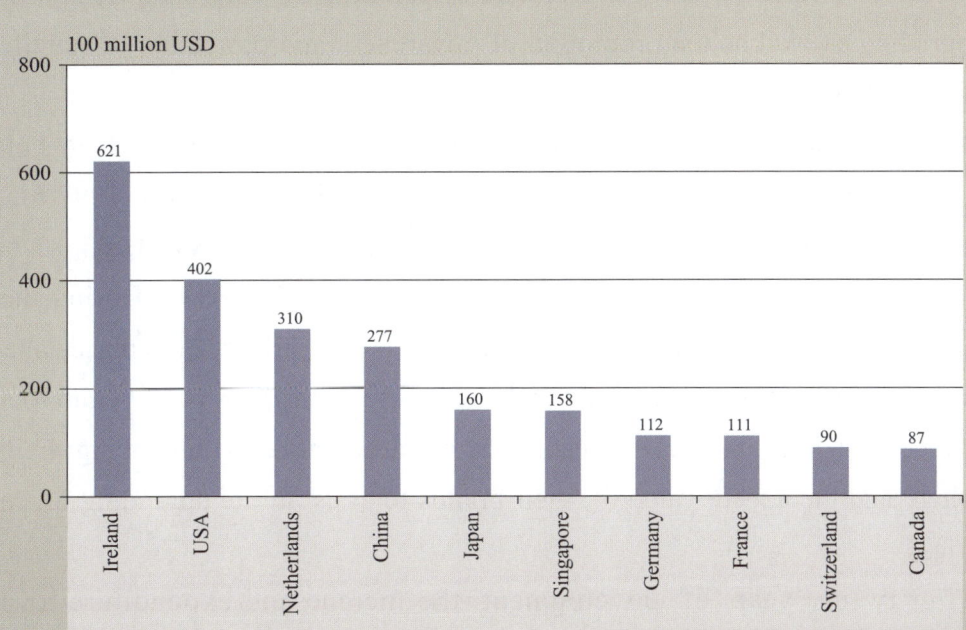

The Top Ten Countries in Terms of Global Expenditures on Intellectual Property during the First Three Quarters of 2018

Source: IMF.

The purpose of the import of intellectual property in China is mainly to introduce advanced technology and concessions, with computers, communications, and automobile enterprises as the main users and the United States, Germany, and Japan as the main partners. According to the *Handbook of Statistics on Trade in Services* (2010), expenditures on intellectual property can be divided into five categories: royalties for licensing and trademarks, royalties for research and development achievements, royalties for copying or distributing computer software, royalties for copying or distributing audio-visual and related products, and royalties for other intellectual property. In terms of the details, more than 80 percent of China's expenditures on intellectual property in 2018 was spent on importing foreign scientific research results and concessions; in terms of industries, the top three were "computers, communications, and other electronic equipment manufacturing industries," the "automobile manufacturing industry" and "railway, ship, aerospace, and other transport equipment manufacturing industries," with a total expenditure of more than 40 percent of total expenditures on intellectual property. The United States, Germany, and Japan rank among the top three counter-party countries. The characteristics of intellectual property imports reflect the demand for advanced technology for China's economic development, transformation and upgrading as well as the promotion of awareness and protection of intellectual property in China.

Income from intellectual property royalties in China has grown rapidly, along with improving the innovation ability of enterprises. From 1997 to 2018, income from intellectual property royalties in China increased from USD 0.1 billion to USD 5.6 billion, with an average annual growth of 25 percent. During the first three quarters of 2018, China ranked number eleven globally, twelve places ahead of its position in 2007. The proceeds show that Chinese enterprises have begun to attach importance to increasing R&D investments and are constantly enhancing their own technology and the added-value of their brands to assist in the upgrading of related industries.

After twenty years of development, the income and expenditure levels of intellectual property royalties in China have increased substantially, while the relatively large deficit shows that although China is a big country, it is not a powerful country in terms of intellectual property. Research and innovation still have a long way to go. Long-term adherence to and strengthening of intellectual property protection will not only enhance China's reputation in the field of international intellectual property but will also promote the high-quality development of the Chinese economy.

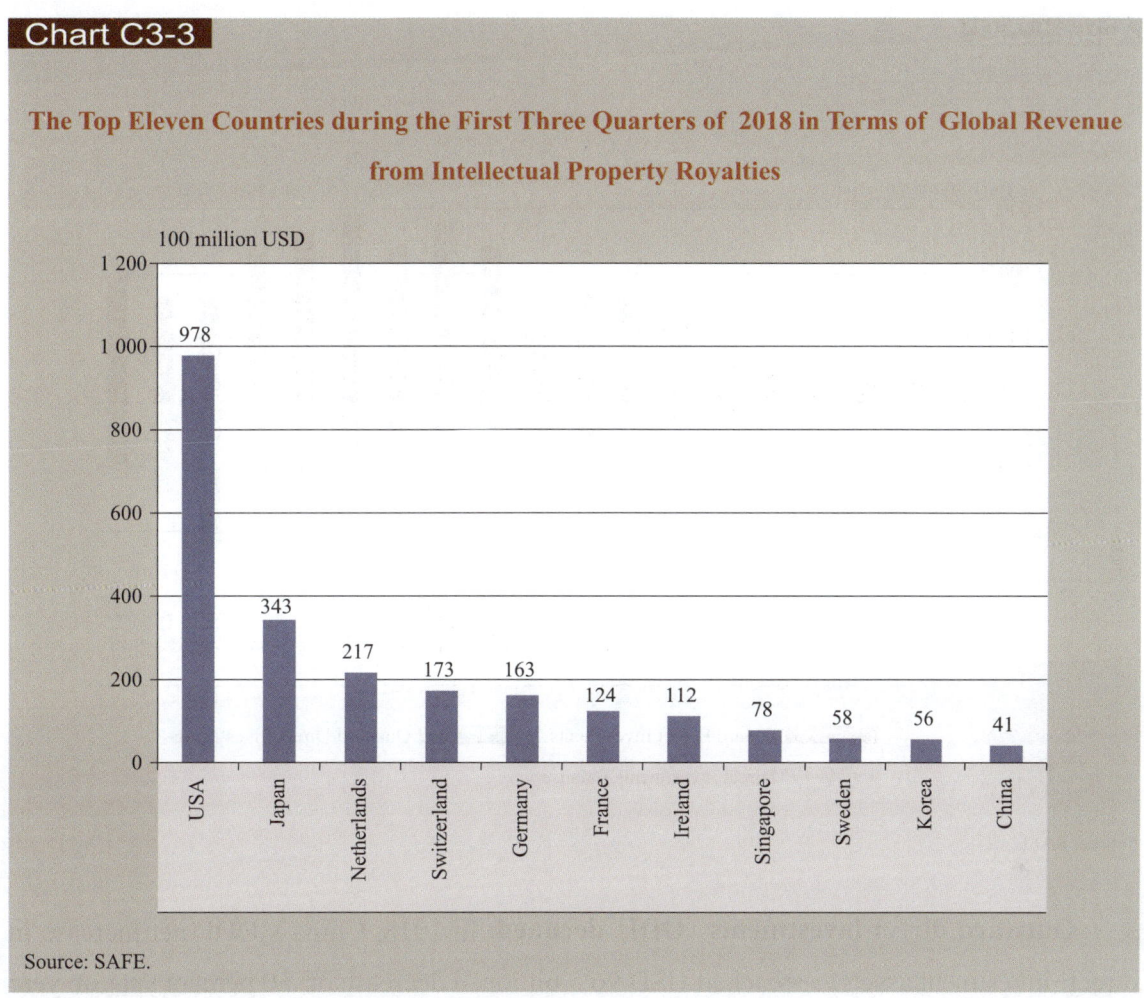

Chart C3-3

The Top Eleven Countries during the First Three Quarters of 2018 in Terms of Global Revenue from Intellectual Property Royalties

Source: SAFE.

(III) Direct Investments

Direct investments① recorded a large net inflow. In 2018, net inflows of direct investments in China's balance of payments totaled USD 107 billion (see Chart 2–9), an increase of 2.9 times year on year.

---

① The net flow of direct investments refers to the gap between the net increase in direct-investment assets (net outflow of funds) and the net increase in direct-investment liabilities (net inflow of funds). When the net increase in direct-investment assets is more than the net increase in direct-investment liabilities, a net outflow is recorded, and vice versa.

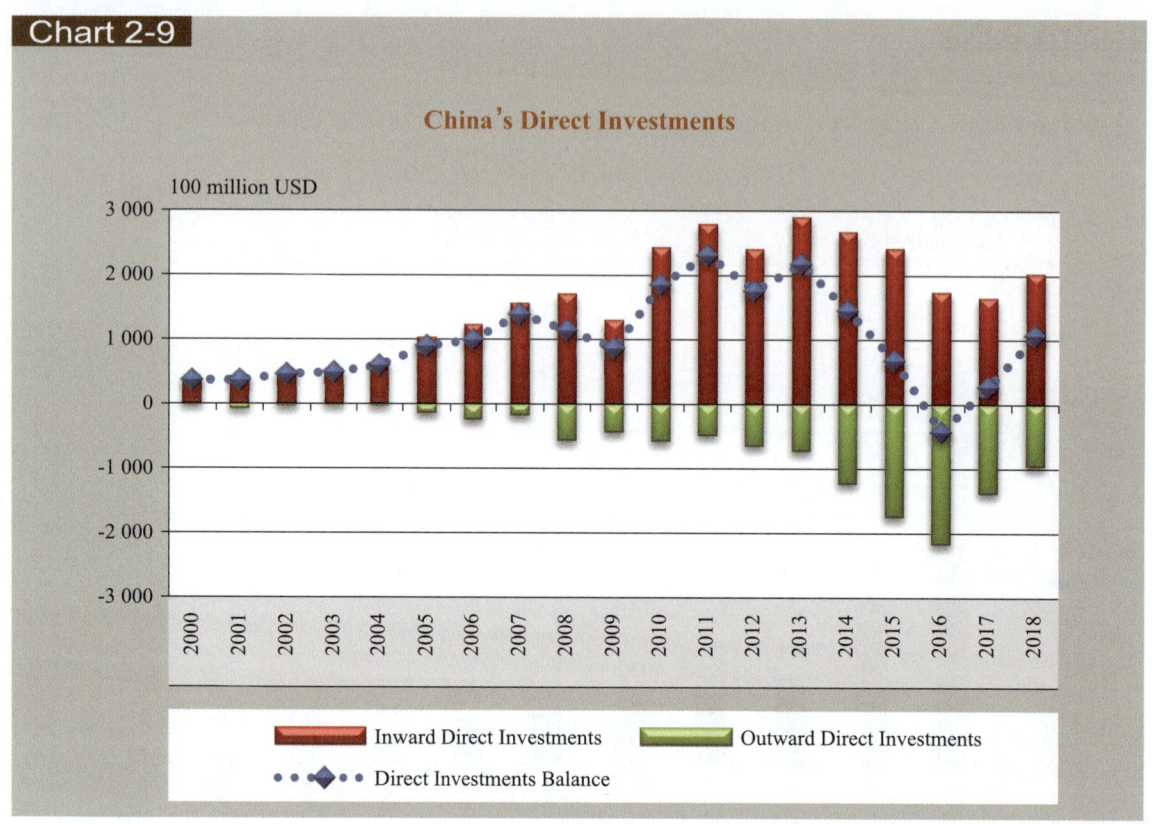

Chart 2-9

China's Direct Investments

Source: SAFE.

Outward direct investments (ODI) declined. In 2018, China's ODI (net increase in direct-investment assets) ① reached USD 96.5 billion, a decrease of 30 percent year on year (see Chart 2-10). Outward direct investments by Chinese enterprises remained rational and stable.

---

① A major component of direct-investment assets is outward direct investments. In addition, reverse investments by domestic foreign-funded enterprises to their parent companies are also included. The net increase in direct-investment asset transactions, which is negative in the balance of payments statement, represents a net outflow.

Chart 2-10

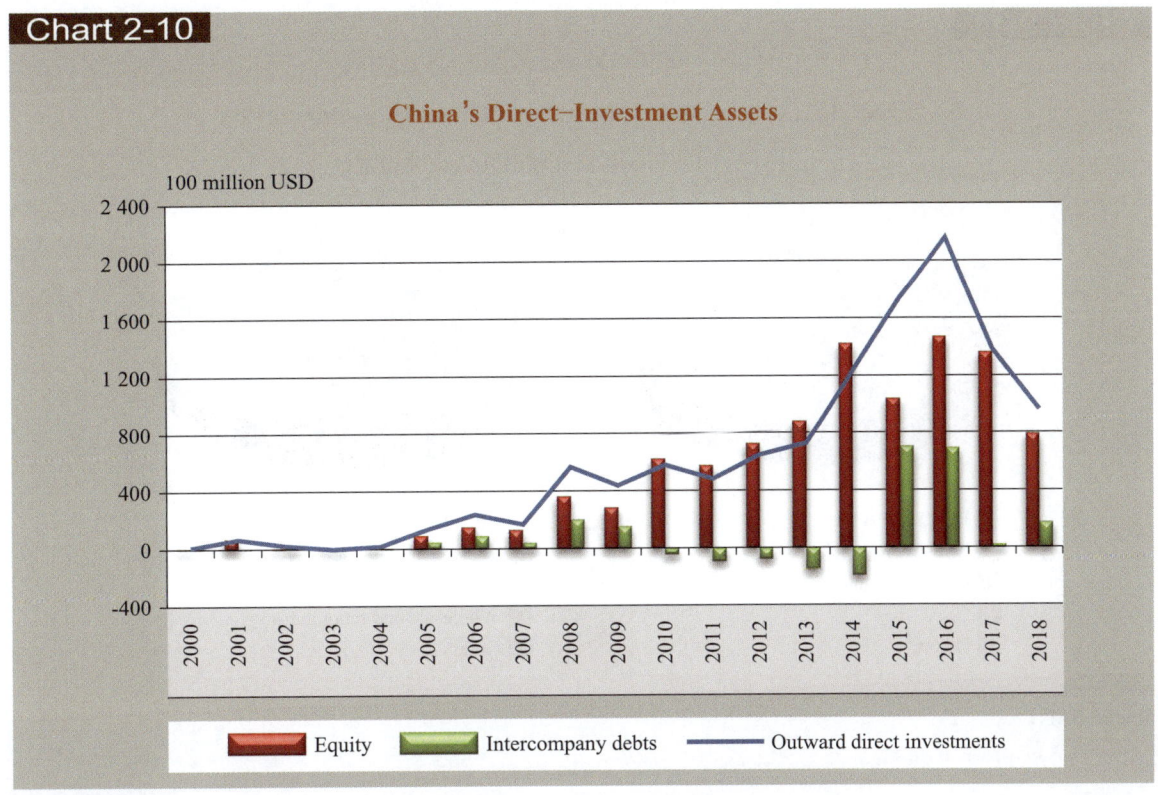

China's Direct–Investment Assets

Source: SAFE.

In terms of the composition of direct investments, equity investments dropped and loan assets rose. First, equity investments reached USD 79 billion, a 42 percent decline year on year. The decline indicates that domestic enterprises tended to be more cautious about their long–term outward investments and asset allocations due to instabilities and uncertainties in the international environment. Second, loans to foreign affiliates recorded USD 17.5 billion, a more rapid increase than that in 2017, reflecting the fact that domestic investors preferred cross–border lending.

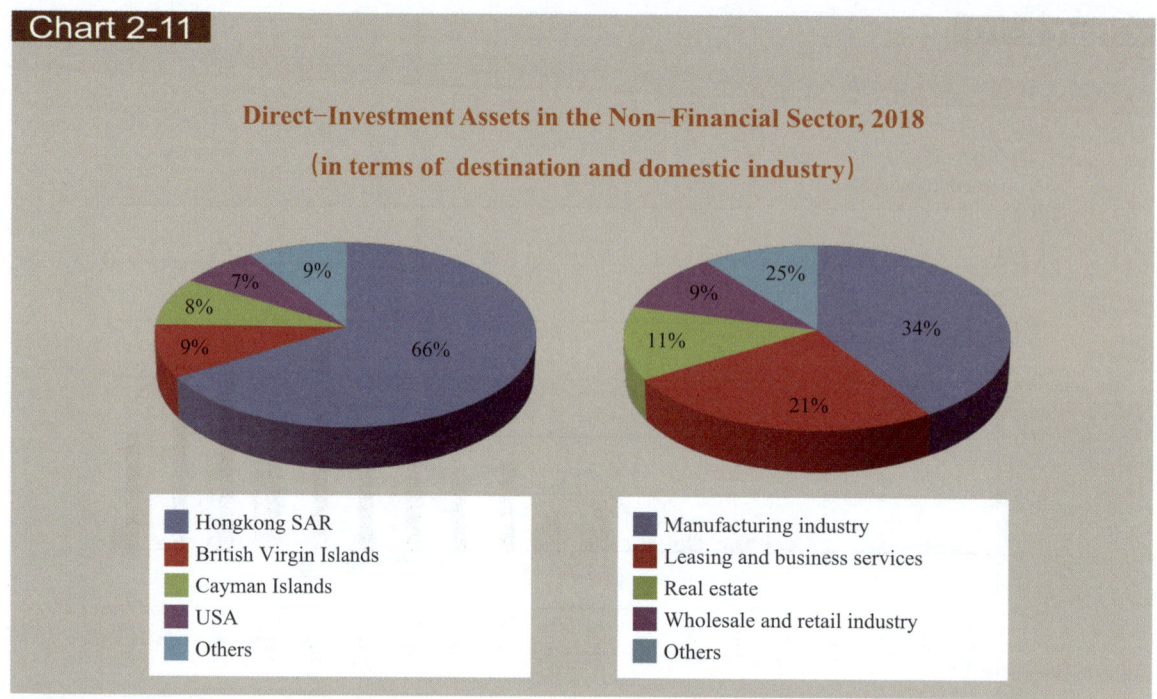

Source: SAFE.

In terms of sectors, outward direct investments by China's non-financial sector dropped, and outward direct investments by China's financial sector increased. First, direct−investment assets by the non−financial sector recorded a net increase of USD 75.7 billion, down 37 percent year on year, mainly due to a 50 percent drop inequity in vestments, including reinvestments of earnings, while loan assets increased eight fold. The Hong Kong SAR, the British Virgin Islands, and the Cayman Islands, where management of capital inflows and outflows is relatively loose, were the major outward direct−investment destinations. In terms of the investors' industries, manufacturing continued to rank as the largest industry, accounting for 34 percent of the total (see Chart 2−11). Second, direct−investment assets by the financial sector recorded a net increase of USD 20.8 billion, up 17 percent year on year. More than 80 percent of the investments were contributed by the banking sector.

Inward foreign direct investments in China maintained large net inflows. Net inflows of inward direct investments (net increase in direct−investment liabilities[①]) in

---

① Direct−investment liabilities are mainly composed of foreign direct investments. This includes reverse investments to domestic parent companies by overseas subsidiaries. The net increase in direct−investment liability transactions, which is positive in the balance of payments statement, represents a net inflow.

China reached USD 203.5 billion in 2018, up 23 percent year on year, and net inflows were the highest during the period from 2016 to 2018.

In terms of the composition, both equity and loan liabilities of inward direct investments increased. First, net inflows of equity investments in China amounted to USD 154.4 billion, up 10 percent year on year (see Chart 2−12).Among these, equity investments in the form of capital increased relatively rapidly during the first half of 2018. Despite a slowdown during the second half of 2018, the inflows of capital exceeded those during the same period of 2017. Overall, equity investments in China were maintained at a high level, indicating that foreign investors have confidence in China's economic prospects. Second, loans from foreign affiliates recorded a net increase of USD 49.1 billion, up 92 percent year on year. In quarterly terms, during the first and second quarters a large net inflow was recorded. During the third and fourth quarters, net inflows dropped significantly, indicating that foreign−invested enterprises were flexibly using both domestic and international markets and resources.

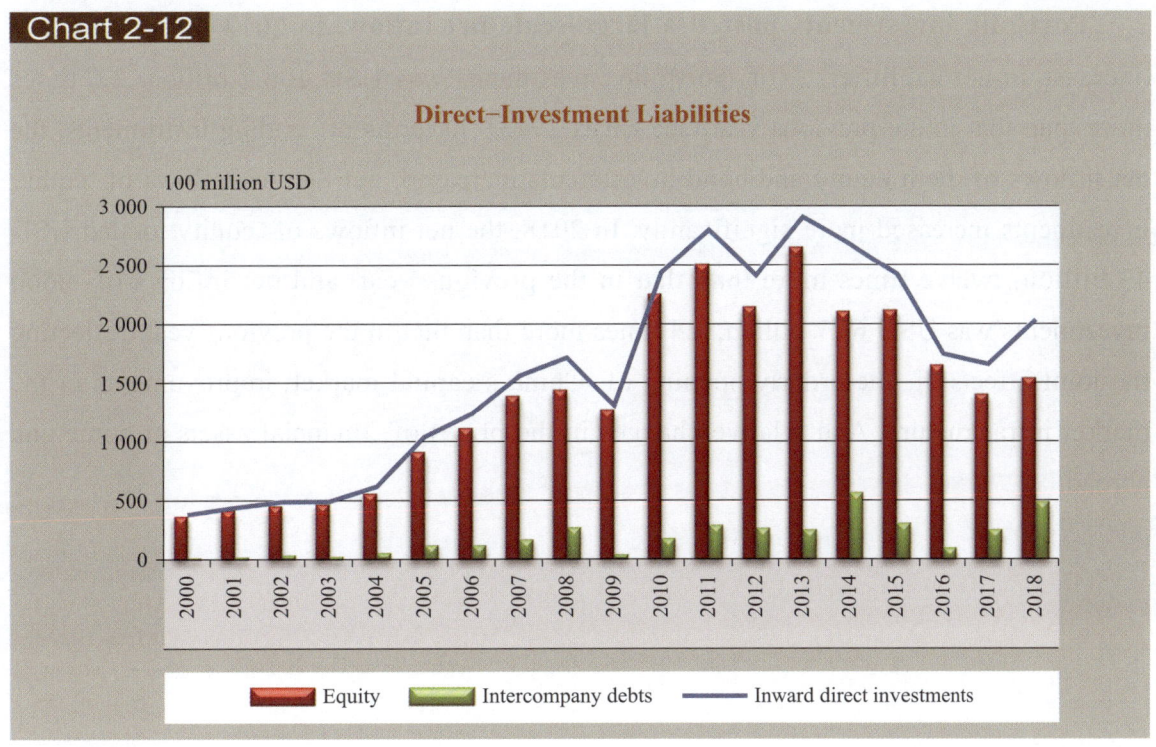

Chart 2-12

Direct−Investment Liabilities

100 million USD

Equity   Intercompany debts   Inward direct investments

Source: SAFE.

In terms of sectors, inward direct investments in both the non-financial sector and the financial sector increased. First, direct−investment liabilities in the non−financial sector recorded a net increase of USD 185.9 billion, up 21 percent year on year, accounting for 90 percent of the total net inflows of direct investments to China. In 2018, FDI inflows into the manufacturing industries accounted for 19 percent of the total, roughly the same as that in 2017. The inflows increased by nearly 40 percent year on year, making manufacturing the second largest absorber of FDI in recent years. The leasing and business services industry absorbed the most direct investments, accounting for 22 percent of the total. In the meantime, the main source of FDI remained the Hong Kong SAR, accounting for more than 70 percent of the total. The Hong Kong SAR was followed by the Cayman Islands, Singapore, and Korea, accounting for 11 percent of the total. Second, direct-investment liabilities in the financial sector recorded a net inflow of USD 17.6 billion, up 45 percent year on year, mainly due to the reinvestment of earnings in the banking and insurance sectors.

（IV）Portfolio investments

Portfolio investments posted a large-scale net inflow. In 2018 the net inflows (increase in net liabilities) [1] of portfolio investments was USD 106.7 billion, 2.6 times more than that in the previous year (see Chart 2-13). In terms of trading instruments, the net inflows of both equity and bond investments increased, but the net inflows of equity investments increased more significantly. In 2018, the net inflows of equity totaled USD 43 billion, twelve times more than that in the previous year, and net inflows of bond investments was USD 63.7 billion, 1.4 times more than that in the previous year, reflecting the joint effects of the orderly opening of China's capital market, improvements in the market infrastructure. And relative changes in the prices of financial assets at home and abroad.

---

[1] In the balance-of-payments statement, positive liabilities indicatea net inflow.

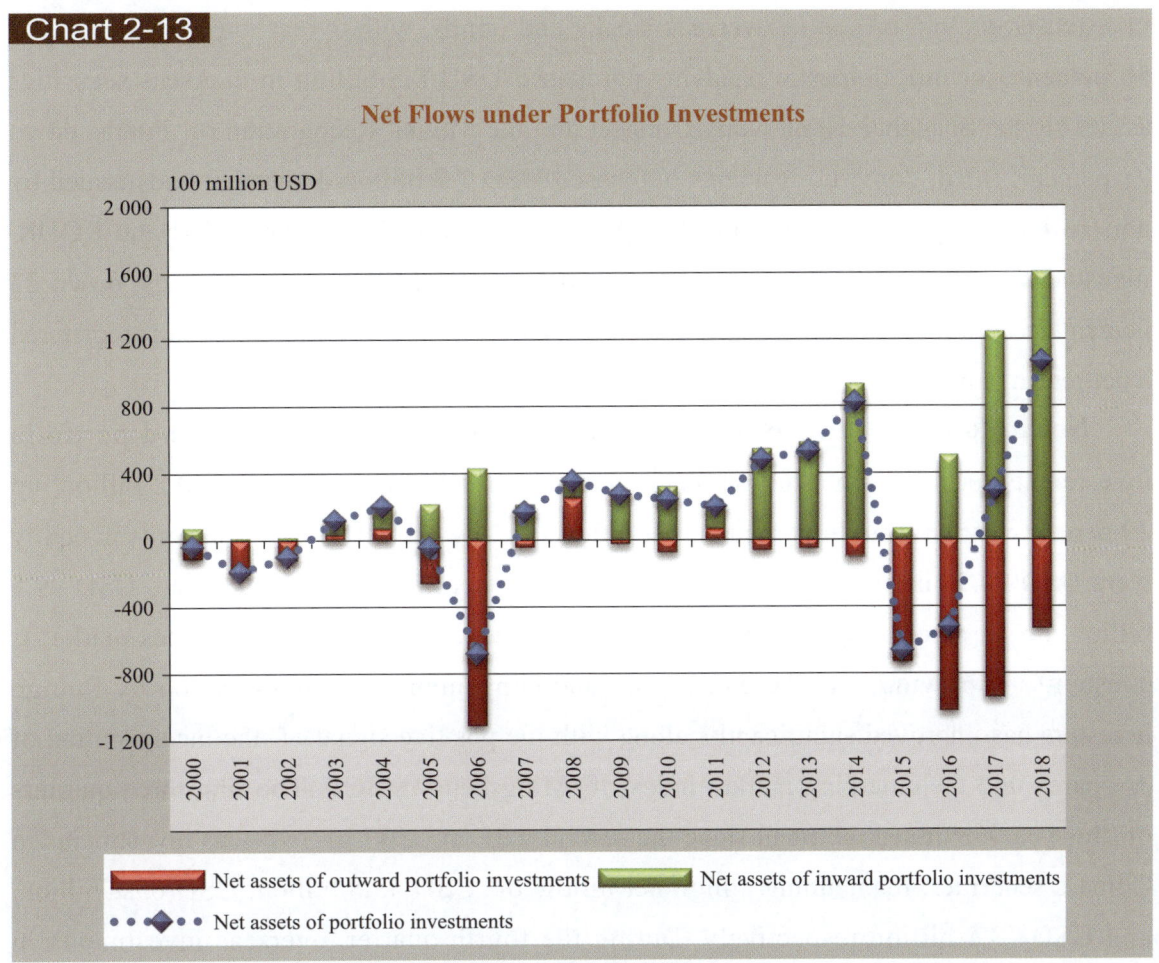

Chart 2-13

Net Flows under Portfolio Investments

100 million USD

Legend:
Net assets of outward portfolio investments   Net assets of inward portfolio investments
Net assets of portfolio investments

Note: Positive outward portfolio investments indicate a decrease in equity and bond of outward investments, and vice versa. Positive inward portfolio investments indicate an increase in equity and bond inward investments, and vice versa.
Source: SAFE.

China's outward portfolio investments declined. In 2018 China's net outward portfolio investments (net increase in assets①) was USD 53.5 billion, with a year-on-year decline of 44 percent. In particular Equity investments were USD 17.7 billion, down nearly 50 percent, and bond investments were USD 35.8 billion, down about 40 percent, mainly due to the slowdown in investments in overseas bond markets by domestic financial institutions and the weakening demand among Chinese residents for cross-border allocations of overseas stock assets. On a quarterly basis, outward portfolio investments in the first quarter fell to USD 33.5 billion, and in the second to fourth quarters they fell to USD 4.3 billion, USD 9.2 billion, and USD 6.6 billion respectively.

In terms of major channels, **first**, domestic banks and other financial institutions

---

① In the balance-of-payments statement, negative liabilities indicatea net outflow.

invested USD 36.6 billion in overseas stocks and bonds, with a year-on-year decline of 50 percent; **second**, domestic residents purchased USD 8.5 billion in overseas securities assets via the Shanghai–Hong Kong Connect and the Mutual Recognition of Funds, down 78 percent; **third**, domestic residents purchased USD 7.2 billion domestic bonds issued by non-residents, up fifteen fold; **fourth**, domestic institutional investors (QDII and RQDII) invested a total of USD 3.5 billion in non-resident-issued stocks and bonds, down 23 percent. In addition, outstanding acceptances of letters of credit by foreign banks registered a net return (a net inflow) of USD 2.3 billion, down 70 percent.

Net inflows of inward portfolio investments rose. In 2018 inward portfolio investments recorded a net inflow (net increase in liabilities[①]) of USD 160.2 billion, up 29 percent year on year. In particular, net inflows of inward portfolio investments in equity were USD 99.5 billion, up 13 percent year on year; net inflows of bonds were USD 99.5 billion, up 13 percent. This shows that the attractiveness of China's securities market is constantly improving, and the enthusiasm and convenience of participation by foreign investors has improved significantly, along with the positive signal of the incorporation of A-shares into the emerging market index of Mingsheng (MSCI). The first three quarters of this year continued the trend since the second half of 2017 of overseas investments in China's securities, maintaining a high net inflow of USD 43.8 billion, USD 65.2 billion, and USD 43.1 billion respectively. During the fourth quarter, overseas investments in securities fell to USD 8.1 billion.

In terms of the main channels, **first**, foreign institutions invested USD 96.2 billion in the domestic securities market, a year-on-year increase of 79 percent, with foreign central banks increasing their holdings of bonds issued by the Chinese government; **second**, capital inflows via the Shanghai–Hong Kong Connect and the Shenzhen–Hong Kong Connect totaled USD 44.7 billion, up 80 percent; **third**, non-residents purchased USD 27.4 billion in overseas stocks and bonds issued by Chinese institutions, which were mainly H-stocks issued by Chinese institutions in the Hong Kong stock market, down 38 percent. **In addition**, bank acceptances of forward letters of credit (with drafts) recorded a net outflow of USD 8 billion.

(Ⅴ) Other Investments

Other investments posted a deficit. In 2018, other investments registered a net

---

① In the balance-of-payments statement, positive liabilities indicate a net inflow.

outflow (an increase in net assets) of USD 77.0 billion, whereas in 2017 other investments recorded an inflow (an increase in net liabilities) of USD 51.9 billion (see Chart 2−14). In particular, currency and deposits recorded a net outflow of USD 21.7 billion, loans recorded a net outflow of USD 49.7 billion, trade credits recorded a net inflow of USD 24.5 billion, and other accounts payables and receivables recorded a net inflow of USD 19.3 billion.

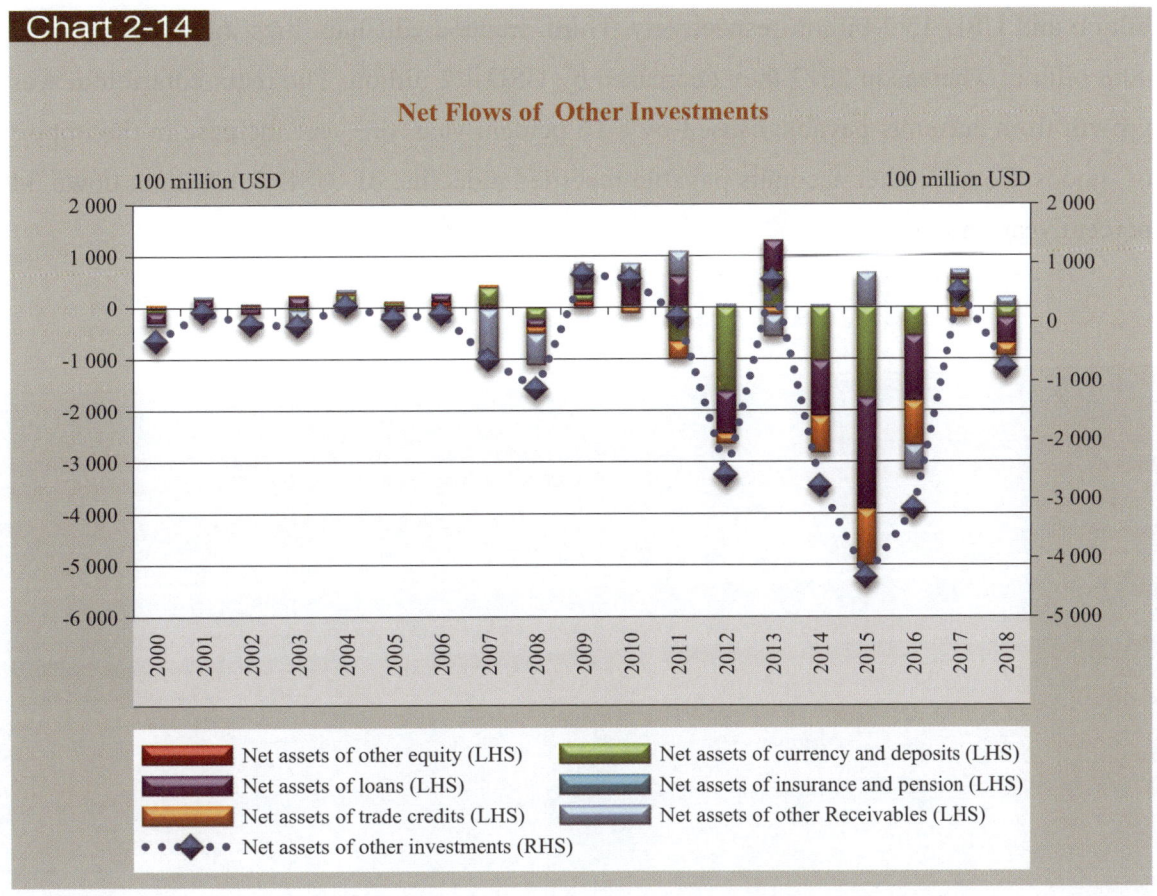

Chart 2-14

Net Flows of Other Investments

Net assets of other equity (LHS)
Net assets of currency and deposits (LHS)
Net assets of loans (LHS)
Net assets of insurance and pension (LHS)
Net assets of trade credits (LHS)
Net assets of other Receivables (LHS)
Net assets of other investments (RHS)

Source: SAFE.

Assets under other investments climbed. In 2018, external assets under other investments grew by USD 198.4 billion, up 97 percent year on year. In particular, overseas loans extended mainly by domestic banks to their own overseas subsidiaries and branches grew by USD 81.8 billion. Overseas deposits grew by USD 73.1 billion, suggesting that domestic entities were actively participating in international business. Trade−credit assets grew by USD 65.3 billion, mainly driven by growth in the export of goods, while other accounts receivable recorded a decline of USD 22.4 billion.

The growth of liabilities of other investments fell. In 2018, the growth of liabilities of other investments amounted to USD 121.4 billion, down 21 percent year on year. The main changes included: first, external loans borrowed by domestic enterprises recorded USD 32.1 billion, down 36 percent year on year, suggesting that domestic enterprises took the initiative to adjust the amount of overseas borrowing. Second, currency and deposits increased by USD 51.4 billion, with foreign currency and RMB increasing by USD 36.2 billion and USD 15.2 billion respectively. Third, trade−credit liabilities increased by USD 40.8 billion, whereas in 2017 they decreased by USD 1.2 billion. The main contributor was growth from accounts payable caused by a 16 percent year−on−year increase in the import of goods. Fourth, other accounts payable recorded a decline of USD 3.1 billion, down 34 percent year on year.

III. International Investment Position

China's external assets and liabilities① **were both on the rise.** At end−December 2018, China's external financial assets reached USD 7 324.2 billion, representing growth of 2.5 percent compared to end−December 2017; external liabilities reached USD 5 194.1 billion, up 2.9 percent; and net assets reached USD 2 130.1 billion, up 1.4 percent (see Chart 3−1).

Chart 3-1

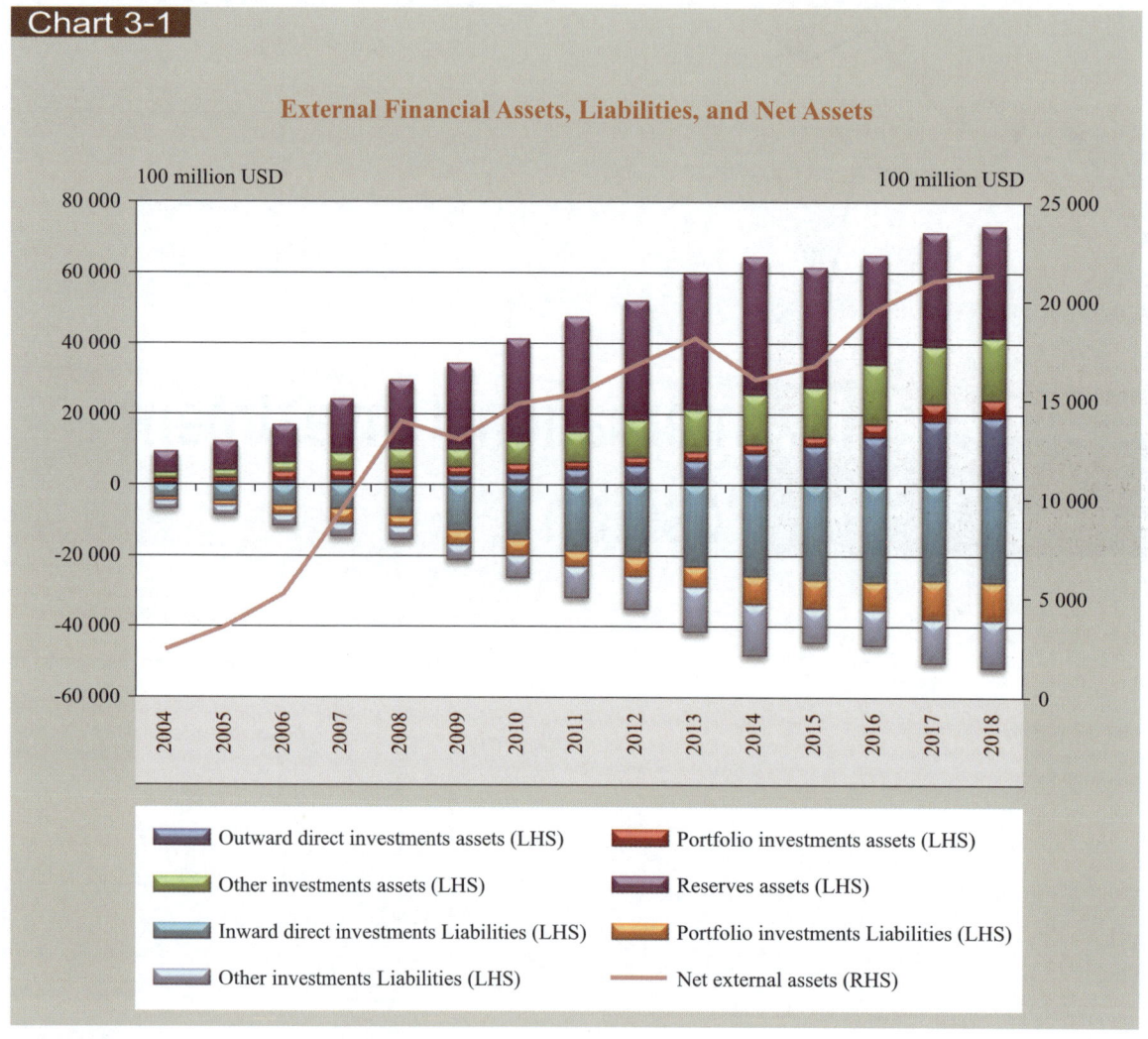

External Financial Assets, Liabilities, and Net Assets

Source: SAFE.

Reserve assets remained the largest component in total external assets, but the ratio of private-sector holdings continued to increase. Among external financial assets, at end−December 2018 reserve assets amounted to USD 3 168.0 billion, down

---

①   External financial assets and liabilities include direct investments, portfolio investments, and other investments, such as loans and deposits. Outward direct investments are included as financial assets because the equity issued by non−resident direct−investment enterprises and held by domestic investors is the same type of financial instrument as the equity investments in portfolio investments. The difference is that direct investments require a higher threshold of equity holdings to reflect a significant influence or control over the production and operations of the enterprises. Inward direct investments belong to external financial liabilities because foreign investors hold equity in foreign−owned companies.

by 2.1percent, of which USD 18.9 billion was due to BOP transactions and USD 86.8 billion was due to changes in exchange rates and in prices other than BOP transactions. As the largest component, reserve assets accounted for 43 percent of total external assets, 2 percentage points less than that at end-December 2017 and a historical low since China's first IIP statement at end-December 2004. Direct-investment assets amounted to USD 1 899.0 billion, accounting for 26 percent of total assets, up by 0.6 percentage point. Portfolio-investment assets amounted to USD 498.0 billion, accounting for 7 percent. Financial-derivative assets amounted to USD 6.2 billion, accounting for 0.1 percent. Other investments, such as loans and deposits, amounted to USD 1 753.0 billion, accounting for 24 percent, up by 1.5 percentage points (see Chart 3-2) .

Chart 3-2

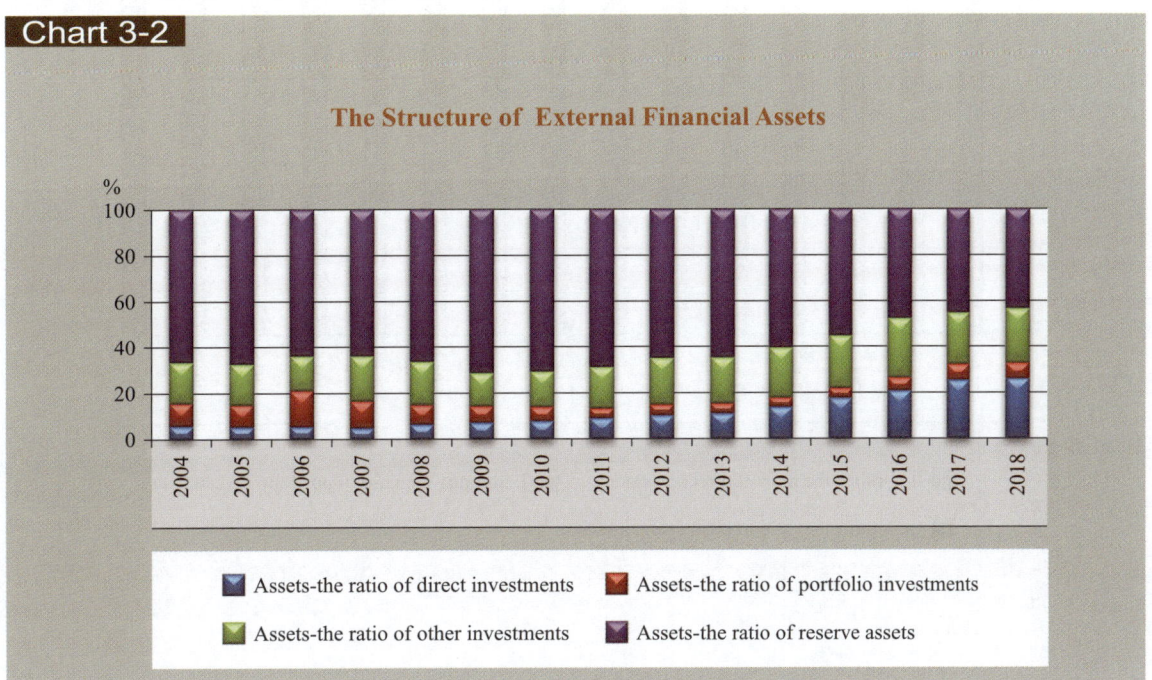

The Structure of External Financial Assets

Source: SAFE.

Although foreign direct investments remained the major item in external liabilities, the proportion of other types of investments such as debt securities investments grew. Among external liabilities, FDI totaled USD 2 762.3 billion at end-December 2018,[①] up 1.3 percent. Continuing as the largest component, FDI accounted for 53 percent of total external liabilities, 0.8 percentage point less than that at end-December 2017. Debt securities under portfolio-investment liabilities amounted to USD 412.2 billion,

① The inward FDI position includes FDI stocks of both the non-financial sector and the financial sector. The position includes inter-company lending as well as other debt positions among the relevant offices. The statistics also reflect the impact of revaluations. The statistical coverage of inward FDI is different from the cumulative statistics of the Ministry of Commerce. Over the years, the latter used the cumulative FDI equity investment flows as the inward FDI position.

accounting for 8 percent, 1.3 percentage points more than that at end–December 2017. Other investments, such as loans and deposits, amounted to USD 1 329.4 billion, accounting for 26 percent, 1.4 percentage points more than that at end–December 2017 (see Chart 3–3).

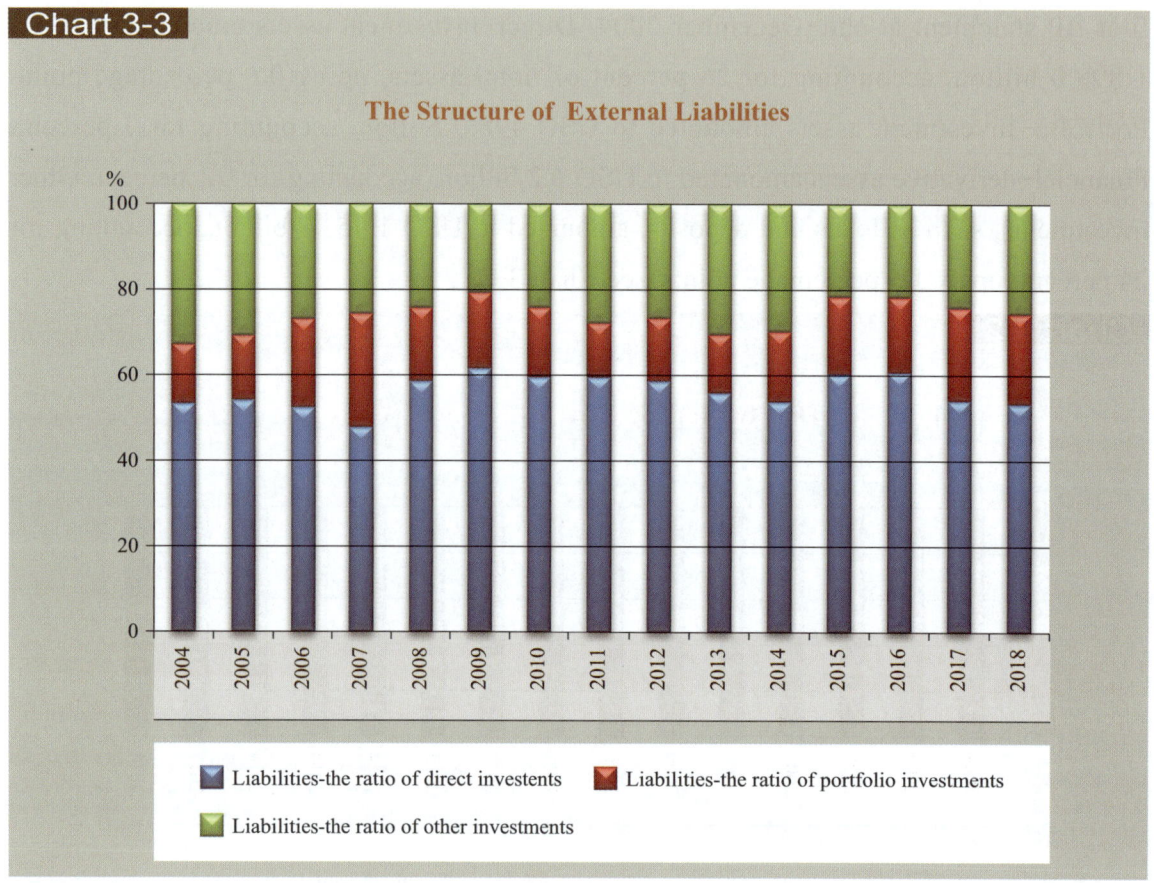

Chart 3-3

The Structure of External Liabilities

Source: SAFE.

The deficit in the investment-income account continued. In 2018, China's net investment income recorded a deficit of USD 61.4 billion. In particular, revenue from outward investments totaled USD 214.6 billion, a year–on–year decrease of 19 percent. Income payments for inward investments totaled USD 276.0 billion, a year–on–year decrease of 5 percent. The annualized yield difference between assets and liabilities was –2.4 percentage points, 0.2 percentage point less than that in 2017 (see Chart 3–4). The structure of external financial assets and liabilities determined the deficit in the investment–income account. At end–December 2018, reserve assets accounted for more than 40 percent of total assets, which were invested in assets with high liquidity. As a result, the average annualized yield of China's external assets from 2005 to end–December 2018 was 3.3

percent. Among the external liabilities, inward FDI was the major component, accounting for more than one-half. As long-term and stable investments, the return on investment from inward FDI is generally higher than other forms of assets. From 2005 to end-December 2018, the average annualized yield of external liabilities was 6.0 percent. Continuous inflows of FDI and high investment returns reveal that the long-term investment environment in China still has great attraction for foreign investors.

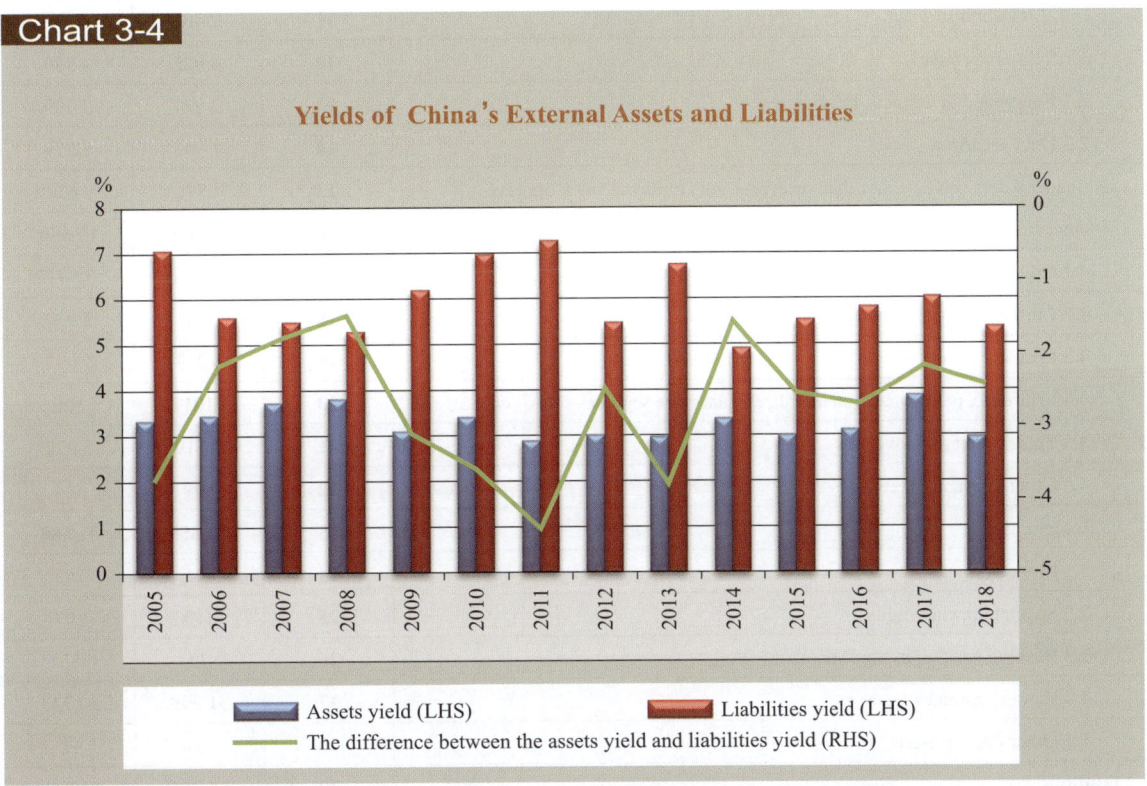

Chart 3-4

Yields of China's External Assets and Liabilities

- Assets yield (LHS)
- Liabilities yield (LHS)
- The difference between the assets yield and liabilities yield (RHS)

Notes: 1. Yields of assets (liabilities) = $\dfrac{\text{annualized revenue (payments) of investment income}}{(\text{positionsat the reference year-end+positionsat the previous year-end})/2}$

2. The difference between the yields of assets and liabilities = the yield of assets- the yield of liabilities

Source: SAFE.

Table 3-1   China's International Investment Position

Unit: 100 million USD

	Line No.	2017	2018
Net International Investment Position[①]	1	21 007	21 301
Assets	2	71 488	73 242
1 Direct investment	3	18 090	18 990
1.1 Equity and investment fund shares	4	15 590	16 316
1.2 Debt instruments	5	2 501	2 674

---

① The net position is the result of assets minus liabilities: A "+"sign indicates net assets, whereas "−"sign indicates net liabilities. The data employ rounded-off numbers.

(Continue)

	Line No.	2017	2018
1.a Financial sector	6	2 371	2 518
1.1.a Equity and investment fund shares	7	2 276	2 416
1.2.a Debt instruments	8	95	102
1.b Non-financial sector	9	15 719	16 472
1.1.b Equity and investment fund shares	10	13 314	13 900
1.2.b Debt instruments	11	2 405	2 572
2 Portfolio investment	12	**4 925**	**4 980**
2.1 Equity and investment fund shares	13	2 977	2 700
2.2 Debt securities	14	1 948	2 279
3 Financial derivatives (other than reserves) and employee stock options	15	**59**	**62**
4 Other investment	16	**16 055**	**17 530**
4.1 Other equity	17	54	54
4.2 Currency and deposits	18	3 611	3 937
4.3 Loans	19	6 373	7 097
4.4 Insurance, pension, and standardized guarantee schemes	20	101	106
4.5 Trade credit and advances	21	5 319	5 972
4.6 Other accounts receivable	22	597	364
5 Reserve assets	23	**32 359**	**31 680**
5.1 Monetary gold	24	765	763
5.2 Special drawing rights	25	110	107
5.3 Reserve position in the IMF	26	79	85
5.4 Foreign currency reserves	27	31 399	30 727
5.5 Other reserve assets	28	5	−2
Liabilities	29	**50 481**	**51 941**
1 Direct investment	30	**27 257**	**27 623**
1.1 Equity and investment fund shares	31	25 150	25 386
1.2 Debt instruments	32	2 107	2 237
1.a Financial sector	33	1 351	1 422
1.1.a Equity and investment fund shares	34	1 241	1 277
1.2.a Debt instruments	35	110	145
1.b Non-financial sector	36	25 906	26 201
1.1.b Equity and investment fund shares	37	23 909	24 109
1.2.b Debt instruments	38	1 997	2 092
2 Portfolio investment	39	**10 994**	**10 964**
2.1 Equity and investment fund shares	40	7 623	6 842
2.2 Debt securities	41	3 370	4 122

(Continue)

	Line No.	2017	2018
3 Financial derivatives (other than reserves) and employee stock options	42	34	60
4 Other investment	43	12 197	13 294
4.1 Other equity	44	0	0
4.2 Currency and deposits	45	4 365	4 833
4.3 Loans	46	3 922	4 169
4.4 Insurance, pension, and standardized guarantee schemes	47	100	109
4.5 Trade credit and advances	48	3 523	3 931
4.6 Other accounts payable	49	188	154
4.7 Special drawing rights	50	100	97

Source: SAFE.

Box 4

External Assets and Liabilities in China's Banking Sector at end-December 2018

By end-December 2018, the scale of external assets and liabilities in China's banking sector increased, whereas net liabilities decreased. External assets reached USD 1 116.4 billion,[1] a year-on-year increase of 12 percent and accounting for 15 percent of China's external assets.[2] The external liabilities of China's banking sector reached USD 1 297.6 billion, a year-on-year increase of 1 percent and accounting for 25 percent of China's external liabilities. China's net liability position was USD 181.2 billion, down 36 percent year on year.

Among the external financial assets, loans and deposits accounted for over 70 percent of the outstanding claims. The percentage share of debt securities was the same as that of other assets. External loans and deposit assets of China's banks totaled USD 831.5 billion, up 11 percent year on year, mainly consisting of loans assets. Investment in overseas bonds was USD 136.5 billion, up 17 percent, accounting for 12 percent of the banks' total external assets, but with growth slowing down since 2017. Other assets such as investments in overseas equity and

[1] The data are derived from the *Statistical Report on External Assets and Liabilities* of the State Administration of Foreign Exchange. Since end-December 2015, China has participated in the international banking statistics of the Bank for International Settlements and it began to submit the cross-border financial assets and liabilities of Chinese banks on a quarterly basis. This box is based on data reported at end-December 2018.

[2] The positions of external assets include international reserve assets. If international reserve assets are excluded, the banks' external assets constitute 27 percent of China's total external assets.

financial derivatives totaled USD 148.5 billion, up 12 percent and accounting for 12 percent of the banks' total external assets, which is slightly higher than that of bond assets.

Among the external liabilities, more than one-half were deposits and loans. The portion of debt securities was the same as that in the previous year and the portion of other investments declined. Loans and deposits in China's banking sector amounted to USD 728.7 billion, a year–on–year increase of 5 percent and accounting for more than one–half of the banks' external liabilities. Among these, deposits from overseas non–banking sectors constituted a major component. Debt securities amounted to USD 184.8 billion, an increase of 0.5 percent and accounting for 14 percent of external liabilities. Other investments such as financial derivatives and equity liabilities amounted to USD 384.1 billion, a year–on–year decrease of 5 percent and accounting for one–third of external liabilities. (See Chart C4–1.)

Chart C4-1

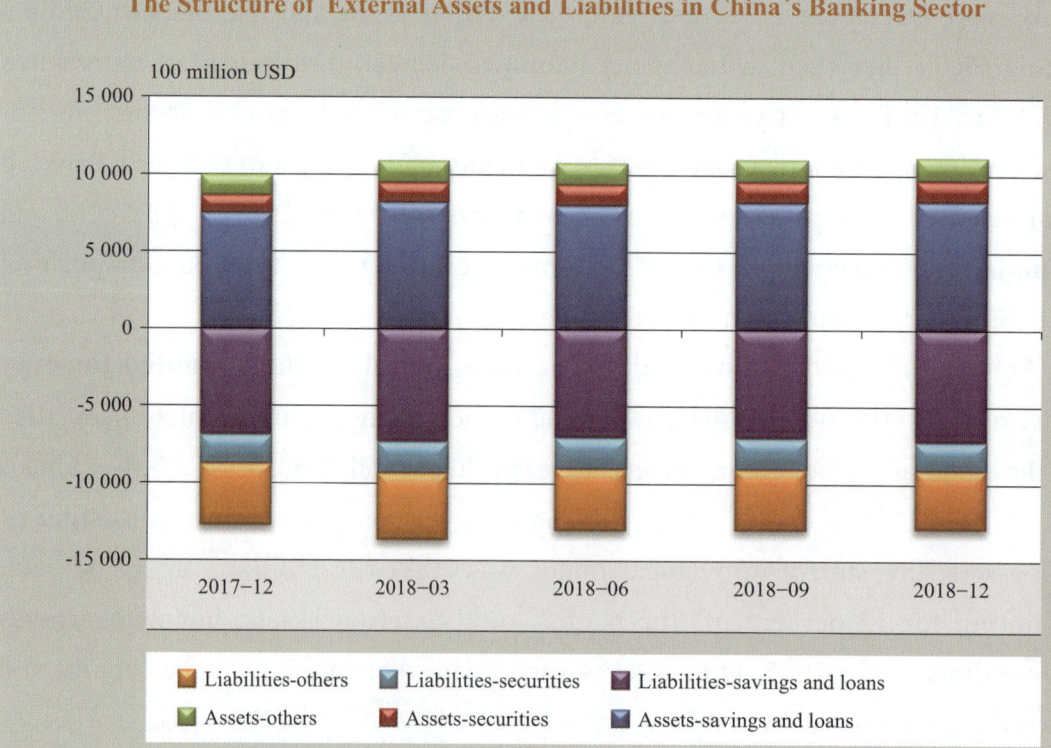

The Structure of External Assets and Liabilities in China's Banking Sector

Source: SAFE.

In terms of currency, China's banking sector recorded net foreign-

exchange external assets and net RMB liabilities. At end–December 2018, the banks' external USD assets amounted to USD 775.9 billion, a year–on–year increase of 15 percent and accounting for the largest proportion of the banks' total external assets. The major contributors were the expansion of USD debt securities and other investment instruments. RMB assets amounted to USD 121.4 billion, an increase of 3 percent year on year. The increase in RMB bond investments played a major role. External assets in other foreign currencies amounted to USD 219.2 billion, 20 percent of the external assets. USD liabilities amounted to USD 505.2 billion, an increase of 7 percent year on year and accounting for a major component of the external liabilities. RMB liabilities amounted to USD 406.1 billion, an increase of 1 percent and accounting for one–third of the external liabilities. External liabilities in other foreign currencies amounted to USD 386.3 billion and accounted for the remaining one–third of the external liabilities. In terms of net assets and liabilities, Chinese banks recorded net liabilities of USD 284.7 billion in RMB, holding at the same level as that in the previous year, and net assets of USD 103.5 billion in foreign currencies, compared to USD 3.5 billion at end–December 2017 (see Chart C4–2).

Chart C4-2

The Structure of External Assets and Liabilities in China's Banking Sector by Currency

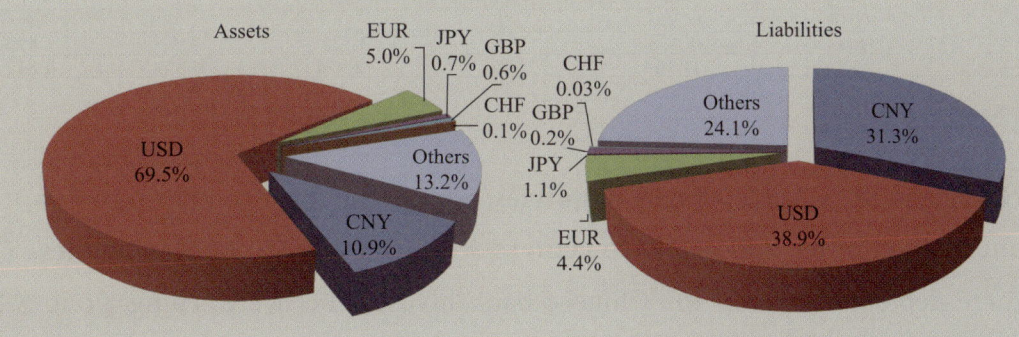

Source: SAFE.

In terms of the counter–party sectors, the non–bank sectors dominated. At end–December 2018, Chinese banks' external assets vis–à–vis the overseas banking sector and the non–banking sector were basically at the same scale. Among them, external assets in the overseas banking sector amounted to USD 547.7 billion, an increase of 20 percent year on year. The increase was due to the increase in loans and deposits to overseas banks. External assets of overseas non-banking sectors amounted to USD 568.7 billion, an increase of 5 percent. The increase was mainly due to the increase in bonds issued by overseas non-banking sectors. Chinese banks absorbed more liabilities from overseas non-banking sectors. Among these, external liabilities in overseas banks amounted to USD 575.7 billion, up 6 percent year on year. External liabilities in overseas non-banking sectors amounted to USD 721.9 billion, down 2 percent, mainly due to changes in the market value of domestic banks' bonds held by overseas non-banking sectors. From the perspective of net assets and liabilities, Chinese banks have net liabilities of USD 2.8 billion to overseas banks, a decrease of 68 percent year on year, and net liabilities of USD 153.2 billion to overseas non-banking sectors, a decrease of 21 percent (see Table C4-1).

Table C4-1　Table on the Structure of External Assets and Liabilities in China's Banking Industry at End-2018

Unit: 100 million of USD

Item		Assets		Libilities		Net Assets
		Amounts	Occupation Ratio	Amounts	Occupation Ratio	Amount
By Tools	Deposit and Loans	8 315	74%	7 287	56%	1 027
	Debt Securities	1 365	12%	1 848	14%	−483
	Other	1 485	13%	3 841	30%	−2 356
By Sectors	Bank	5 477	49%	5 757	44%	−280
	Non Bank	5 687	51%	7 219	56%	−1 532
By Currencies	CNY	1 214	11%	4 061	31%	−2 847
	USD	7 759	69%	5 052	39%	2 707
	EUR	561	5%	571	4%	−10
	JPY	74	1%	146	1%	−71
	GBP	70	1%	21	0%	49
	Other	1 486	13%	3 125	24%	−1 639
Total		11 164	100%	12 976	100%	−1 812

Source: SAFE.

In terms of counter-party countries/regions in the external position, the advanced economies and offshore centers were the major counter-parties. The top three debtor economies of Chinese bank investments were: Hong Kong SAR (USD 334.7 billion) , the U. S. (USD 123.2 billion) , and the UK (USD 44 billion) . They received a total of 45 percent of Chinese bank investments. The top three creditor economies of the external liabilities of Chinese banks were: Hong Kong SAR (USD 691.8 billion) , Singapore (USD 107.4 billion) , and Taiwan of China (USD 77.5 billion) . They contributed 67 percent of the total investments to Chinese banks (see Chart C4-3) .

Chart C4-3

The Structure of the External Assets and Liabilities of China's Banking Sector by Country/Region

Assets

- Hongkong SAR 30%
- USA 11%
- UK 4%
- Others 55%

Liabilities

- Hongkong SAR 53%
- Singapore 8%
- Taiwan of China 6%
- Others 33%

IV. Operation of the Foreign-Exchange Market and the RMB Exchange Rate

（I）Trends in the RMB Exchange Rate

The RMB exchange rate was relatively stable against the USD. At end-December 2018, the mid-price of the RMB exchange rate against the USD was 6.8632, adepreciation of 4.79 percent from the end of 2017. The RMB spot exchange rate against the USD in the inter-bank foreign-exchange market（CNY）and in the offshore market（CNH）each depreciated by 5.33 percent respectively（see Chart 4-1）. The average daily spread between the CNH and the CNY was 102 bps, lower than the 130 bps in 2017. During all of 2018, with the appreciation of the USD, the decline of the RMB against the USD was comparable to that of the developed countriesʼ currencies, such as the EUR and the GBP, and was much lower than that of most of the emerging market currencies. The RMB has become a stable currency in the global monetary system.

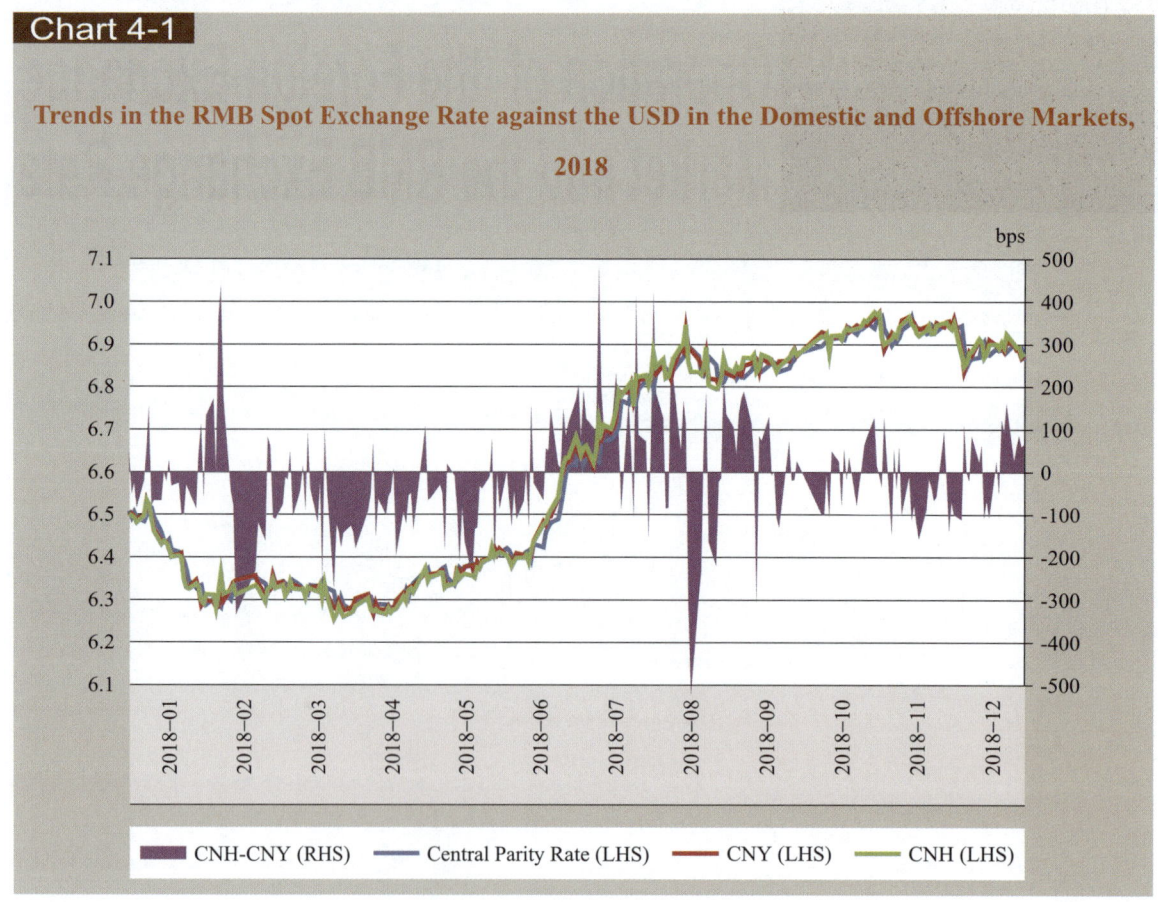

Chart 4-1

Trends in the RMB Spot Exchange Rate against the USD in the Domestic and Offshore Markets, 2018

Sources: CFETS, Reuters.

The RMB exchange rate was mixed against other major currencies. At the end of

2018, the mid-price of the RMB exchange rate against the EUR, 100 JPY, GBP, AUD, and CAD stood at 7.8473，6.1887，8.6762，4.8250, and 5.0381 respectively, a depreciation of 0.57 percent, 6.47 percent respectively, and an appreciation of 1.19 percent, 5.55 percent, and 3.23 percent respectively（see Chart 4-2）.

Chart 4-2

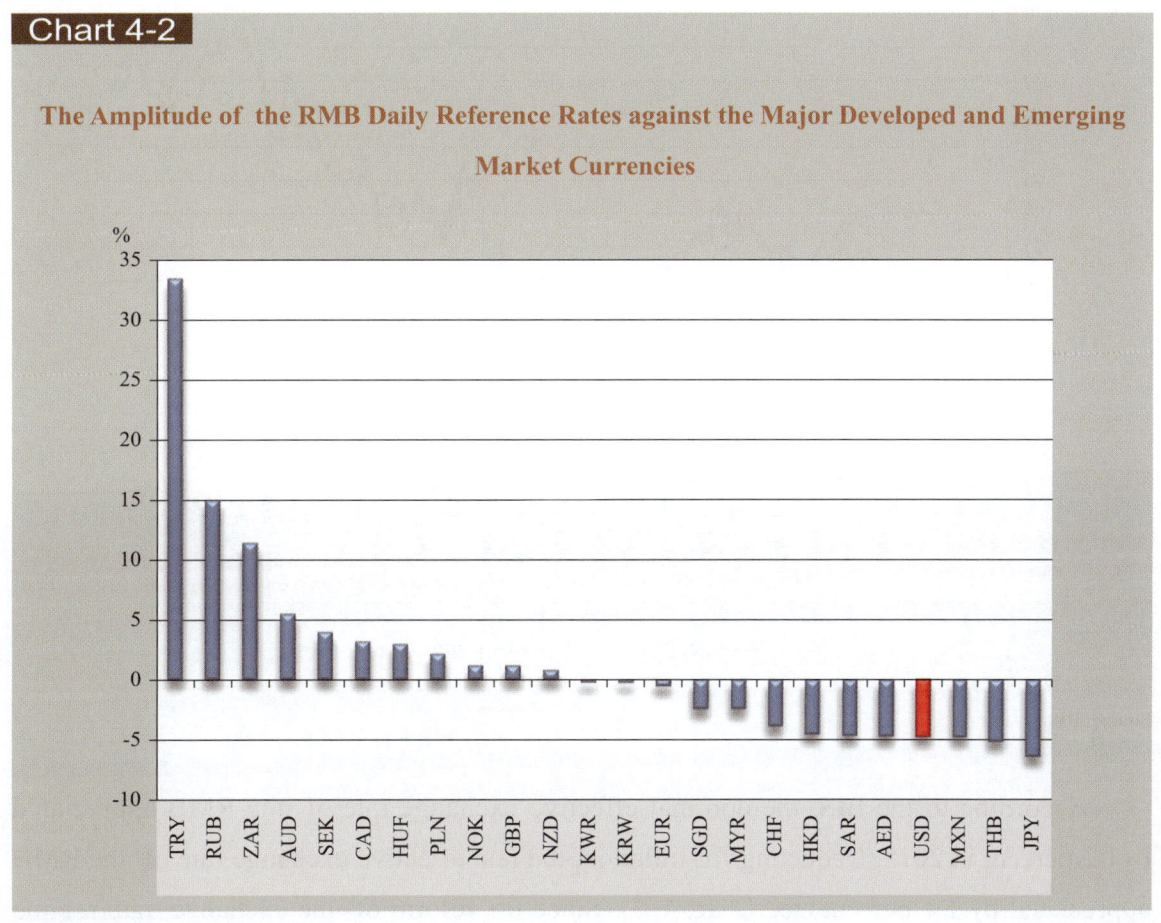

The Amplitude of the RMB Daily Reference Rates against the Major Developed and Emerging Market Currencies

Source: CFETS.

The RMB exchange rate was basically stable against the basket of currencies. According to CFETS data, at the end of 2018 the RMB exchange-rate indexes of the CFETS, the BIS basket of currencies, and the SDR basket of currencies were 93.28, 96.78, and 93.14 respectively, a depreciation of 1.66 percent, an appreciation of 0.89 percent, and a depreciation of 2.97 percent respectively, from the end of the previous year.

Chart 4-3

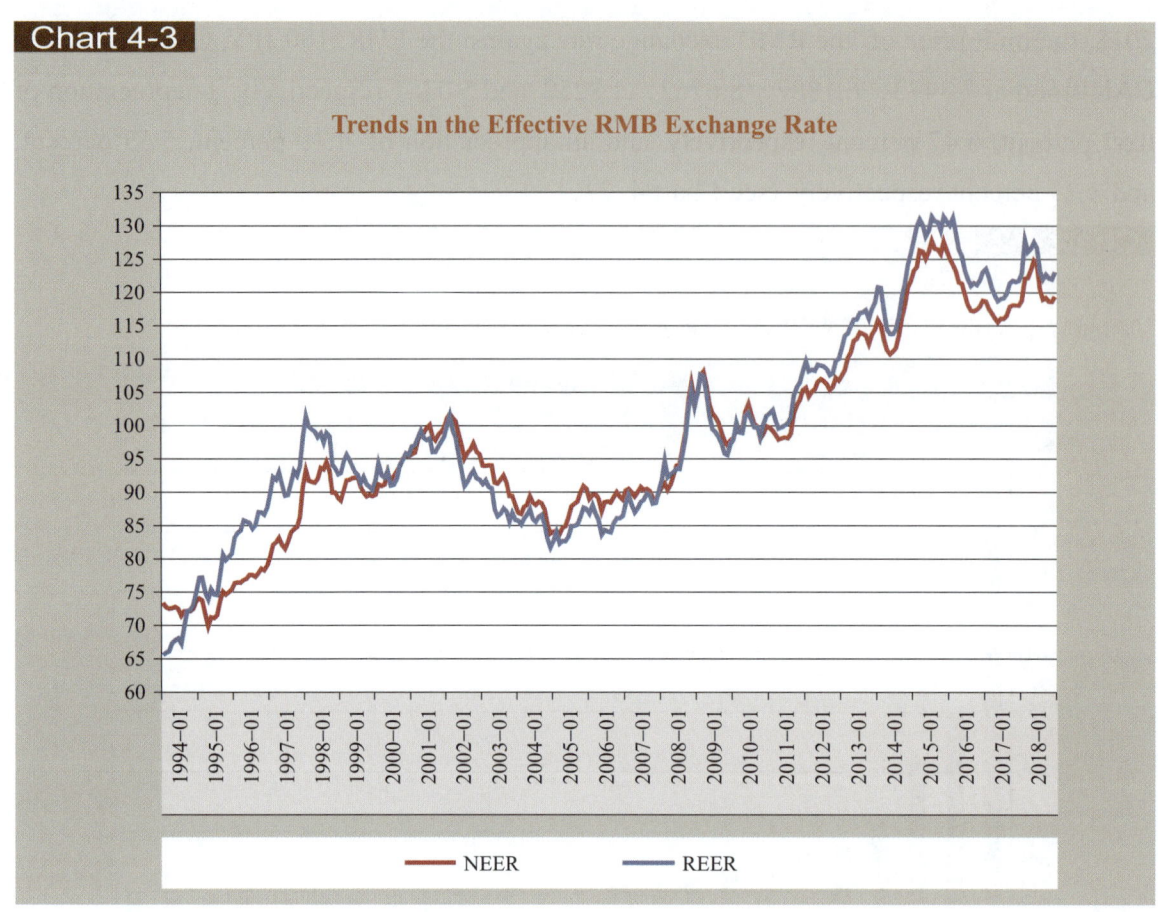

Trends in the Effective RMB Exchange Rate

— NEER   — REER

Source: BIS.

According to the BIS, the nominal effective exchange rate of the RMB appreciated by1.2 percent in 2018. Deducting for inflation, the real effective exchange rate of the RMB appreciated by 1.1 percent (see Chart 4-3). Since the reform of the exchange-rate regime in 2005, the nominal and real effective exchange rates of the RMB appreciated by 38.1 percent and 47.2 percent respectively.

The RMB exchange rate fluctuated in both directions and flexibility increased. In 2018, the closing price fluctuation of the RMB exchange rate against the USD reached 11.3 percent, which is higher than that in the previous year. On the one hand, the domestic economy and cross-border capital flows stabilized, and the economic structure continued to be optimized. All these factors supported the fundamentals in the RMB exchange rate. On the other hand, due to Sino-US trade frictions, USD interest-rate increases, and narrowed spreads, in order to conform to market changes the RMB exchange rate, with a more flexible exchange mechanism, fluctuated between rising and falling.

At the end of 2018, the one-year historic volatility of the RMB exchange rate in the domestic and offshore markets stood at 4.3 percent and 5.4 percent, up1.2 percent and 1.7 percent from the beginning of 2018 respectively. The implied volatilities in the domestic and offshore options markets reached 5.2 percent and 6.1 percent, up 1.2 percent and 0.6 percent from the beginning of 2018 respectively (see Chart 4-4).

Chart 4-4

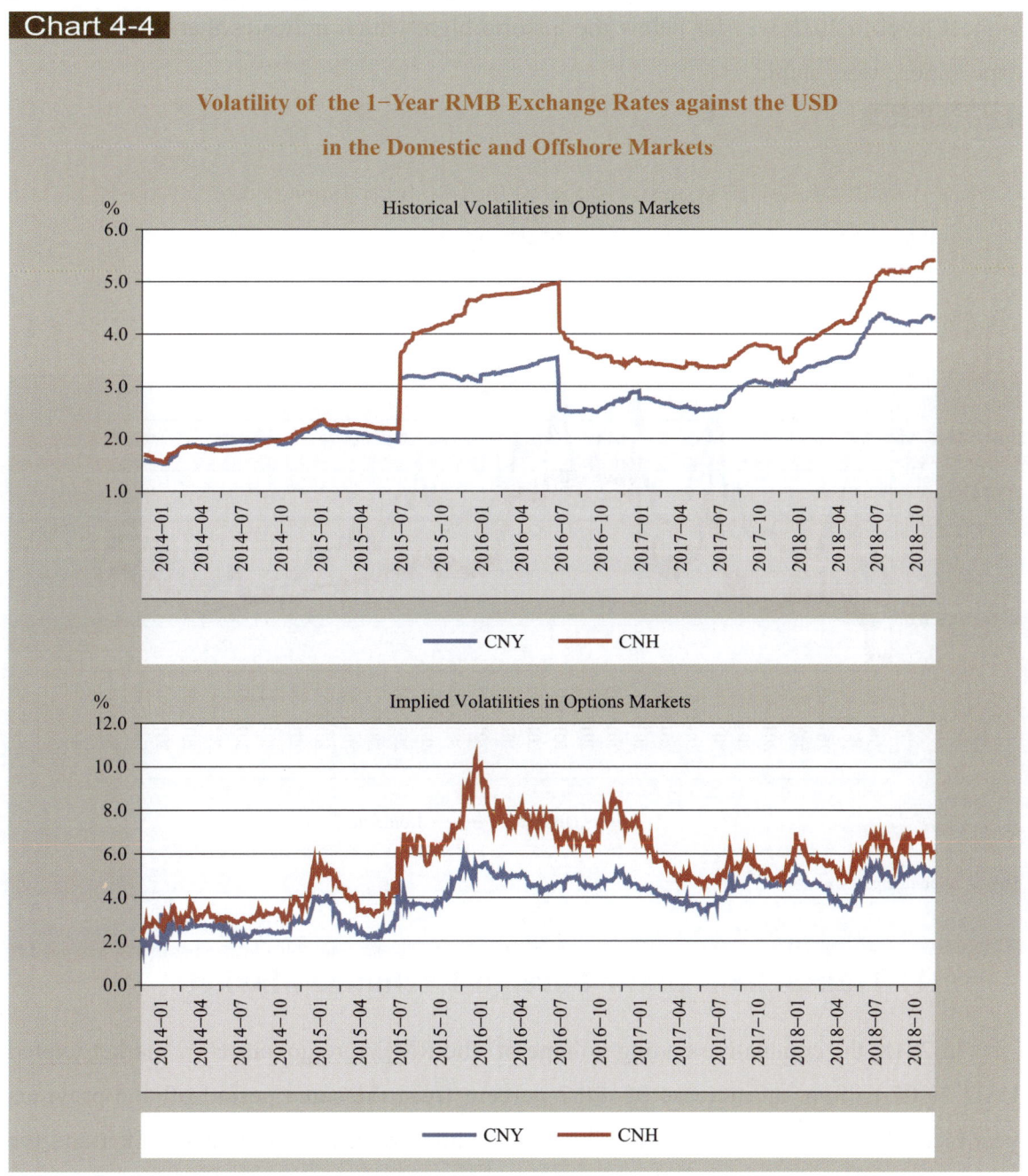

Volatility of the 1-Year RMB Exchange Rates against the USD
in the Domestic and Offshore Markets

Source: Bloomberg.

In 2018, domestic and offshore risk reversals (the difference between the volatility of the USD call / RMB put options and the USD put / RMB call options) were 0.92 percent and 0.93 percent respectively, up slightly from the end of the last year, but they persisted in their decline beginning in November (see Chart 4-5). During the entire year of 2018 the domestic risk reversals first declined, then went up, and finally declined, while the highest level in 2018 was far below the historic high, which indicates that exchange-rate expectations were stable.

Chart 4-5

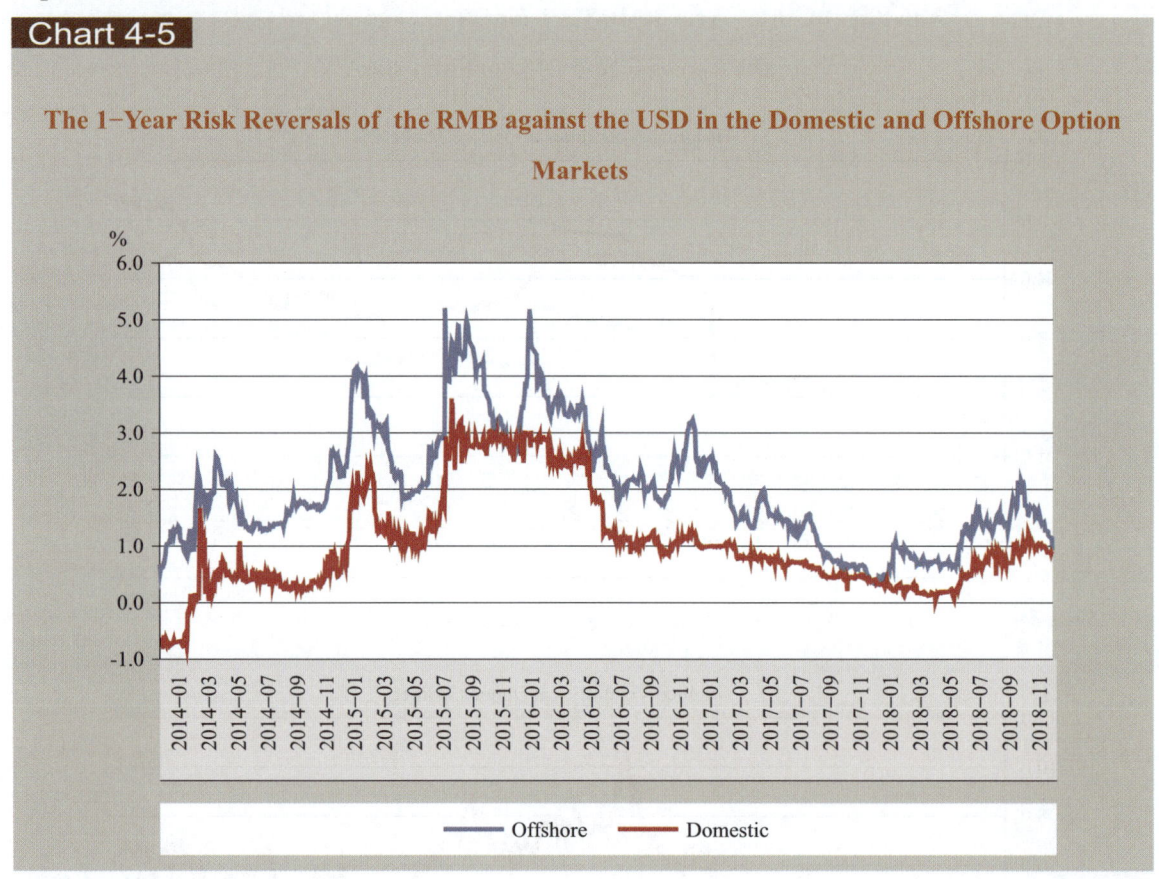

The 1-Year Risk Reversals of the RMB against the USD in the Domestic and Offshore Option Markets

Source: Bloomberg.

(II) Transactions in the Foreign-Exchange Market

In 2018, the cumulative trading volume of the RMB/foreign-currency market totaled USD 29.07 trillion, an increase of 20.7 percent from the same period of the previous year (see Chart 4-6), among these. The total trading volume in the client market and the inter-bank market were USD 4.23 trillion and USD 24.85 trillion respectively. [1] Spot and

---

[1] The client market uses the total volume of both purchases and sales of foreign exchange. The inter-bank market uses the unilateral trading volume. The same as below.

derivative transactions witnessed a trading volume of USD 11.06 trillion and USD 18.01 trillion respectively (see Table 4-6). Derivatives accounted for 61.9 percent of the share of the total transactions in the foreign-exchange market. This structure was closer to that of the global foreign-exchange market (see Chart 4-7).

Chart 4-6

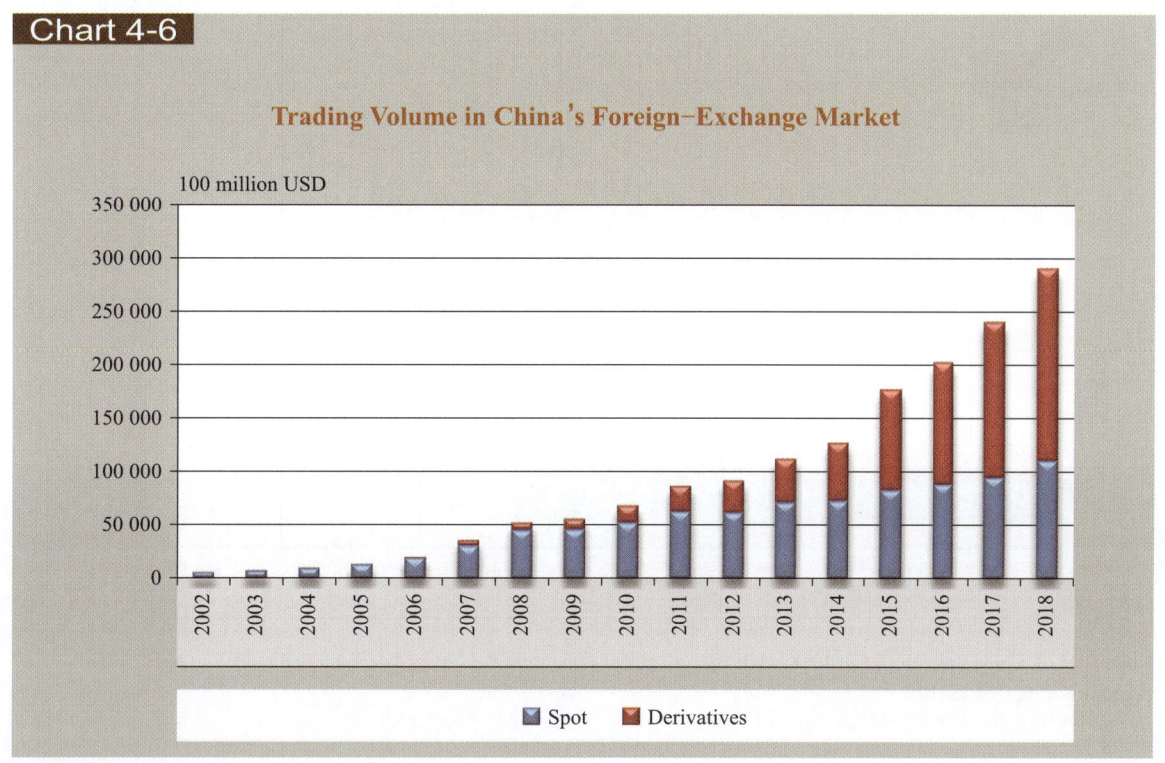

Trading Volume in China's Foreign-Exchange Market

Sources: SAFE, CFETS.

Steady growth of foreign-exchange spot transactions. In 2018, the spot foreign-exchange market saw a trading volume of USD 11.06 trillion, up 16.6 percent from the same period of the previous year. Spot purchases and sales of foreign exchange in the client market totaled USD 3.43 trillion (including banks, but excluding implementation of forwards), up 11.0 percent from the previous year. The spot inter-bank foreign-exchange market saw a trading volume of USD 7.63 trillion, up 19.3 percent from the previous year. The share of USD transactions was 96.8 percent.

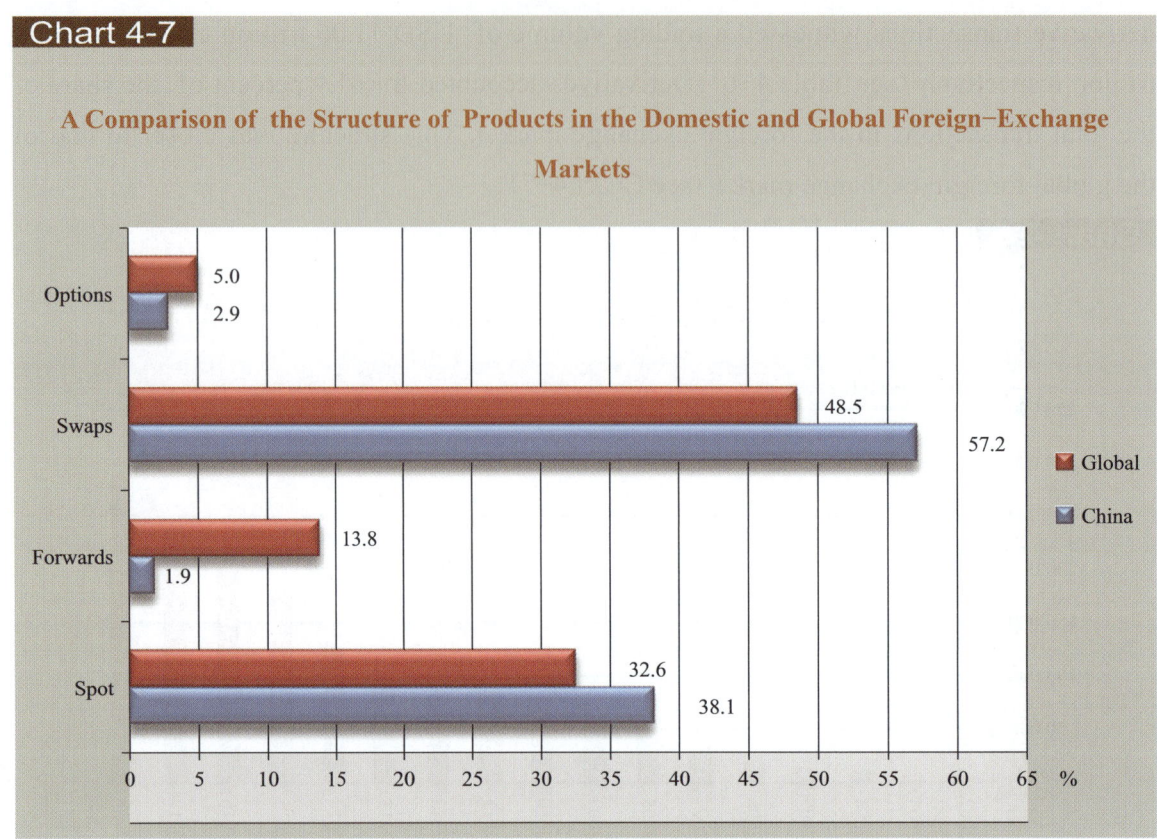

Chart 4-7

A Comparison of the Structure of Products in the Domestic and Global Foreign–Exchange Markets

Note: Date of China was colected in 2018, while date of global came from the survey date published by BIS in April, 2016.

Sources: SAFE, CFETS, BIS.

Foreign-exchange forward transactions continued to rise. In 2018, the forward market saw a trading volume of USD 541.9 billion, up 27.2 percent from the previous year. In the client market, purchases and sales of forwards in foreign exchange totaled USD 454.3 billion, up 40.9 percent from the previous year. Purchases and sales of forwards were USD 213.0 billion and USD 241.3 billion, up 43.7 percent and 38.5 percent respectively （see Chart4–8）. Short–term 6–month transactions accounted for 65 percent of the total transactions, down 2 percent from the previous year. In the inter–bank foreign–exchange market, forwards totaled USD 87.5 billion, down 15.3 percent from the previous year.

Swap transactions continued to rise. In 2018, cumulative foreign–exchange and currency–swap transactions totaled USD 16.62 trillion, up 22.6 percent from the previous year. Cumulative foreign–exchange and currency–swap transactions in the client market reached USD 103.6 billion, up 0.4 percent from the previous year. Spot purchases/forward sales and spot sales/forward purchases stood at USD 91.9 billion and USD 11.7 billion respectively, up 5.7 percent and down 28.1 percent from the previous year respectively. The cumulative foreign-exchange and currency-swap transactions in the inter-bank market reached USD 16.51 trillion, up 22.6 percent from the previous year. Swap transactions are an important tool for banks to manage liquidity in domestic and foreign currencies.

Chart 4-8

The Trading Volume of Purchases and Sales of Forward Foreign-Exchange Transactions in the Client Market

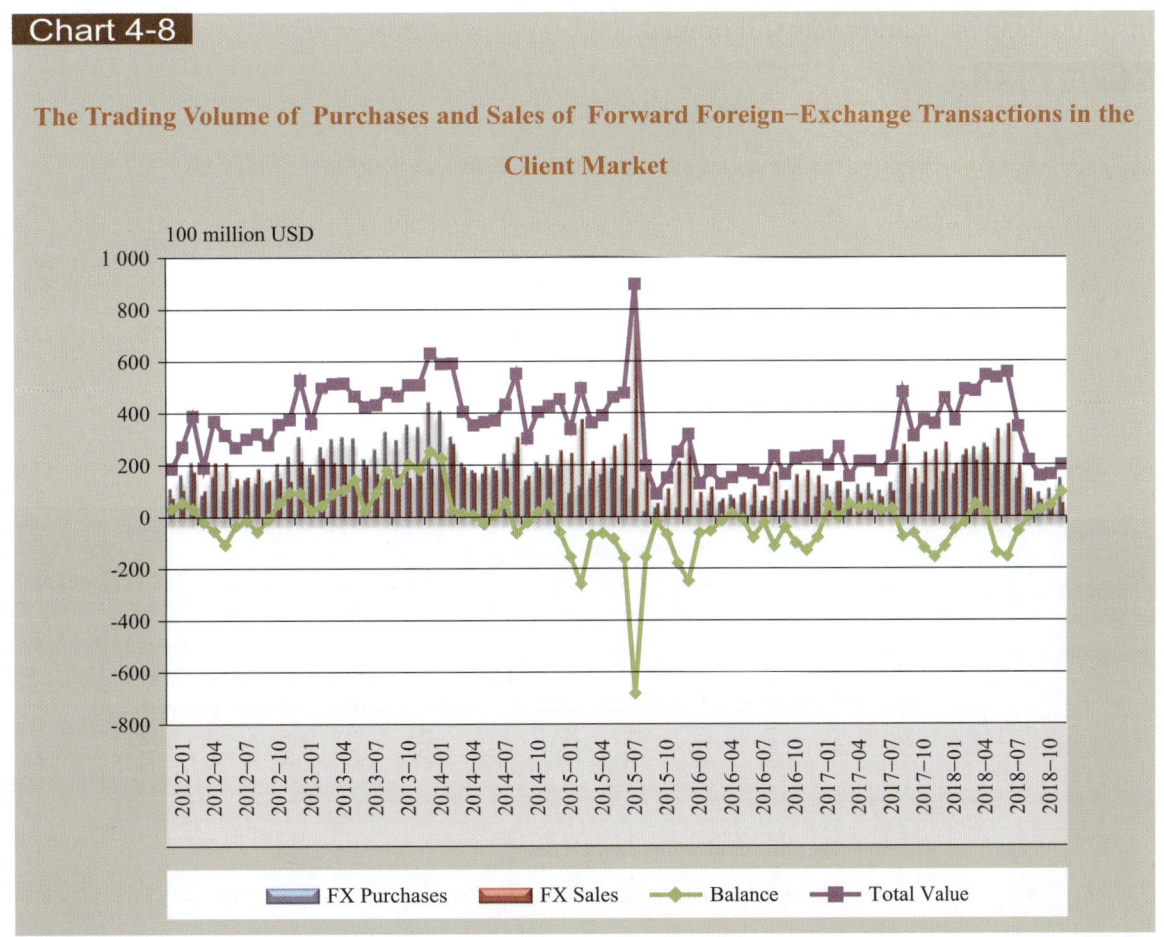

Source: SAFE.

Faster growth in options transactions. In 2018 the trading volume of options totaled USD 847.4 billion, up 40.7 percent from the previous year. The client market saw a total trading volume of USD 236.3 billion, up 2.4 percent from the previous year. The inter-bank market saw a total trading volume of USD 611.1 billion, up 64.6 percent from the previous year.

Foreign-exchange market participants remained stable. Proprietary transactions by banks continued to dominate (see Chart 4-9). In 2018, the share of inter-bank transactions among all foreign-exchange transactions, which were 83.9 percent in 2017, was up to 84.8 percent. The share of bank transactions with non-financial customers declined from 15.3

percent to 14.4 percent. This may be due to the substitution effect of cross–border RMB settlement business. The share of non–banking financial institutions was 0.8 percent, basically the same as that in 2016 and 2017, indicating that participation by non–banking institutions in the market was still limited.

Chart 4-9

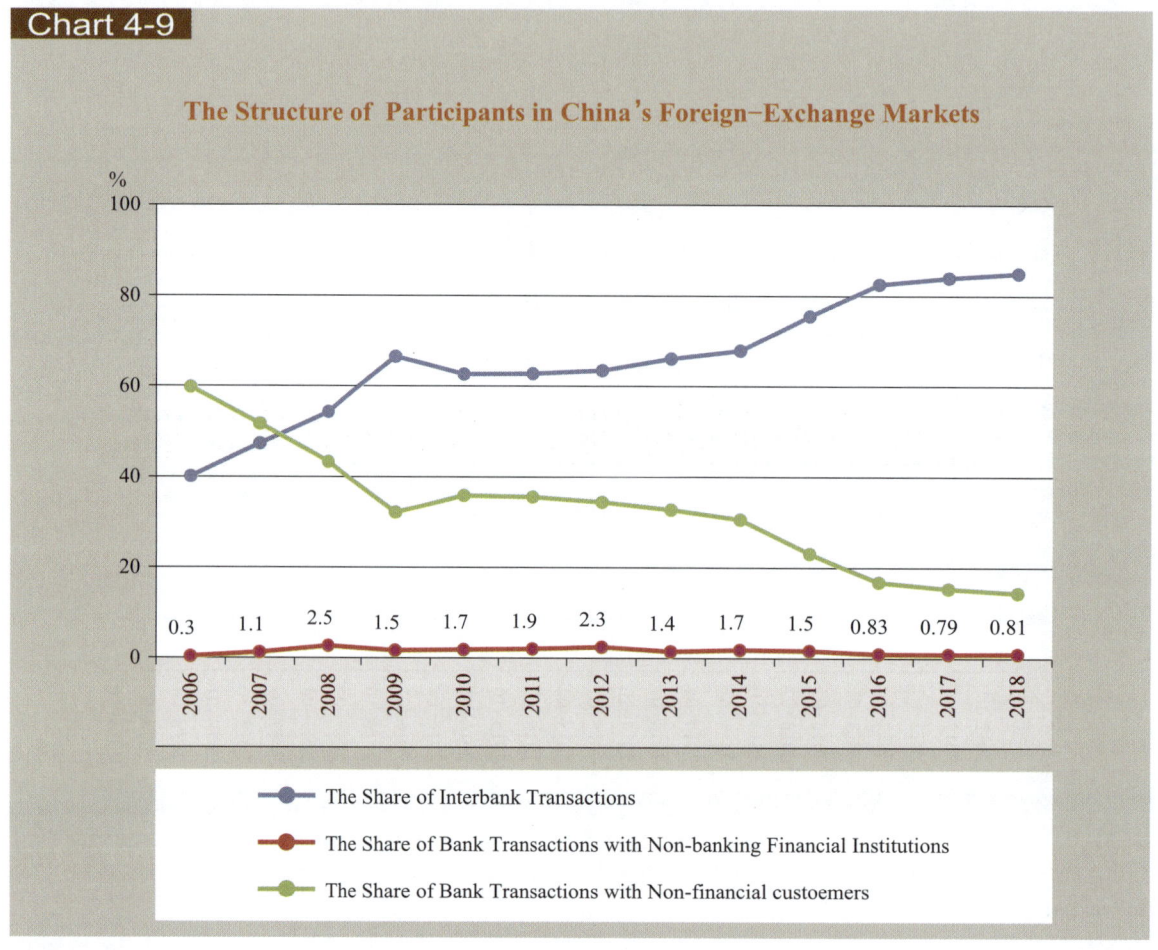

The Structure of Participants in China's Foreign–Exchange Markets

- The Share of Interbank Transactions
- The Share of Bank Transactions with Non-banking Financial Institutions
- The Share of Bank Transactions with Non-financial custoemers

Sources: SAFE, CFETS.

Table 4–1   Transactions in the RMB/Foreign–Exchange Market, 2018

Product	Trading Volume (100 million USD)
Spot	**110 647**
Client Market	**34 315**
Interbank Foreign Exchange Market	**76 332**
Forward	**5 419**
Client Market	**4 543**
Less than 3 months (including 3 months)	2 048
3 months to 1 year (including 1 year)	2 144
More than 1 year	352
Interbank Foreign Exchange Market	**875**
Less than 3 months (including 3 months)	552
3 months to 1 year (including 1 year)	293

(Continue)

Product	Trading Volume (100 million USD)
More than 1 year	31
Foreign Exchange and Currency Swaps	**166 171**
Client Market	**1 036**
Interbank Foreign Exchange Market	**165 135**
Less than 3 months (including 3 months)	141 448
3 months to 1 year (including 1 year)	22 864
More than 1 year	823
Options	**8 474**
Client Market	**2 363**
Foreign Exchange Call Options/RMB Put Options	1 146
Foreign Exchange Put Options/RMB Call Options	1 217
Less than 3 months (including 3 months)	980
3 months to 1 year (including 1 year)	1 187
More than 1 year	196
Interbank Foreign Exchange Market	**6 111**
Less than 3 months (including 3 months)	4 359
3 months to 1 year (including 1 year)	1 735
More than 1 year	17
Total	**290 711**
Client Market	**42 257**
Interbank Foreign Exchange Market	**248 454**
Including: Spots	110 647
Forwards	5 419
Foreign Exchange and Currency Swaps	166 171
Options	8 474

Note: The trading volumes here are all unilateral transactions and the data employ rounded-off numbers.

Sources: SAFE, CFETS.

Ⅴ. Outlook for the balance of Payments

In 2019 the international environment is still complex and changeable. There are some uncertainties, including the slowdown of global economic growth, the impact of trade protectionism on international trade development and market confidence, and the possibility that international political instability may promote market risk aversion. However, domestic fundamentals, such as the economy, policy, and the market, will still play a cornerstone role. It is expected that China will continue to be characterized by a basic balance in the current account, overall stability of cross-border capital flows, and an autonomous equilibrium in the balance of payments.

The internal basis for the stability in Chinaʹs balance of payments remains solid. First, the trend of long-term Chinese economic development will not change. Chinaʹs economy still has sufficient resilience and a huge potential. Chinese economic growth will remain at a high global level, which will be achieved on the basis of a larger economic aggregate, which will provide a solid economic basis for China to effectively react to changes in the external environment. In 2019, China will strengthen counter-cyclical regulation in macro-economic policy and will continue to implement an active fiscal policy and a sound monetary policy. As the macro-leverage rate will stabilize, a virtuous cycle in the national economy will gradually take shape. Second, the process of promoting an all-round opening-up in China will remain unchanged. In 2019, China will provide greater support and conveniences for market access, intellectual property protection, trade and investment facilitation, and capital market opening, which will provide a solid policy basis for overseas capital to invest in the domestic market. Third, the trend of improving Chinese mechanisms for the operation of the balance of payments will not change. At present, the two-way floating of the RMB exchange rate is being strengthened, which is conducive to consolidating more diversified and rational market expectations. The combination of the macro-prudential and micro-supervision framework for cross-border capital flows is conducive to maintaining healthy order in the foreign-exchange market, which will provide a good market basis for promoting the smooth operation of cross-border capital flows and an autonomous equilibrium in the balance of payments.

The current account will remain basically balanced. First, both export and import growth of trade in goods are likely to stabilize, and trade in goods will retain a certain surplus. On the one hand, Chinaʹs export demand has fallen, but its export competitiveness is still strong. According to the latest International Monetary Fund forecast, global economic growth in 2019 is projected to be 3.5 percent, 0.2 percentage point slower than that in 2018. At the same time, China's manufacturing industry is characterized by a mature infrastructure, a complete industrial chain, a large number of skilled workers, and large markets both at home and abroad, and it is coupled with the continuous promotion of transformation and upgrading, which helps to maintain strong international competitiveness of related products. On the other hand, against the backdrop that China pays attention to high-quality economic development with relatively stable internal demand, import growth will be more stable. Second, the trade deficit in services will gradually stabilize. The travel deficit is still the main source of the deficit in services trade. At present, the demand for overseas tourism and study has stabilized. For example, in recent years the growth rate of the tourism deficit has fallen to a single digit, which shows that the space for further growth has begun to narrow after reaching a historically high level. This is a natural law and process. In addition, with improvements in the quality of the domestic service industry and the enhancement of soft power, such as the ecological environment and system, cross-border consumption by domestic residents will become more rational and stable.

Capital inflows for mid-and long-term investments under the capital account have greater room for improvement. In terms of direct investments, China's actual utilization of foreign capital remains relatively large. In the future, with the further expansion of the opening and the increasing importance of the domestic market, China will have a great potential to attract direct investments. According to UNCTAD statistics, at the end of 2017 the ratio of FDI stock to GDP was 12 percent, the global average was 39 percent, and the average level of the developing countries was 33 percent. In terms of securities investments, in 2018 foreign central banks and other institutions had more capital inflows for the purpose of mid-and long-term asset allocations. At present, the proportion of foreign investors in the domestic capital market is still low. In the future, as China's stock market and bond market become more deeply integrated into the major international indexes, under the policy of further opening and facilitation, China will become an important destination for the diversification of asset allocations of international capital.

Box 5

The Securities Market has become an Important Channel for Overseas Investors to Invest in China

In recent years, the opening up of the inter-bank bond market in China has accelerated, the reform of the Qualified Foreign Institutional Investors (QFII) system has been deepened, and the Shanghai–Hong Kong Stock Connect, the Shenzhen–Hong Kong Stock Connect, and the Bond Connect have been implemented in succession. It is now more convenient for foreign investors to invest in China's securities market. At the same time, with the inclusion of China's bonds and stocks in the leading international indices, demand by foreign investors to invest in China's bonds and stocks has been increasing. According to SAFE statistics, in recent years foreign institutions have continuously increased their holdings of China's bonds and listed stocks (including funds, the same below). The total size of their holdings has increased from USD 219.2 billion at the end of 2014 to USD 444.8 billion at the end of 2018, an increase of 103 percent. Among these, bond holdings rose from USD 108.5 billion to USD 263.8 billion, an increase of 143 percent, and stock holdings rose from USD 110.7 billion to USD 181 billion, an increase of 64 percent. In the future, China's securities market will still have a great potential to attract foreign investors.

In terms of market size, China's bond market and China's stock market both rank among the top three in the world in terms of having a large market capacity. According to statistics of the Bank for International Settlements (BIS), at the end of the third quarter of 2018 the top five countries in market value among the global bond markets were the United States (USD 41 trillion), Japan (USD 12.6 trillion), China (USD 12.4 trillion), the UK (USD 5.8 trillion), and France (USD 4.6 trillion). The market value of China's bond market was only USD 0.2 trillion smaller than that of Japan (see Chart C5−1). According to Bloomberg, at the end of February 2019, the US stock market ranked first in the world, with a market value of USD 30 trillion, China ranked second (USD 6.7 trillion), and Japan ranked third (USD 5.73 trillion) (see Chart C5−2).

Chart C5-1

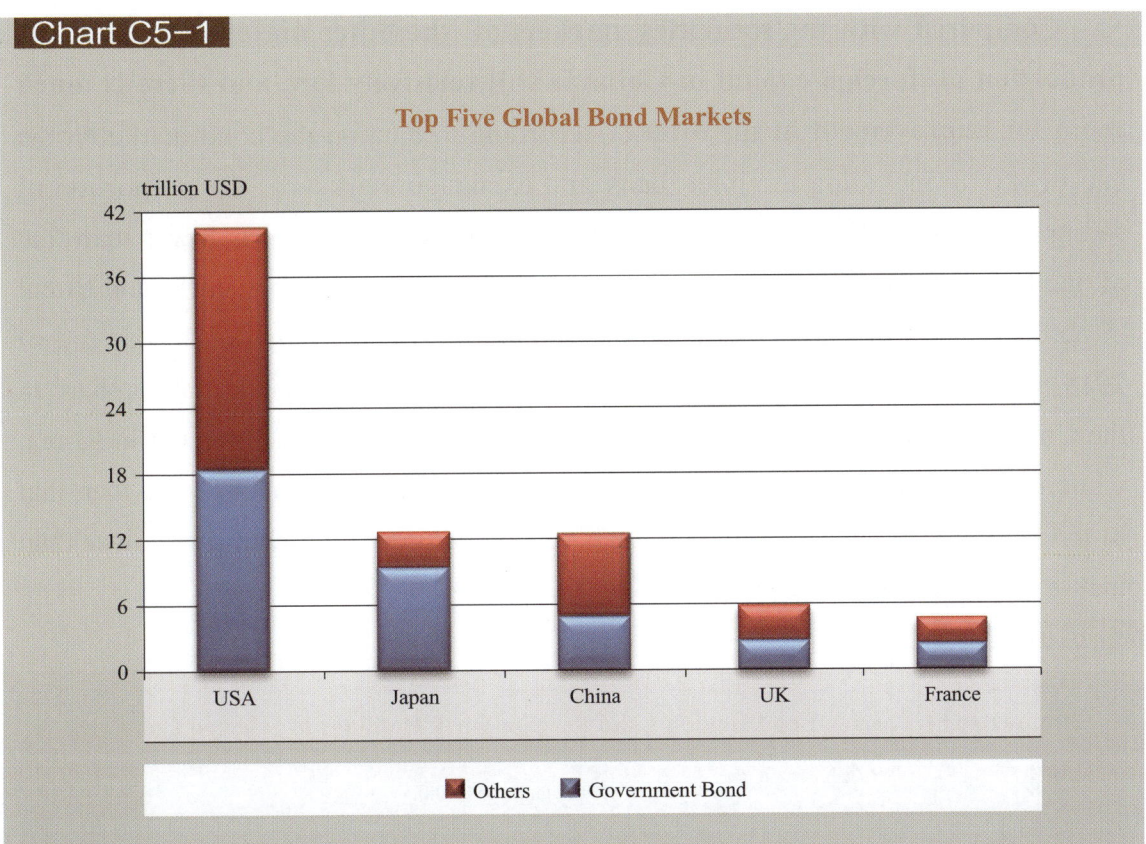

Top Five Global Bond Markets

Note: As of the end of the third quarter of 2018.

Source: BIS.

Chart C5-2

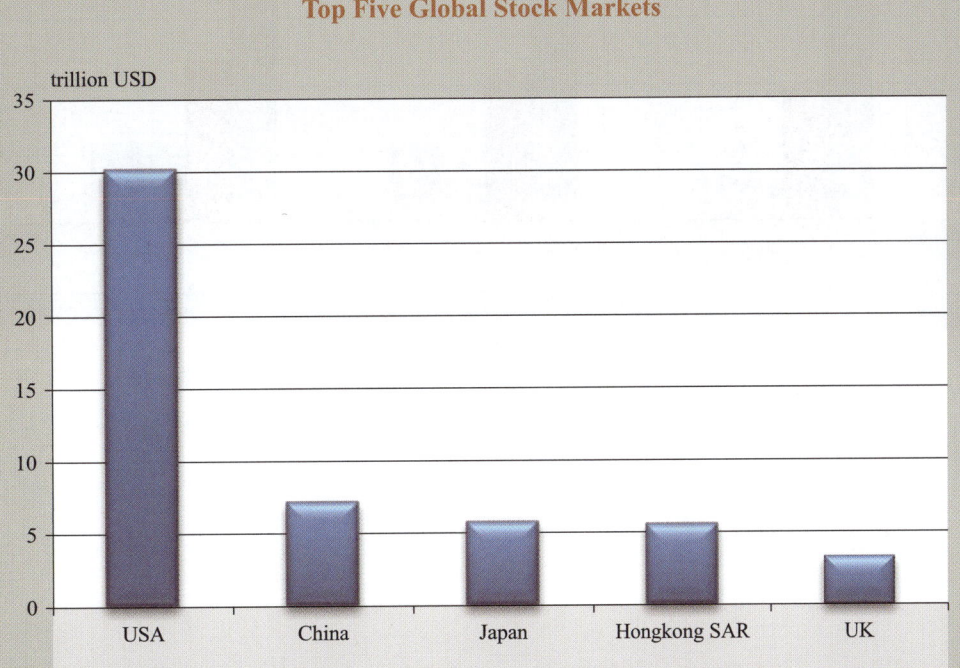

Top Five Global Stock Markets

Note: As of the end of February 2019.

Source:Bloomberg.

Compared with the securities markets of the other major countries, the proportion of foreign capital in China is still relatively low, and there is much room for improvement in the future. According to data on the bond market at the end of 2018 (including the inter-bank and exchange markets), the proportion of foreign capital in China's bond market was 2.1 percent, which was lower than that of the United States (25 percent), Japan (12 percent), Korea (6 percent), and Brazil (5 percent) (see Chart C5-3). According to data on the stock market at the end of 2018, foreign ownership accounted for 15 percent of the total stock market share in the United States, 30 percent in Japan, 21 percent in Brazil, and 33 percent in Korea, while the figure was 3.5 percent in China, which was not only much lower than that in the developed countries such as Japan and the United States but also lower than that in the emerging markets such as Korea and Brazil.

Chart C5-3

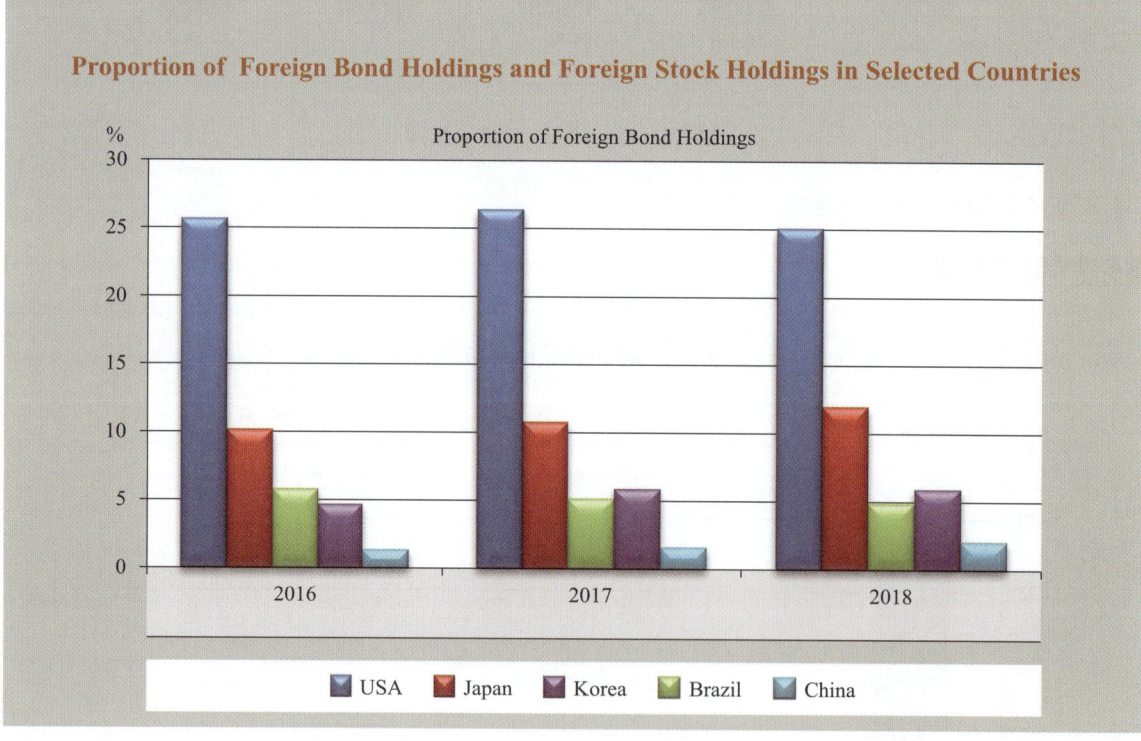

Proportion of Foreign Bond Holdings and Foreign Stock Holdings in Selected Countries

Proportion of Foreign Bond Holdings

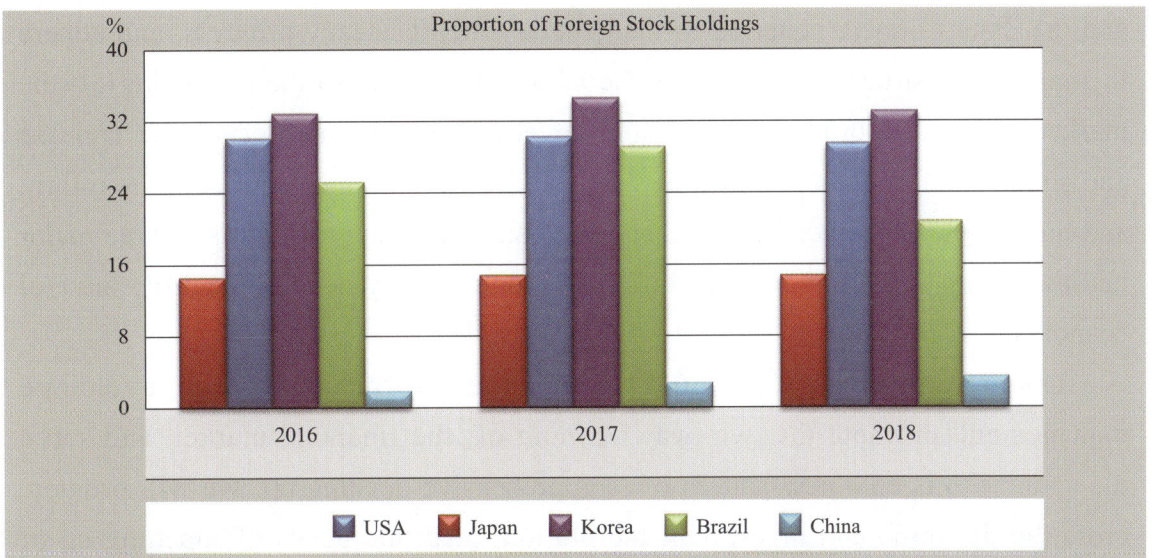

Sources: Bloomberg, CEIC, BIS, US Treasury, US Federal Reserve, Ministry of Finance of Japan, Bank of Japan, Tokyo Stock Exchange, PBC, SAFE, Shanghai Stock Exchange, Shenzhen Stock Exchange. Calculated by the staff in the SAFE.

Note: Japan's foreign stock holdings at the end of 2018 are based on the equity securities of the liabilities in the IIP at the end of 2018; the foreign bond holdings of Japan, Korea, and Brazil at the end of 2018 have been replaced by the data at the end of the third quarter. Among these, Japan's foreign bond holdings are based on the debt securities of liabilities in the IIP.

At present, the economic environment for the development and opening of China's securities market remains stable, and the institutional environment is improving day by day. On the one hand, the domestic economy is maintaining a generally stable and positive trend, with relatively rapid economic growth worldwide, good sovereign credit, and a relatively stable exchange rate, which establishes a foundation for the sound development of the securities market. Moreover, the overall income level of China's bond market is still higher than that of the major developed markets, and its stock market also has a potential for development. On the other hand, financial services in China's securities market are more complete, and the level of liberalization and facilitation of foreign investments is constantly improving. For example, in 2018, net purchases of China's bonds and stocks by foreign investors totaled USD 139.2 billion, an increase of 73 percent over 2017. Among these, purchases were USD 897.7 billion, up 51 percent, and sales were USD 758.5 billion, up 48 percent, showing that both capital inflows and capital outflows involved in foreign investments are very smooth.

In 2019, the foreign-exchange management authorities will conscientiously implement the decision-making arrangements of the Central Committee of the Party and the State Council, adhering to the general tone of steady progress, and adhere to supply-side structural reforms as the main line, adhere to the deepening of the market-oriented reforms, expand a high level of opening up, deepen the "release and control" reforms, implement the "six stability" requirements, deepen the reform and opening-up in the foreign-exchange sector, to continue to fight the three major battles, and to actively serve the sustainable and healthy development of the real economy.

On the one hand, we should deepen the reform of foreign-exchange management, promote the two-way opening of the financial market, and serve the country to open a new pattern of comprehensive opening up. We will promote cross-border trade and investment facilitation, meet the needs of opening up of the Chinese economy and financial market, and further optimize foreign-exchange management policies to support innovative trade modes; we will optimize financial services and the business environment, promote stable growth of foreign direct investment in China, and actively support domestic enterprises with the ability and conditions to carry out genuine and compliant foreign investments; we will promote capital investments in a sound and orderly manner, promote the opening of the domestic stock and bond markets; establish and improve an open and competitive foreign-exchange market, increase the depth of the foreign- exchange market, expand trading subjects, enrich trading tools, expand the trading scope, promote the market opening, and meet the hedging needs of different subjects. We will actively support the reform of foreign-exchange management in the free trade pilot areas of Guangdong, Hong Kong, Macao, Dawan District, and the Xiong'an New Area, and support Hainan to deepen the reform and opening up in an all-round way.

On the other hand, we must adhere to bottom line thinking, maintain the stability of the foreign-exchange market, guard against the risks of cross-border capital flows, safeguard the security, flow, and value-added of the foreign- exchange reserves, and safeguard national economic and financial security. We will continue to improve the exchange-rate formation mechanism and maintain the basic stability of the RMB exchange rate at a reasonable and balanced level. We will improve the "macro prudential + micro supervision" management framework for cross-border capital flows, improve the monitoring, early warning, and response mechanism for the macro-prudential management of cross-border capital flows, enrich the policy toolbox for macro-prudential management of cross-border capital flows, regulate cross-border capital flows counter-cyclically in a market-oriented manner, maintain the stability, consistency, and predictability of cross-cyclical micro-regulation of foreign exchange, and strictly crack down on foreign-exchange violations.

2018 中 国 国 际 收 支 报 告
China's Balance of Payments Report

附 录 统计资料
Appendix Statistics

一、国际收支 [①]
I. Balance of Payments

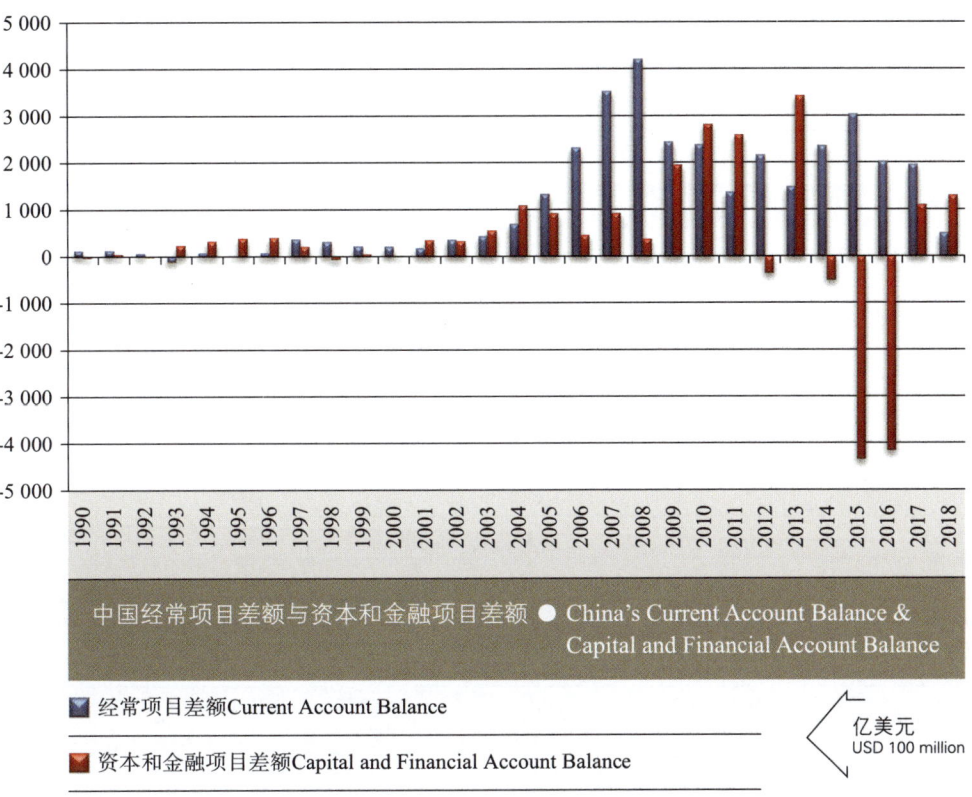

中国经常项目差额与资本和金融项目差额 ● China's Current Account Balance & Capital and Financial Account Balance

■ 经常项目差额Current Account Balance

■ 资本和金融项目差额Capital and Financial Account Balance

亿美元
USD 100 million

---

① 资料来源：国家外汇管理局；IMF《国际收支统计》《国际金融统计》；环亚经济数据库。
Sources: State Administration of Foreign Exchange; IMF, Balance of Payments Statistics, International Financial Statistics; CEIC Database.

中国国际收支概览表 (1)

China's Balance of Payments Abridged (1)

项目 / 年份 Item/Year	1983	1984	1985	1986	1987	1988
1. 经常账户 Current account	42	20	−114	−70	3	−38
贷方 Credit	240	273	276	276	354	470
借方 Debit	−198	−253	−390	−347	−351	−508
A. 货物和服务 Goods and services	26	1	−125	−74	3	−41
贷方 Credit	220	248	258	262	341	449
借方 Debit	−194	−247	−383	−336	−338	−490
a. 货物 Goods	18	−2	−131	−90	−13	−56
贷方 Credit	192	217	227	223	300	398
借方 Debit	−174	−219	−358	−313	−313	−454
b. 服务 Services	8	2	6	16	16	15
贷方 Credit	28	31	31	39	41	51
借方 Debit	−20	−29	−25	−23	−25	−36
B. 初次收入 Primary income	12	15	8	0	−2	−2
贷方 Credit	15	19	14	9	10	15
借方 Debit	−3	−4	−5	−9	−12	−16
C. 二次收入 Secondary income	5	4	2	4	2	4
贷方 Credit	6	6	4	5	4	6
借方 Debit	−1	−2	−2	−1	−2	−1
2. 资本和金融账户 Capital and financial account	−41	−32	139	83	11	48
2.1 资本账户 Capital account	0	0	0	0	0	0
贷方 Credit	0	0	0	0	0	0
借方 Debit	0	0	0	0	0	0
2.2 金融账户 Financial account	−41	−32	139	83	11	48
资产 Assets	−54	−58	50	13	−58	−45
负债 Liabilities	13	25	89	70	69	93
2.2.1 非储备性质的金融账户 Financial account excluding reserve assets	−14	−38	85	65	27	53
资产 Assets	−27	−63	−4	−4	−42	−40

单位：亿美元
Unit: USD 100 million

续表 (Continue)

项目 / 年份 Item/Year	1983	1984	1985	1986	1987	1988
负债 Liabilities	13	25	89	70	69	93
直接投资 Direct investment	8	13	13	18	17	23
资产 Assets	−1	−1	−6	−5	−6	−9
负债 Liabilities	9	14	20	22	23	32
证券投资 Portfolio investment	−6	−16	30	16	11	9
资产 Assets	−6	−17	23	0	−1	−3
负债 Liabilities	0	1	8	16	12	12
金融衍生工具 Financial derivatives (other than reserves) and employee stock options	0	0	0	0	0	0
资产 Assets	0	0	0	0	0	0
负债 Liabilities	0	0	0	0	0	0
其他投资 Other investment	−16	−34	41	32	0	20
资产 Assets	−19	−44	−20	1	−34	−28
负债 Liabilities	4	10	62	31	34	49
2.2.2 储备资产 Reserve assets	−27	5	54	17	−17	−5
其中：外汇储备 Foreign exchange reserves	−19	7	56	12	−15	−4
3. 净误差与遗漏 Net errors and omissions	**−2**	**12**	**−25**	**−12**	**−14**	**−10**

中国国际收支概览表 (2)

China's Balance of Payments Abridged (2)

项目 / 年份 Item/Year	1989	1990	1991	1992	1993	1994
1. 经常账户 Current account	−43	120	133	64	−119	77
贷方 Credit	436	525	602	736	800	1, 121
借方 Debit	−479	−405	−469	−672	−919	−1, 045
A. 货物和服务 Goods and services	−49	107	116	50	−118	74
贷方 Credit	412	491	555	668	743	1, 046
借方 Debit	−461	−385	−439	−618	−861	−973
a. 货物 Goods	−72	70	62	19	−143	35
贷方 Credit	350	411	460	543	597	844
借方 Debit	−422	−341	−398	−524	−740	−810
b. 服务 Services	23	37	54	31	25	39
贷方 Credit	62	81	95	126	146	202
借方 Debit	−39	−44	−41	−94	−120	−163
B. 初次收入 Primary income	2	11	8	2	−13	−10
贷方 Credit	19	30	37	56	44	57
借方 Debit	−17	−20	−29	−53	−57	−68
C. 二次收入 Secondary income	4	3	8	12	12	13
贷方 Credit	5	4	9	12	13	18
借方 Debit	−1	−1	−1	−1	−1	−4
2. 资本和金融账户 Capital and financial account	42	−89	−65	19	217	21
2.1 资本账户 Capital account	0	0	0	0	0	0
贷方 Credit	0	0	0	0	0	0
借方 Debit	0	0	0	0	0	0
2.2 金融账户 Financial account	42	−89	−65	19	217	21
资产 Assets	−15	−138	−160	−59	−109	−367
负债 Liabilities	58	49	94	77	326	389
2.2.1 非储备性质的金融账户 Financial account excluding reserve assets	64	−28	46	−3	235	326
资产 Assets	7	−77	−49	−80	−91	−62

单位：亿美元
Unit: USD 100 million

续表 (Continue)

项目 / 年份 Item/Year	1989	1990	1991	1992	1993	1994
负债 Liabilities	58	49	94	77	326	389
直接投资 Direct investment	26	27	35	72	231	318
资产 Assets	−8	−8	−9	−40	−44	−20
负债 Liabilities	34	35	44	112	275	338
证券投资 Portfolio investment	−2	−2	2	−1	31	35
资产 Assets	−3	−2	−3	−5	−6	−4
负债 Liabilities	1	0	6	4	36	39
金融衍生工具 Financial derivatives (other than reserves) and employee stock options	0	0	0	0	0	0
资产 Assets	0	0	0	0	0	0
负债 Liabilities	0	0	0	0	0	0
其他投资 Other investment	40	−52	9	−74	−27	−27
资产 Assets	18	−66	−36	−35	−41	−38
负债 Liabilities	22	14	45	−38	14	12
2.2.2 储备资产 Reserve assets	−22	−61	−111	21	−18	−305
其中：外汇储备 Foreign exchange reserves	−22	−55	−106	23	−18	−304
3. 净误差与遗漏 Net errors and omissions	**1**	**−31**	**−68**	**−83**	**−98**	**−98**

中国国际收支概览表 (3)

China's Balance of Payments Abridged (3)

项目 / 年份 Item/Year	1995	1996	1997	1998	1999	2000
1. 经常账户 Current account	16	72	370	315	211	204
贷方 Credit	1 389	1 645	1 986	1 990	2 124	2 725
借方 Debit	−1 373	−1 573	−1 617	−1 675	−1 913	−2 521
A. 货物和服务 Goods and services	120	176	428	438	306	288
贷方 Credit	1 319	1 548	1 874	1 888	1 987	2 531
借方 Debit	−1 199	−1 373	−1 446	−1 449	−1 681	−2 243
a. 货物 Goods	128	122	366	456	329	299
贷方 Credit	1 074	1 268	1 532	1 637	1 693	2 181
借方 Debit	−947	−1 147	−1 167	−1 181	−1 364	−1 881
b. 服务 Services	−8	54	63	−18	−23	−11
贷方 Credit	244	280	342	251	294	350
借方 Debit	−252	−226	−280	−268	−317	−362
B. 初次收入 Primary income	−118	−124	−110	−166	−145	−147
贷方 Credit	52	73	57	56	83	126
借方 Debit	−170	−198	−167	−222	−228	−272
C. 二次收入 Secondary income	14	21	51	43	49	63
贷方 Credit	18	24	55	47	54	69
借方 Debit	−4	−2	−3	−4	−4	−5
2. 资本和金融账户 Capital and financial account	162	83	−147	−127	−33	−86
2.1 资本账户 Capital account	0	0	0	0	0	0
贷方 Credit	0	0	0	0	0	0
借方 Debit	0	0	0	0	0	0
2.2 金融账户 Financial account	162	83	−147	−127	−33	−86
资产 Assets	−247	−357	−788	−479	−452	−666
负债 Liabilities	409	440	641	352	419	580
2.2.1 非储备性质的金融账户 Financial account excluding reserve assets	387	400	210	−63	52	20
资产 Assets	−22	−40	−431	−415	−367	−561

单位：亿美元
Unit: USD 100 million

续表 (Continue)

项目 / 年份 Item/Year	1995	1996	1997	1998	1999	2000
负债 Liabilities	409	440	641	352	419	580
直接投资 Direct investment	338	381	417	411	370	375
资产 Assets	−20	−21	−26	−26	−18	−9
负债 Liabilities	358	402	442	438	388	384
证券投资 Portfolio investment	8	17	69	−37	−112	−40
资产 Assets	1	−6	−9	−38	−105	−113
负债 Liabilities	7	24	78	1	−7	73
金融衍生工具 Financial derivatives (other than reserves) and employee stock options	0	0	0	0	0	0
资产 Assets	0	0	0	0	0	0
负债 Liabilities	0	0	0	0	0	0
其他投资 Other investment	40	2	−276	−437	−205	−315
资产 Assets	−3	−13	−396	−350	−244	−439
负债 Liabilities	43	15	120	−86	39	123
2.2.2 储备资产 Reserve assets	−225	−317	−357	−64	−85	−105
其中：外汇储备 Foreign exchange reserves	−220	−315	−349	−51	−97	−109
3. 净误差与遗漏 Net errors and omissions	**−178**	**−155**	**−223**	**−187**	**−178**	**−119**

中国国际收支概览表 (4)

China's Balance of Payments Abridged (4)

项目 / 年份 Item/Year	2001	2002	2003	2004	2005	2006
1. 经常账户 Current account	174	354	431	689	1 324	2 318
贷方 Credit	2 906	3 551	4 825	6 522	8 403	10 779
借方 Debit	−2 732	−3 197	−4 395	−5 833	−7 080	−8 460
A. 货物和服务 Goods and services	281	374	358	512	1 246	2 089
贷方 Credit	2 721	3 330	4 480	6 074	7 733	9 917
借方 Debit	−2 440	−2 956	−4 121	−5 562	−6 487	−7 828
a. 货物 Goods	282	377	398	594	1 301	2 157
贷方 Credit	2 329	2 868	3 966	5 429	6 949	8 977
借方 Debit	−2 047	−2 491	−3 568	−4 835	−5 647	−6 820
b. 服务 Services	−1	−3	−40	−82	−55	−68
贷方 Credit	392	462	513	645	785	941
借方 Debit	−393	−465	−553	−727	−840	−1 008
B. 初次收入 Primary income	−192	−149	−102	−51	−161	−51
贷方 Credit	94	83	161	206	393	546
借方 Debit	−286	−233	−263	−257	−554	−597
C. 二次收入 Secondary income	85	130	174	229	239	281
贷方 Credit	91	138	185	243	277	316
借方 Debit	−6	−8	−10	−14	−39	−35
2. 资本和金融账户 Capital and financial account	−125	−432	−513	−819	−1 553	−2 355
2.1 资本账户 Capital account	−1	0	0	−1	41	40
贷方 Credit	0	0	0	0	42	41
借方 Debit	−1	0	0	−1	−1	−1
2.2 金融账户 Financial account	−125	−432	−512	−818	−1 594	−2 395
资产 Assets	−541	−932	−1 212	−1 916	−3 352	−4 519
负债 Liabilities	416	500	699	1 098	1 758	2 124
2.2.1 非储备性质的金融账户 Financial account excluding reserve assets	348	323	549	1 082	912	453
资产 Assets	−67	−177	−150	−16	−845	−1 671

续表 (Continue)

项目 / 年份 Item/Year	2001	2002	2003	2004	2005	2006
负债 Liabilities	416	500	699	1 098	1 758	2 124
直接投资 Direct investment	374	468	494	601	904	1 001
资产 Assets	−69	−25	0	−20	−137	−239
负债 Liabilities	442	493	495	621	1 041	1 241
证券投资 Portfolio investment	−194	−103	114	197	−47	−684
资产 Assets	−207	−121	30	65	−262	−1 113
负债 Liabilities	12	18	84	132	214	429
金融衍生工具 Financial derivatives (other than reserves) and employee stock options	0	0	0	0	0	0
资产 Assets	0	0	0	0	0	0
负债 Liabilities	0	0	0	0	0	0
其他投资 Other investment	169	−41	−60	283	56	136
资产 Assets	208	−31	−180	−61	−447	−319
负债 Liabilities	−39	−10	120	345	502	455
2.2.2 储备资产 Reserve assets	−473	−755	−1 061	−1 901	−2 506	−2 848
其中：外汇储备 Foreign exchange reserves	−466	−742	−1 060	−1 904	−2 526	−2 853
3. 净误差与遗漏 Net errors and omissions	**−49**	**78**	**82**	**130**	**229**	**36**

中国国际收支概览表 (5)

China's Balance of Payments Abridged (5)

项目 / 年份 Item/Year	2007	2008	2009	2010	2011	2012
1. 经常账户 Current account	**3 532**	**4 206**	**2 433**	**2 378**	**1 361**	**2 154**
贷方 Credit	13 832	16 597	14 006	17 959	22 087	23 933
借方 Debit	−10 300	−12 391	−11 574	−15 581	−20 726	−21 779
A. 货物和服务 Goods and services	**3 080**	**3 488**	**2 201**	**2 230**	**1 819**	**2 318**
贷方 Credit	12 571	14 953	12 497	16 039	20 089	21 751
借方 Debit	−9 490	−11 465	−10 296	−13 809	−18 269	−19 432
a. 货物 Goods	**3 117**	**3 599**	**2 435**	**2 464**	**2 287**	**3 116**
贷方 Credit	11 316	13 500	11 272	14 864	18 078	19 735
借方 Debit	−8 199	−9 901	−8 836	−12 400	−15 791	−16 619
b. 服务 Services	**−37**	**−111**	**−234**	**−234**	**−468**	**−797**
贷方 Credit	1 254	1 453	1 226	1 175	2 010	2 016
借方 Debit	−1 291	−1 564	−1 460	−1 409	−2 478	−2 813
B. 初次收入 Primary income	**80**	**286**	**−85**	**−259**	**−703**	**−199**
贷方 Credit	835	1 118	1 083	1 424	1 443	1 670
借方 Debit	−754	−832	−1 168	−1 683	−2 146	−1 869
C. 二次收入 Secondary income	**371**	**432**	**317**	**407**	**245**	**34**
贷方 Credit	426	526	426	495	556	512
借方 Debit	−55	−94	−110	−88	−311	−477
2. 资本和金融账户 Capital and financial account	**−3 665**	**−4 394**	**−2 019**	**−1 849**	**−1 223**	**−1 283**
2.1 资本账户 Capital account	**31**	**31**	**39**	**46**	**54**	**43**
贷方 Credit	33	33	42	48	56	45
借方 Debit	−2	−3	−3	−2	−2	−3
2.2 金融账户 Financial account	**−3 696**	**−4 425**	**−2 058**	**−1 895**	**−1 278**	**−1 326**
资产 Assets	−6 371	−6 087	−4 283	−6 536	−6 136	−3 996
负债 Liabilities	2 676	1 662	2 225	4 641	4 858	2 670
2.2.1 非储备性质的金融账户 Financial account excluding reserve assets	911	371	1 945	2 822	2 600	−360
资产 Assets	−1 764	−1 291	−280	−1 819	−2 258	−3 030

单位：亿美元
Unit: USD 100 million

续表 (Continue)

项目 / 年份 Item/Year	2007	2008	2009	2010	2011	2012
负债 Liabilities	2 676	1 662	2 225	4 641	4 858	2 670
直接投资 Direct investment	1 391	1 148	872	1 857	2 317	1 763
资产 Assets	−172	−567	−439	−580	−484	−650
负债 Liabilities	1 562	1 715	1 311	2 437	2 801	2 412
证券投资 Portfolio investment	164	349	271	240	196	478
资产 Assets	−45	252	−25	−76	62	−64
负债 Liabilities	210	97	296	317	134	542
金融衍生工具 Financial derivatives (other than reserves) and employee stock options	0	0	0	0	0	0
资产 Assets	0	0	0	0	0	0
负债 Liabilities	0	0	0	0	0	0
其他投资 Other investment	−644	−1 126	803	724	87	−2 601
资产 Assets	−1 548	−976	184	−1 163	−1 836	−2 317
负债 Liabilities	904	−150	619	1 887	1 923	−284
2.2.2 储备资产 Reserve assets	−4 607	−4 795	−4 003	−4 717	−3 878	−966
其中：外汇储备 Foreign exchange reserves	−4 609	−4 783	−3 821	−4 696	−3 848	−987
3. 净误差与遗漏 Net errors and omissions	**133**	**188**	**−414**	**−529**	**−138**	**−871**

中国国际收支概览表 (6)

China's Balance of Payments Abridged (6)

项目 / 年份 Item/Year	2013	2014	2015	2016	2017	2018
1. 经常账户 Current account	**1 482**	**2 360**	**3 042**	**2 022**	**1 951**	**491**
贷方 Credit	25 927	27 434	26 193	24 546	27 450	29 136
借方 Debit	−24 445	−25 074	−23 151	−22 524	−25 499	−28 645
A. 货物和服务 Goods and services	**2 354**	**2 213**	**3 579**	**2 557**	**2 170**	**1 029**
贷方 Credit	23 556	24 629	23 602	21 979	24 293	26 510
借方 Debit	−21 202	−22 416	−20 023	−19 422	−22 123	−25 481
a. 货物 Goods	**3 590**	**4 350**	**5 762**	**4 889**	**4 759**	**3 952**
贷方 Credit	21 486	22 438	21 428	19 895	22 162	24 174
借方 Debit	−17 896	−18 087	−15 666	−15 006	−17 403	−20 223
b. 服务 Services	**−1 236**	**−2 137**	**−2 183**	**−2 331**	**−2 589**	**−2 922**
贷方 Credit	2 070	2 191	2 174	2 084	2 131	2 336
借方 Debit	−3 306	−4 329	−4 357	−4 415	−4 720	−5 258
B. 初次收入 Primary income	**−784**	**133**	**−411**	**−440**	**−100**	**−514**
贷方 Credit	1 840	2 394	2 232	2 258	2 876	2 348
借方 Debit	−2 624	−2 261	−2 643	−2 698	−2 976	−2 862
C. 二次收入 Secondary income	**−87**	**14**	**−126**	**−95**	**−119**	**−24**
贷方 Credit	532	411	359	309	282	278
借方 Debit	−619	−397	−486	−404	−400	−302
2. 资本和金融账户 Capital and financial account	**−853**	**−1 692**	**−912**	**272**	**179**	**1 111**
2.1 资本账户 Capital account	31	0	3	−3	−1	−6
贷方 Credit	45	19	5	3	2	3
借方 Debit	−14	−20	−2	−7	−3	−9
2.2 金融账户 Financial account	**−883**	**−1 691**	**−915**	**276**	**180**	**1 117**
资产 Assets	−6 517	−5 806	95	−2 320	−4 239	−3 721
负债 Liabilities	5 633	4 115	−1 010	2 596	4 419	4 838
2.2.1 非储备性质的金融账户 Financial account excluding reserve assets	**3 430**	**−514**	**−4 345**	**−4 161**	**1 095**	**1 306**
资产 Assets	−2 203	−4 629	−3 335	−6 756	−3 324	−3 532

单位：亿美元
Unit: USD 100 million

续表 (Continue)

项目 / 年份 Item/Year	2013	2014	2015	2016	2017	2018
负债 Liabilities	5 633	4 115	−1 010	2 596	4 419	4 838
直接投资 Direct investment	2 180	1 450	681	−417	278	1 070
资产 Assets	−730	−1 231	−1 744	−2 164	−1 383	−965
负债 Liabilities	2 909	2 681	2 425	1 747	1 661	2 035
证券投资 Portfolio investment	529	824	−665	−523	295	1 067
资产 Assets	−54	−108	−732	−1 028	−948	−535
负债 Liabilities	582	932	67	505	1 243	1 602
金融衍生工具 Financial derivatives (other than reserves) and employee stock options	0	0	−21	−54	4	−62
资产 Assets	0	0	−34	−65	15	−48
负债 Liabilities	0	0	13	12	−12	−13
其他投资 Other investment	722	−2 788	−4 340	−3 167	519	−770
资产 Assets	−1 420	−3 289	−825	−3 499	−1 008	−1 984
负债 Liabilities	2 142	502	−3 515	332	1 527	1 214
2.2.2 储备资产 Reserve assets	−4 314	−1 178	3 429	4 437	−915	−189
其中：外汇储备 Foreign exchange reserves	−4 327	−1 188	3 423	4 487	−930	−182
3. 净误差与遗漏 Net errors and omissions	**−629**	**−669**	**−2 130**	**−2 295**	**−2 130**	**−1 602**

2018 年中国国际收支平衡表

China's Balance of Payments in 2018

项　目	行次	2018
1. 经常账户 Current account	1	**491**
贷方 Credit	2	29 136
借方 Debit	3	−28 645
1.A 货物和服务 Goods and services	4	**1 029**
贷方 Credit	5	26 510
借方 Debit	6	−25 481
1.A. a 货物 Goods	7	**3 952**
贷方 Credit	8	24 174
借方 Debit	9	−20 223
1.A. b 服务 Services	10	**−2 922**
贷方 Credit	11	2 336
借方 Debit	12	−5 258
1.A. b.1 加工服务 Manufacturing services on physical inputs owned by others	13	172
贷方 Credit	14	174
借方 Debit	15	−3
1.A. b.2 维护和维修服务 Maintenance and repair services n.i.e	16	46
贷方 Credit	17	72
借方 Debit	18	−25
1.A. b.3 运输 Transport	19	−669
贷方 Credit	20	423
借方 Debit	21	−1 092
1.A. b.4 旅行 Travel	22	−2 370
贷方 Credit	23	404
借方 Debit	24	−2 773
1.A. b.5 建设 Construction	25	49
贷方 Credit	26	136
借方 Debit	27	−86
1.A. b.6 保险和养老金服务 Insurance and pension services	28	−66
贷方 Credit	29	49

续表 (Continue)

项　目	行次	2018
借方 Debit	30	−116
1.A. b.7 金融服务 Financial services	31	12
贷方 Credit	32	33
借方 Debit	33	−21
1.A. b.8 知识产权使用费 Charges for the use of intellectual property	34	−302
贷方 Credit	35	56
借方 Debit	36	−358
1.A. b.9 电信、计算机和信息服务 Telecommunications, computer, and information services	37	65
贷方 Credit	38	300
借方 Debit	39	−235
1.A. b.10 其他商业服务 Other business services	40	191
贷方 Credit	41	662
借方 Debit	42	−470
1.A. b.11 个人、文化和娱乐服务 Personal, cultural, and recreational services	43	−24
贷方 Credit	44	10
借方 Debit	45	−34
1.A. b.12 别处未提及的政府服务 Government goods and services n.i.e	46	−27
贷方 Credit	47	18
借方 Debit	48	−45
1.B 初次收入 Primary income	49	**−514**
贷方 Credit	50	2 348
借方 Debit	51	−2 862
1.B.1 雇员报酬 Compensation of employees	52	82
贷方 Credit	53	181
借方 Debit	54	−99
1.B.2 投资收益 Investment income	55	−614
贷方 Credit	56	2 146
借方 Debit	57	−2 760

单位：亿美元
Unit: USD 100 million

续表 (Continue)

项　目	行次	2018
1.B.3 其他初次收入 Other primary income	58	18
贷方 Credit	59	21
借方 Debit	60	−3
1.C 二次收入 Secondary income	61	**−24**
贷方 Credit	62	278
借方 Debit	63	−302
2. 资本和金融账户 Capital and financial account	64	**1 111**
2.1 资本账户 Capital account	65	**−6**
贷方 Credit	66	3
借方 Debit	67	−9
2.2 金融账户 Financial account	68	**1 117**
资产 Assets	69	−3 721
负债 Liabilities	70	4 838
2.2.1 非储备性质的金融账户 Financial account excluding reserve assets	71	**1 306**
资产 Assets	72	−3 532
负债 Liabilities	73	4 838
2.2.1.1 直接投资 Direct investment	74	**1 070**
2.2.1.1.1 直接投资资产 Assets	75	−965
2.2.1.1.1.1 股权 Equity and investment fund shares	76	−790
2.2.1.1.1.2 关联企业债务 Debt instruments	77	−175
2.2.1.1.2 直接投资负债 Liabilities	78	2 035
2.2.1.1.2.1 股权 Equity and investment fund shares	79	1 544
2.2.1.1.2.2 关联企业债务 Debt instruments	80	491
2.2.1.2 证券投资 Portfolio investment	81	**1 067**
2.2.1.2.1 资产 Assets	82	−535
2.2.1.2.1.1 股权 Equity and investment fund shares	83	−177
2.2.1.2.1.2 债券 Debt securities	84	−358
2.2.1.2.2 负债 Liabilities	85	1 602
2.2.1.2.2.1 股权 Equity and investment fund shares	86	607

单位：亿美元
Unit: USD 100 million

续表 (Continue)

项　目	行次	2018
2.2.1.2.2.2 债券 Debt securities	87	995
2.2.1.3 金融衍生工具 **Financial derivatives (other than reserves) and employee stock options**	88	**−62**
2.2.1.3.1 资产 Assets	89	−48
2.2.1.3.2 负债 Liabilities	90	−13
2.2.1.4 其他投资 Other investment	91	**−770**
2.2.1.4.1 资产 Assets	92	−1 984
2.2.1.4.1.1 其他股权 Other equity	93	0
2.2.1.4.1.2 货币和存款 Currency and deposits	94	−731
2.2.1.4.1.3 贷款 Loans	95	−818
2.2.1.4.1.4 保险和养老金 Insurance, pension, and standardized guarantee schemes	96	−6
2.2.1.4.1.5 贸易信贷 Trade credit and advances	97	−653
2.2.1.4.1.6 其他应收款 Other accounts receivable	98	224
2.2.1.4.2 负债 Liabilities	99	1 214
2.2.1.4.2.1 其他股权 Other equity	100	0
2.2.1.4.2.2 货币和存款 Currency and deposits	101	514
2.2.1.4.2.3 贷款 Loans	102	321
2.2.1.4.2.4 保险和养老金 I nsurance, pension, and standardized guarantee schemes	103	2
2.2.1.4.2.5 贸易信贷 Trade credit and advances	104	408
2.2.1.4.2.6 其他应付款 Other accounts payable	105	−31
2.2.1.4.2.7 特别提款权 Special drawing rights	106	0
2.2.2 储备资产 Reserve assets	107	**−189**
2.2.2.1 货币黄金 Monetary gold	108	0
2.2.2.2 特别提款权 Special drawing rights	109	0
2.2.2.3 在国际货币基金组织的储备头寸 Reserve position in the IMF	110	−7
2.2.2.4 外汇储备 Foreign exchange reserves	111	−182
2.2.2.5 其他储备资产 Other reserve assets	112	0
3. 净误差与遗漏 Net errors and omissions	113	**−1 602**

美国国际收支概览表

Balance of Payments Abridged of United States

项目 / 年份 Item/Year	2010	2011	2012	2013	2014	2015	2016	2017	2018
一、经常项目差额 Current Account Balance	−430.70	−444.59	−426.20	−349.54	−365.19	−407.77	−432.87	−449.14	−488.48
贷方 Credit	2 624.55	2 982.62	3 095.67	3 212.24	3 341.77	3 207.29	3 183.79	3 433.24	3 701.69
借方 Debit	3 055.26	3 427.21	3 521.87	3 561.79	3 706.96	3 615.06	3 616.66	3 882.38	4 190.17
A. 货物和服务差额 Goods and Services Balance	−494.66	−548.63	−536.77	−461.88	−489.58	−498.53	−502.00	−552.27	−622.12
贷方 Credit	1 853.60	2 127.02	2 218.99	2 293.45	2 376.66	2 266.69	2 215.85	2 351.07	2 500.76
借方 Debit	2 348.26	2 675.65	2 755.76	2 755.33	2 866.24	2 765.22	2 717.85	2 903.34	3 122.87
a. 货物差额 Goods Balance	−648.68	−740.64	−741.17	−702.24	−749.92	−761.87	−751.05	−807.49	−891.32
贷方 Credit	1 290.27	1 499.24	1 562.58	1 592.00	1 635.56	1 511.38	1 456.96	1 553.39	1 672.33
借方 Debit	1 938.95	2 239.88	2 303.75	2 294.25	2 385.48	2 273.25	2 208.01	2 360.88	2 563.65
b. 服务差额 Services Balance	154.02	192.02	204.40	240.37	260.34	263.33	249.05	255.22	269.21
贷方 Credit	563.33	627.78	656.41	701.45	741.09	755.31	758.89	797.69	828.42
借方 Debit	409.31	435.76	452.01	461.08	480.76	491.97	509.84	542.47	559.22
B. 初次收入差额 Primary Income Balance	168.22	211.08	207.47	205.98	218.40	203.61	193.02	221.73	244.30
贷方 Credit	680.17	755.94	767.97	792.82	824.55	810.08	830.18	928.12	1 060.36
借方 Debit	511.95	544.86	560.50	586.84	606.15	606.47	637.15	706.39	816.06
C. 二次收入差额 Secondary Income Balance	−104.26	−107.05	−96.90	−93.64	−94.01	−112.85	−123.90	−118.60	−110.66
贷方 Credit	90.78	99.66	108.71	125.97	140.57	130.52	137.77	154.05	140.58
借方 Debit	195.05	206.71	205.61	219.62	234.58	243.37	261.66	272.65	251.24
二、资本项目差额 Capital Account Balance	−0.16	−1.19	6.90	−0.41	−0.05	−0.04	−0.06	24.75	9.41
三、金融项目净贷出 (+) / 净借入 (−) Financial Account Net Lending(+)/Net Borrow(−)	−448.25	−541.51	−453.31	−400.88	−293.67	−319.65	−387.17	−330.17	−524.55
1. 直接投资差额 Direct Investment Balance	85.79	173.12	126.90	104.67	135.67	−202.03	−181.48	24.39	−317.72
1.1 资产 Assets	349.83	436.62	377.24	392.80	387.53	307.06	312.98	379.22	−50.63
1.2 负债 Liabilities	264.04	263.50	250.35	288.13	251.86	509.09	494.46	354.83	267.08

单位：10亿美元
Unit: USD billions

续表 (Continue)

项目 / 年份 Item/Year	2010	2011	2012	2013	2014	2015	2016	2017	2018
2. 证券投资差额 Portfolio Investment Balance	−620.82	−226.26	−498.25	−30.69	−114.93	−53.50	−195.06	−212.49	−109.68
2.1 资产 Assets	199.62	85.36	248.76	481.30	582.68	160.41	36.29	586.69	210.33
2.2 负债 Liabilities	820.43	311.63	747.01	511.98	697.60	213.91	231.35	799.18	320.01
3. 金融衍生产品（储备除外）和雇员认股权差额 Derivatives (other than reserves) and Employee Stock Options Balance	−14.08	−35.01	7.06	2.22	−54.34	−27.04	7.83	23.07	−20.26
4. 其他投资差额 Other Investment Balance	100.85	−453.36	−89.02	−477.08	−260.08	−37.09	−18.45	−165.15	−76.90
4.1 资产 Assets	407.42	−45.33	−453.70	−221.41	−100.10	−258.97	−2.72	218.52	136.93
4.2 负债 Liabilities	306.57	408.04	−364.68	255.67	159.98	−221.88	15.72	383.67	213.83
5. 储备资产差额 Reserve Assets Balance	1.83	15.98	4.46	−3.09	−3.58	−6.30	2.10	−1.70	5.00
四、净误差与遗漏 Net Errors and Omissions	−15.57	−79.75	−29.56	−54.01	67.99	81.85	47.87	92.52	−40.47

德国国际收支概览表

Balance of Payments Abridged of Germany

项目 / 年份 Item/Year	2010	2011	2012	2013	2014	2015	2016	2017	2018
一、经常项目差额 Current Account Balance	193.03	228.67	248.92	253.03	278.34	288.11	293.67	296.17	291.44
贷方 Credit	1 765.77	2 060.93	1 959.39	2 041.46	2 109.35	1 878.55	1 903.85	2 052.33	2 208.09
借方 Debit	1 572.74	1 832.27	1 710.47	1 788.42	1 831.01	1 590.44	1 610.18	1 756.16	1 916.65
A. 货物和服务差额 Goods and Services Balance	178.33	182.97	215.61	227.64	258.04	255.19	256.57	260.55	239.75
贷方 Credit	1 444.67	1 685.00	1 629.56	1 708.02	1 772.72	1 574.27	1 595.87	1 737.11	1 869.99
借方 Debit	1 266.35	1 502.04	1 413.95	1 480.37	1 514.68	1 319.09	1 339.31	1 476.56	1 630.24
a. 货物差额 Goods Balance	213.74	227.28	257.42	282.43	291.40	275.49	279.91	285.63	262.68
贷方 Credit	1 217.09	1 432.93	1 377.08	1 434.69	1 469.88	1 293.90	1 304.24	1 418.34	1 527.22
借方 Debit	1 003.34	1 205.65	1 119.65	1 152.27	1 178.49	1 018.41	1 024.33	1 132.70	1 264.54
b. 服务差额 Services Balance	−35.41	−44.32	−41.81	−54.78	−33.36	−20.30	−23.34	−25.08	−22.93
贷方 Credit	227.59	252.07	252.48	273.32	302.84	280.37	291.64	318.77	342.77
借方 Debit	263.00	296.39	294.30	328.10	336.20	300.68	314.98	343.85	365.70
B. 初次收入差额 Primary Income Balance	68.08	94.02	83.49	83.39	74.61	75.75	82.11	91.44	107.81
贷方 Credit	264.98	305.14	261.96	253.73	253.30	224.75	235.21	240.02	257.34
借方 Debit	196.90	211.12	178.48	170.34	178.69	148.99	153.10	148.59	149.52
C. 二次收入差额 Secondary Income Balance	−53.37	−48.32	−50.18	−58.00	−54.31	−42.83	−45.00	−55.81	−56.12
贷方 Credit	56.11	70.80	67.87	79.71	83.33	79.53	72.77	75.20	80.76
借方 Debit	109.49	119.12	118.05	137.71	137.64	122.36	117.78	131.01	136.89
二、资本项目差额 Capital Account Balance	1.62	0.60	−0.61	−0.82	4.00	−0.02	2.27	−2.15	2.32
三、金融项目净贷出（+）/净借入（−） Financial Account Net Lending(+)/ Net Borrow(−)	121.61	163.79	192.55	298.82	321.10	261.81	284.94	321.37	266.63
1. 直接投资差额 Direct Investment Balance	60.64	10.35	33.65	26.04	87.81	68.40	46.54	53.98	53.80
1.1 资产 Assets	146.69	107.83	99.11	93.45	107.59	130.86	109.16	137.40	159.08
1.2 负债 Liabilities	86.05	97.48	65.46	67.41	19.78	62.46	62.62	83.42	105.28

单位：10亿美元
Unit: USD billions

续表 (Continue)

项目 / 年份 Item/Year	2010	2011	2012	2013	2014	2015	2016	2017	2018
2. 证券投资差额 Portfolio Investment Balance	**154.11**	**−51.41**	**66.85**	**209.55**	**177.67**	**209.94**	**220.26**	**224.47**	**133.81**
2.1 资产 Assets	230.22	25.56	136.16	181.57	201.45	138.65	107.95	120.14	82.43
2.2 负债 Liabilities	76.11	76.97	69.32	−27.98	23.79	−71.29	−112.31	−104.33	−51.38
3. 金融衍生产品（储备除外）和雇员认股权差额 Derivatives (other than reserves) and Employee Stock Options Balance	**17.57**	**39.76**	**30.92**	**31.80**	**50.79**	**33.80**	**32.09**	**13.23**	**27.45**
3.1 资产 Assets	17.57	39.76	30.92	31.80	50.79	33.80	32.09	13.23	27.45
3.2 负债 Liabilities	0.00	0.00	0.00	0.00	0.00	0.00	0.00	0.00	0.00
4. 其他投资差额 Other Investment Balance	**−110.71**	**165.09**	**61.14**	**31.42**	**4.83**	**−50.33**	**−13.95**	**29.69**	**51.57**
4.1 资产 Assets	156.88	194.46	217.56	−226.81	60.62	10.82	195.36	144.18	150.96
4.2 负债 Liabilities	267.59	29.37	156.43	−258.23	55.78	61.15	209.32	114.50	99.39
5. 储备资产差额 Reserve Assets Balance	**2.13**	**3.91**	**1.70**	**1.16**	**−3.30**	**−2.42**	**1.90**	**−1.48**	**0.45**
四、净误差与遗漏 Net Errors and Omissions	**−70.91**	**−61.56**	**−54.06**	**47.77**	**35.46**	**−28.70**	**−9.10**	**25.86**	**−26.67**

英国国际收支概览表

Balance of Payments Abridged of United Kingdom

项目 / 年份 Item/Year	2010	2011	2012	2013	2014	2015	2016	2017	2018
一、经常项目差额 Current Account Balance	−92.50	−62.18	−113.10	−151.90	−161.16	−149.80	−154.87	−106.50	−92.25
贷方 Credit	986.41	1 147.93	1 091.14	1 093.10	1 121.88	1 022.47	959.59	1 052.51	926.31
借方 Debit	1 078.91	1 210.10	1 204.24	1 244.99	1 283.04	1 172.28	1 114.46	1 159.02	1 018.56
A. 货物和服务差额 Goods and Services Balance	−63.76	−40.33	−52.71	−55.55	−60.57	−49.52	−55.09	−36.66	−52.11
贷方 Credit	689.27	799.44	791.50	812.96	854.14	790.17	749.11	801.81	625.33
借方 Debit	753.02	839.77	844.21	868.51	914.70	839.70	804.21	838.47	677.44
a. 货物差额 Goods Balance	−150.42	−151.90	−171.71	−187.58	−202.47	−181.20	−182.92	−174.68	−134.80
贷方 Credit	417.82	493.74	476.43	472.51	489.26	441.16	408.06	441.23	358.66
借方 Debit	568.24	645.64	648.15	660.09	691.73	622.36	590.98	615.91	493.46
b. 服务差额 Services Balance	86.67	111.56	119.00	132.03	141.90	131.68	127.82	138.02	82.70
贷方 Credit	271.45	305.70	315.07	340.45	364.88	349.02	341.05	360.59	266.67
借方 Debit	184.78	194.13	196.07	208.42	222.97	217.34	213.23	222.57	183.98
B. 初次收入差额 Primary Income Balance	1.68	10.56	−28.09	−56.77	−62.25	−65.46	−69.34	−42.87	−17.23
贷方 Credit	276.15	328.47	276.24	252.06	240.16	206.49	185.93	225.88	281.38
借方 Debit	274.48	317.92	304.34	308.82	302.41	271.95	255.27	268.75	298.61
C. 二次收入差额 Secondary Income Balance	−30.42	−32.40	−32.29	−39.58	−38.34	−34.82	−30.44	−26.98	−22.91
贷方 Credit	20.99	20.02	23.39	28.08	27.58	25.81	24.55	24.82	19.60
借方 Debit	51.41	52.42	55.68	67.66	65.93	60.63	54.99	51.79	42.51
二、资本项目差额 Capital Account Balance	−1.13	−1.20	−0.93	−1.90	−3.10	−3.02	−2.17	−1.75	0.38
三、金融项目净贷出（＋）/净借入（－） Financial Account Net Lending(+)/ Net Borrow(−)	−123.20	−55.26	−104.68	−140.04	−158.84	−169.76	−154.99	−96.38	−105.76
1. 直接投资差额 Direct Investment Balance	−12.33	53.82	−34.73	−8.22	−172.81	−114.50	−213.39	84.71	−62.95
1.1 资产 Assets	54.41	80.83	12.02	46.25	−113.92	−56.05	52.42	131.33	−48.40
1.2 负债 Liabilities	66.73	27.01	46.75	54.47	58.89	58.45	265.81	46.62	14.55

单位：10亿美元
Unit: USD billions

续表 (Continue)

项目 / 年份 Item/Year	2010	2011	2012	2013	2014	2015	2016	2017	2018
2. 证券投资差额 Portfolio Investment Balance	−201.02	−214.12	274.40	−284.86	22.87	−213.17	−201.02	−92.48	−214.05
2.1 资产 Assets	−16.20	−149.19	161.02	−107.04	131.56	−48.10	−228.98	105.66	94.29
2.2 负债 Liabilities	184.81	64.93	−113.38	177.82	108.70	165.07	−27.96	198.15	308.34
3. 金融衍生产品（储备除外）和雇员认股权差额 Derivatives (other than reserves) and Employee Stock Options Balance	158.95	97.40	−278.80	90.32	−37.71	285.34	229.13	−100.37	220.31
4. 其他投资差额 Other Investment Balance	397.32	165.51	−430.67	−392.75	134.94	−162.58	219.12	217.09	−470.28
4.1 资产 Assets	238.37	68.12	−151.87	−483.07	172.65	−447.92	−10.01	317.45	−690.59
4.2 负债 Liabilities	10.01	10.87	11.63	6.96	10.14	31.32	8.65	7.53	9.56
5. 储备资产差额 Reserve Assets Balance	−19.56	18.99	20.98	20.72	15.56	14.38	10.71	19.40	−4.33
四、净误差与遗漏 Net Errors and Omissions	158.95	97.40	−278.80	90.32	−37.71	285.34	229.13	−100.37	220.31

巴西国际收支概览表

Balance of Payments Abridged of Brazil

项目 / 年份 Item/Year	2010	2011	2012	2013	2014	2015	2016	2017	2018
一、经常项目差额 Current Account Balance	-75.76	-76.97	-74.06	-74.84	-104.18	-59.43	-23.55	-9.76	-14.51
贷方 Credit	254.52	320.34	294.49	297.51	281.84	240.51	234.57	269.15	239.03
借方 Debit	330.28	397.31	368.55	372.35	386.02	299.95	258.11	278.91	185.45
A. 货物和服务差额 Goods and Services Balance	-11.60	-9.48	-22.59	-45.98	-54.74	-19.28	14.59	30.18	19.64
贷方 Credit	232.06	292.55	281.26	279.59	264.06	223.87	217.75	251.72	273.06
借方 Debit	243.66	302.03	303.85	325.57	318.80	243.15	203.16	221.54	253.42
a. 货物差额 Goods Balance	18.43	27.56	17.26	0.39	-6.63	17.67	45.04	64.03	53.59
贷方 Credit	201.26	255.44	242.12	241.58	224.10	190.09	184.45	217.24	239.03
借方 Debit	182.83	227.88	224.86	241.19	230.73	172.42	139.42	153.21	185.45
b. 服务差额 Services Balance	-30.03	-37.04	-39.85	-46.37	-48.11	-36.95	-30.45	-33.85	-33.95
贷方 Credit	30.80	37.11	39.14	38.01	39.97	33.78	33.30	34.48	34.02
借方 Debit	60.83	74.15	78.98	84.38	88.07	70.72	63.75	68.33	67.97
B. 初次收入差额 Primary Income Balance	-67.05	-70.48	-54.31	-32.54	-52.17	-42.91	-41.08	-42.57	36.67
贷方 Credit	17.70	22.88	8.62	12.13	12.85	11.93	11.53	11.98	27.45
借方 Debit	84.75	93.36	62.93	44.67	65.02	54.84	52.61	54.55	64.12
C. 二次收入差额 Secondary Income Balance	2.90	2.98	2.84	3.68	2.72	2.75	2.94	2.63	2.52
贷方 Credit	4.77	4.91	4.62	5.79	4.93	4.71	5.29	5.45	5.59
借方 Debit	1.87	1.92	1.78	2.11	2.21	1.96	2.34	2.82	3.07
二、资本项目差额 Capital Account Balance	0.24	0.26	0.21	0.32	0.23	0.46	0.27	0.38	0.44
三、金融项目净贷出（+）/净借入（-）Financial Account Net Lending(+)/ Net Borrow(-)	-125.00	-137.61	-92.83	-67.88	-111.43	-56.71	-25.65	-10.32	-12.25
1. 直接投资差额 Direct Investment Balance	-61.69	-85.09	-81.40	-54.74	-71.14	-61.20	-65.43	-64.06	-74.25
1.1 资产 Assets	26.76	16.07	5.21	14.94	26.04	13.52	12.82	6.27	14.06
1.2 负债 Liabilities	88.45	101.16	86.61	69.69	97.18	74.72	78.25	70.33	88.31

单位：10亿美元
Unit: USD billions

续表 (Continue)

项目 / 年份 Item/Year	2010	2011	2012	2013	2014	2015	2016	2017	2018
2. 证券投资差额 Portfolio Investment Balance	−66.91	−41.25	−15.83	−32.28	−38.43	−22.25	19.22	15.14	11.71
2.1 资产 Assets	4.74	−16.86	7.40	8.98	2.82	−3.57	−0.60	14.06	3.30
2.2 负债 Liabilities	71.65	24.39	23.23	41.26	41.25	18.68	−19.81	−1.07	−8.40
3. 金融衍生产品（储备除外）和雇员认股权差额 Derivatives (other than reserves) and Employee Stock Options Balance	0.11	0.00	−0.02	−0.11	1.57	3.45	−0.97	0.71	2.75
3.1 资产 Assets	−0.36	−0.39	−0.30	−0.50	−7.61	−20.66	−13.87	−8.15	−12.08
3.2 负债 Liabilities	−0.47	−0.38	−0.28	−0.39	−9.18	−24.11	−12.90	−8.86	−14.83
4. 其他投资差额 Other Investment Balance	3.49	−11.27	4.42	19.26	−3.43	23.28	21.53	37.90	47.55
4.1 资产 Assets	40.45	36.05	23.87	38.31	50.67	43.97	33.50	44.42	49.96
4.2 负债 Liabilities	36.96	47.33	19.44	19.05	54.10	20.69	11.97	6.52	2.41
5. 储备资产差额 Reserve Assets Balance	48.10	59.65	18.90	−5.92	10.83	1.57	9.23	5.09	2.94
四、净误差与遗漏 Net Errors and Omissions	−1.39	−1.25	−0.08	0.72	3.35	3.83	6.85	4.15	4.76

俄罗斯国际收支概览表

Balance of Payments Abridged of Russia

项目 / 年份 Item/Year	2010	2011	2012	2013	2014	2015	2016	2017	2018
一、经常项目差额 Current Account Balance	67.45	97.27	71.28	33.43	57.51	67.78	24.47	33.16	113.81
贷方 Credit	487.16	629.90	653.99	651.47	627.37	440.32	381.51	468.32	572.46
借方 Debit	419.70	532.63	582.71	618.04	569.85	372.55	357.04	435.16	458.65
A. 货物和服务差额 Goods and Services Balance	120.87	163.40	145.08	122.31	133.65	111.25	66.26	84.19	164.51
贷方 Credit	441.83	573.45	589.77	591.96	562.55	393.03	332.35	411.18	507.83
借方 Debit	320.96	410.05	444.70	469.65	428.90	281.79	266.10	326.99	343.32
a. 货物差额 Goods Balance	146.99	196.85	191.66	180.57	188.93	148.40	90.21	115.42	194.45
贷方 Credit	392.67	515.41	527.43	521.84	496.81	341.42	281.71	353.55	443.07
借方 Debit	245.68	318.55	335.77	341.27	307.88	193.02	191.49	238.13	248.62
b. 服务差额 Services Balance	−26.12	−33.46	−46.59	−58.26	−55.28	−37.15	−23.96	−31.23	−29.94
贷方 Credit	49.16	58.04	62.34	70.12	65.74	51.62	50.64	57.63	64.76
借方 Debit	75.28	91.50	108.93	128.38	121.02	88.77	74.60	88.86	94.70
B. 初次收入差额 Primary Income Balance	−47.10	−60.40	−67.66	−79.60	−67.96	−37.75	−35.50	−42.05	−41.40
贷方 Credit	38.06	42.69	47.76	42.18	47.17	37.27	40.51	46.58	52.99
借方 Debit	85.17	103.09	115.42	121.78	115.13	75.02	76.01	88.63	94.39
C. 二次收入差额 Secondary Income Balance	−6.32	−5.72	−6.13	−9.27	−8.18	−5.72	−6.29	−8.98	−9.30
贷方 Credit	7.26	13.77	16.46	17.33	17.64	10.02	8.64	10.56	11.64
借方 Debit	13.58	19.49	22.59	26.61	25.82	15.74	14.93	19.54	20.94
二、资本项目差额 Capital Account Balance	−0.04	0.13	−5.22	−0.39	−42.01	−0.31	−0.76	−0.19	−1.11
三、金融项目净贷出（＋）/净借入（−）Financial Account Net Lending(+)/ Net Borrow(−)	21.53	76.12	25.67	46.21	130.99	68.62	10.06	12.92	77.06
1. 直接投资差额 Direct Investment Balance	9.45	11.77	−1.77	17.29	35.05	15.23	−10.22	8.20	23.11
1.1 资产 Assets	52.62	66.85	48.82	86.51	57.08	22.09	22.31	36.76	31.93
1.2 负债 Liabilities	43.17	55.08	50.59	69.22	22.03	6.85	32.54	28.56	8.82

单位：10亿美元
Unit: USD billions

续表 (Continue)

项目 / 年份 Item/Year	2010	2011	2012	2013	2014	2015	2016	2017	2018
2. 证券投资差额 Portfolio Investment Balance	1.50	15.28	−17.03	11.01	39.94	26.42	−2.36	−7.98	7.59
2.1 资产 Assets	3.44	9.84	2.28	11.76	16.74	13.55	0.66	1.26	−1.83
2.2 负债 Liabilities	1.95	−5.44	19.31	0.75	−23.20	−12.87	3.02	9.24	−9.42
3. 金融衍生产品（储备除外）和雇员认股权差额 Derivatives (other than reserves) and Employee Stock Options Balance	1.84	1.39	1.36	0.35	5.26	7.12	−0.02	0.36	−0.73
3.1 资产 Assets	−8.84	−16.44	−16.70	−8.49	−16.52	−20.76	−12.84	−13.79	−11.71
3.2 负债 Liabilities	−10.68	−17.83	−18.05	−8.83	−21.78	−27.89	−12.82	−14.15	−10.97
4. 其他投资差额 Other Investment Balance	8.74	47.68	43.11	17.57	50.74	19.85	22.67	12.34	47.09
4.1 资产 Assets	19.24	83.37	83.70	80.82	24.01	−18.41	−5.45	−8.46	22.25
4.2 负债 Liabilities	10.49	35.69	40.59	63.26	−26.73	−38.25	−28.11	−20.80	−24.84
5. 储备资产差额 Reserve Assets Balance	36.75	12.64	30.02	−22.08	−107.55	1.70	8.24	22.63	38.20
四、净误差与遗漏 Net Errors and Omissions	−9.13	−8.65	−10.37	−8.90	7.94	2.86	−5.40	2.58	2.57

中国国际投资头寸表

China's International Investment Position

项 目	2010年末	2011年末	2012年末	2013年末	2014年末	2015年末	2016年末	2017年末	2018年末
净 头 寸 Net International Investment Position	**16 880**	**16 884**	**18 665**	**19 960**	**16 028**	**16 728**	**19 504**	**18 141**	**21 301**
A. 资产 Assets	**41 189**	**47 345**	**52 132**	**59 861**	**64 383**	**61 558**	**65 070**	**69 256**	**73 242**
1. 直接投资 Direct investment	**3 172**	**4 248**	**5 319**	**6 605**	**8 826**	**10 959**	**13 574**	**14 730**	**18 990**
1.1 股权 Equity and investment fund shares	–	–	–	–	7 408	9 123	11 274	12 413	16 316
1.2 关联企业债务 Debt instruments	–	–	–	–	1 418	1 836	2 300	2 317	2 674
2. 证券投资 Portfolio investment	**2 571**	**2 044**	**2 406**	**2 585**	**2 625**	**2 613**	**3 670**	**4 972**	**4 980**
2.1 股权 Equity and investment fund shares	630	864	1 298	1 530	1 613	1 620	2 152	3 075	2 700
2.2 债券 Debt securities	1 941	1 180	1 108	1 055	1 012	993	1 518	1 896	2 279
3. 金融衍生工具 Financial derivatives (other than reserves) and employee stock options	–	–	–	–	0	36	52	60	62
4. 其他投资 Other investment	6 304	8 495	10 527	11 867	13 938	13 889	16 797	17 136	17 530
4.1 其他股权 Other equity	–	–	–	–	0	1	1	54	54
4.2 货币和存款 Currency and deposits	2 051	2 942	3 906	3 751	4 453	3 598	3 653	3 677	3 937
4.3 贷款 Loans	1 174	2 232	2 778	3 089	3 747	4 569	5 768	6 372	7 097
4.4 保险和养老金 Insurance, pension, and standardized guarantee schemes	–	–	–	–	0	172	123	101	106
4.5 贸易信贷 Trade credit and advances	2 060	2 769	3 387	3 990	4 677	5 137	6 145	6 339	5 972
4.6 其他应收款 Other accounts receivable	1 018	552	457	1 038	1 061	412	1 107	593	364
5. 储备资产 Reserve assets	**29 142**	**32 558**	**33 879**	**38 804**	**38 993**	**34 061**	**30 978**	**32 359**	**31 680**
5.1 货币黄金 Monetary gold	481	530	567	408	401	602	679	765	763
5.2 特别提款权 Special drawing rights	123	119	114	112	105	103	97	110	107
5.3 在国际货币基金组织的储备头寸 Reserve position in the IMF	64	98	82	71	57	45	96	79	85

单位：亿美元
Unit: USD 100 million

续表 (Continue)

项　目	2010年末	2011年末	2012年末	2013年末	2014年末	2015年末	2016年末	2017年末	2018年末
5.4 外汇储备 Foreign currency reserves	28 473	31 811	33 116	38 213	38 430	33 304	30 105	31 399	30 727
5.5 其他储备资产 Other reserve assets	–	–	–	–	0	7	2	5	−2
B. 负债 Liabilities	24 308	30 461	33 467	39 901	48 355	44 830	45 567	51 115	51 941
1. 直接投资 Direct investment	15 696	19 069	20 680	23 312	25 991	26 963	27 551	29 014	27 623
1.1 股权 Equity and investment fund shares	–	–	–	–	24 076	24 962	25 370	26 758	25 386
1.2 关联企业债务 Debt instruments	–	–	–	–	1 915	2 002	2 181	2 256	2 237
2. 证券投资 Portfolio investment	2 239	2 485	3 361	3 865	7 962	8 170	8 111	10 439	10 964
2.1 股权 Equity and investment fund shares	2 061	2 114	2 619	2 977	6 513	5 971	5 795	7 166	6 842
2.2 债券 Debt securities	178	371	742	889	1 449	2 200	2 316	3 272	4 122
3. 金融衍生工具 Financial derivatives (other than reserves) and employee stock options	–	–	–	–	0	53	60	34	60
4. 其他投资 Other investment	6 373	8 907	9 426	12 724	14 402	9 643	9 844	11 628	13 294
4.1 其他股权 Other equity	–	–	–	–	0	0	0	0	0
4.2 货币和存款 Currency and deposits	1 650	2 477	2 446	3 466	5 030	3 267	3 166	4 452	4 833
4.3 贷款 Loans	2 389	3 724	3 680	5 642	5 720	3 293	3 205	3 922	4 169
4.4 保险和养老金 Insurance, pension, and standardized guarantee schemes	–	–	–	–	0	93	88	100	109
4.5 贸易信贷 Trade credit and advances	2 112	2 492	2 915	3 365	3 344	2 721	2 883	2 871	3 931
4.6 其他应付款 Other accounts payable	106	106	277	144	207	172	408	184	154
4.7 特别提款权 Special drawing rights	116	107	107	108	101	97	94	100	97

外汇储备

Foreign Exchange Reserves

单位：亿美元
Unit: USD 100 million

年份 Year	外汇储备余额 Foreign Exchange Reserves	外汇储备增加额 Increase of Foreign Exchange Reserves
1990	111	55
1991	217	106
1992	194	−23
1993	212	18
1994	516	304
1995	736	220
1996	1 050	315
1997	1 399	348
1998	1 450	51
1999	1 547	97
2000	1 656	109
2001	2 122	466
2002	2 864	742
2003	4 033	1 168
2004	6 099	2 067
2005	8 189	2 090
2006	10 663	2 475
2007	15 282	4 619
2008	19 460	4 178
2009	23 992	4 531
2010	28 473	4 481
2011	31 811	3 338
2012	33 116	1 304
2013	38 213	5 097
2014	38 430	217
2015	33 304	−5 127
2016	30 105	−3 198
2017	31 399	1 294
2018	30 727	−672

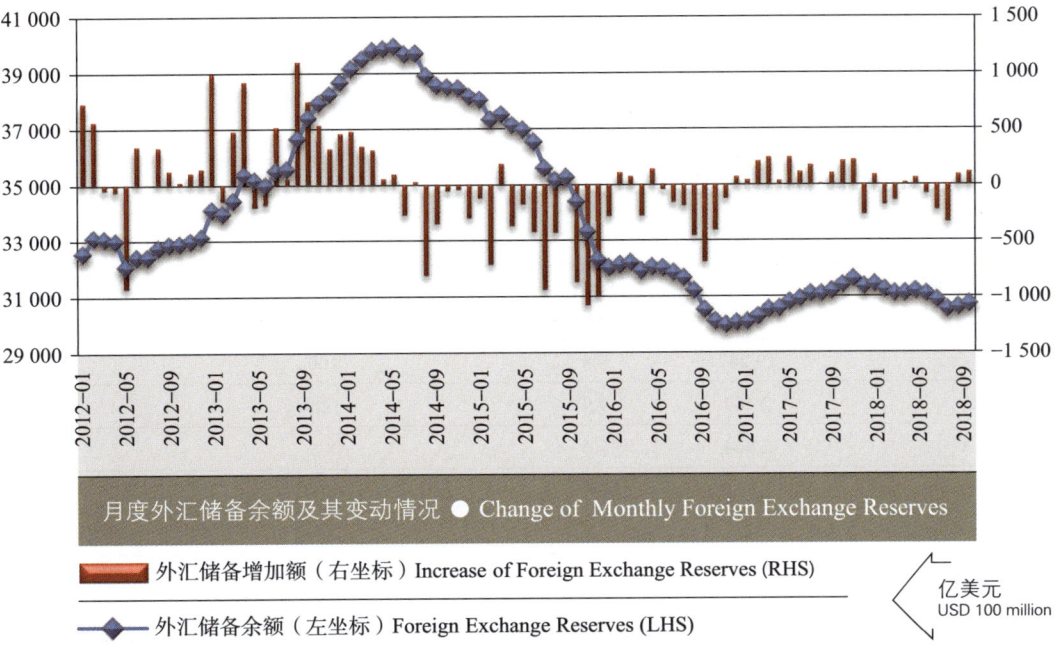

月度外汇储备余额及其变动情况 ● Change of Monthly Foreign Exchange Reserves

▮ 外汇储备增加额（右坐标）Increase of Foreign Exchange Reserves (RHS)

◆ 外汇储备余额（左坐标）Foreign Exchange Reserves (LHS)

亿美元
USD 100 million

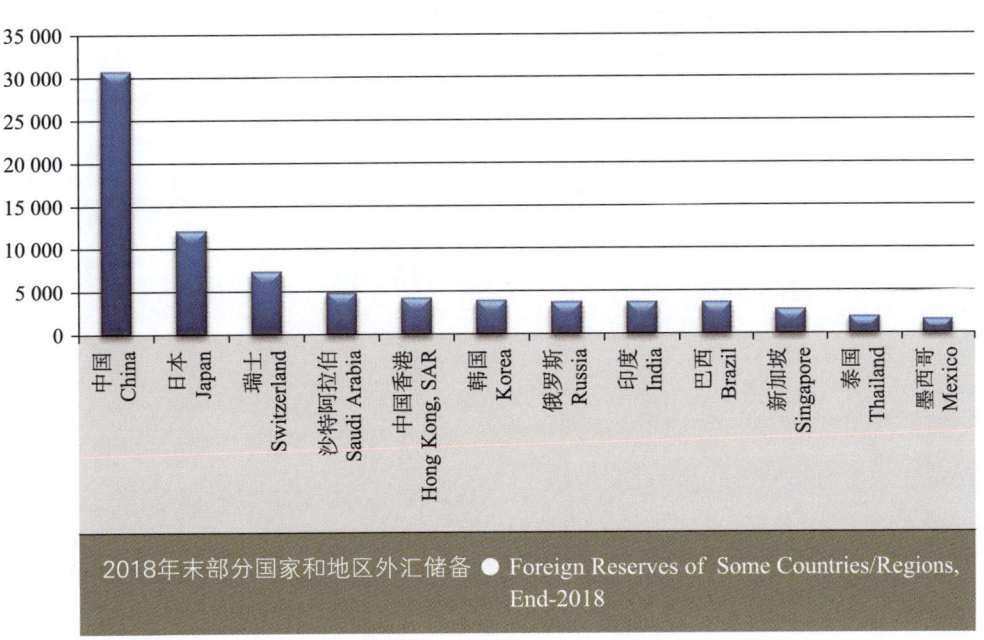

2018年末部分国家和地区外汇储备 ● Foreign Reserves of Some Countries/Regions,
End-2018

亿美元
USD 100 million

二、对外贸易 ①
II. Foreign Trade

2018 年世界货物贸易出口前十名

单位：10亿美元
Unit: USD 100 billions

Top 10 Countries/Regions of Goods Export in 2018

国家 / 地区 Countries/Regions	出口额 Export	增长 Increase（%）	占世界出口总额比重 Ratio to total Export of the world（%）	2017 年排名 Ranking in 2017
世界 World	19 287	8.8	100	
1. 中国 P. R.C	2 487	9.9	12.9	1
2. 美国 U. S.A	1 664	7.6	8.6	2
3. 德国 Germany	1 561	7.8	8.1	3
4. 日本 Japan	738	5.8	3.8	4
5. 荷兰 Netherlands	723	10.8	3.7	5
6. 韩国 Korea	605	5.4	3.1	6
7. 法国 France	582	8.8	3.0	8
8. 中国香港 Hong Kong, SAR	569	3.5	3.0	7
9. 意大利 Italy	547	8.0	2.8	9
10. 英国 UK	486	9.1	2.5	10

① 资料来源：海关总署、世界贸易组织。
Sources: General Administration of Customs; World Trade Organization.

2018 年世界货物贸易进口前十名

单位：10亿美元
Unit: USD 100 billions

Top 10 Countries/Regions of Goods Import in 2018

国家 / 地区 Countries/Regions	进口额 Import	增长 Increase （%）	占世界进口总额比重 Ratio to total Import of the world（%）	2017 年排名 Ranking in 2017
世界 World	18 024	10.2	100	
1. 美国 U. S.A	2 409	8.5%	13.2%	1
2. 中国 P. R.C	1 842	15.8%	10.8%	2
3. 德国 Germany	1 167	10.6%	6.5%	3
4. 日本 Japan	672	11.4%	3.8%	5
5. 英国 UK	644	4.7%	3.4%	4
6. 法国 France	625	8.7%	3.4%	6
7. 荷兰 Netherlands	590	12.4%	3.3%	8
8. 中国香港 Hong Kong, SAR	574	6.4%	3.2%	7
9. 韩国 Korea	478	11.9%	2.7%	9
10. 印度 India	453	13.9%	2.6%	11

中国进出口总值

China's Total Value of Import & Export

年度 /Year	进出口 /Import & Export	出口 /Export	进口 /Import	差额 /Balance
1982	416	223	193	30
1983	436	222	214	8
1984	535	261	274	−13
1985	696	274	423	−149
1986	738	309	429	−120
1987	827	394	432	−38
1988	1 028	475	553	−78
1989	1 117	525	591	−66
1990	1 154	621	534	87
1991	1 357	719	638	81
1992	1 655	849	806	44
1993	1 957	917	1 040	−122
1994	2 366	1 210	1 156	54
1995	2 809	1 488	1 321	167
1996	2 899	1 511	1 388	122
1997	3 252	1 828	1 424	404
1998	3 239	1 837	1 402	435
1999	3 606	1 949	1 657	292
2000	4 743	2 492	2 251	241
2001	5 097	2 661	2 436	225
2002	6 208	3 256	2 952	304
2003	8 510	4 382	4 128	255
2004	11 546	5 933	5 612	321
2005	14 219	7 620	6 600	1 020
2006	17 604	9 689	7 915	1 775
2007	21 746	12 186	9 560	2 627
2008	25 633	14 307	11 326	2 981
2009	22 075	12 016	10 059	1 957
2010	29 740	15 778	13 962	1 815
2011	36 419	18 984	17 435	1 549

单位：亿美元
Unit: USD 100 million

续表 (Continue)

年度 /Year	进出口 /Import & Export	出口 /Export	进口 /Import	差额 /Balance
2012	38 671	20 487	18 184	2 303
2013	41 590	22 090	19 500	2 590
2014	43 015	23 423	19 592	3 831
2015	39 530	22 735	16 796	5 939
2016	36 856	20 976	15 879	5 097
2017	41 071	22 633	18 438	4 196
2018	46 230	24 870	21 359	3 511

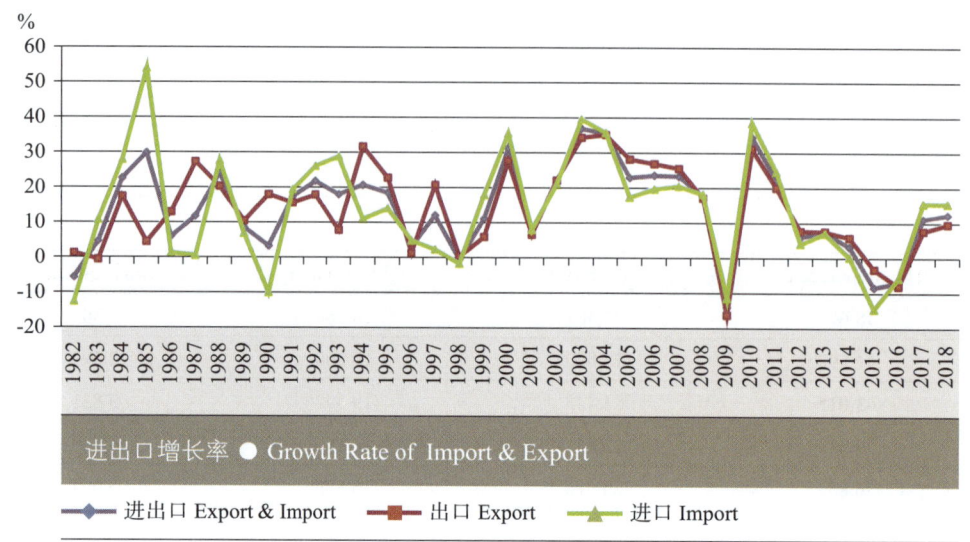

进出口增长率 ● Growth Rate of Import & Export

◆ 进出口 Export & Import　　■ 出口 Export　　▲ 进口 Import

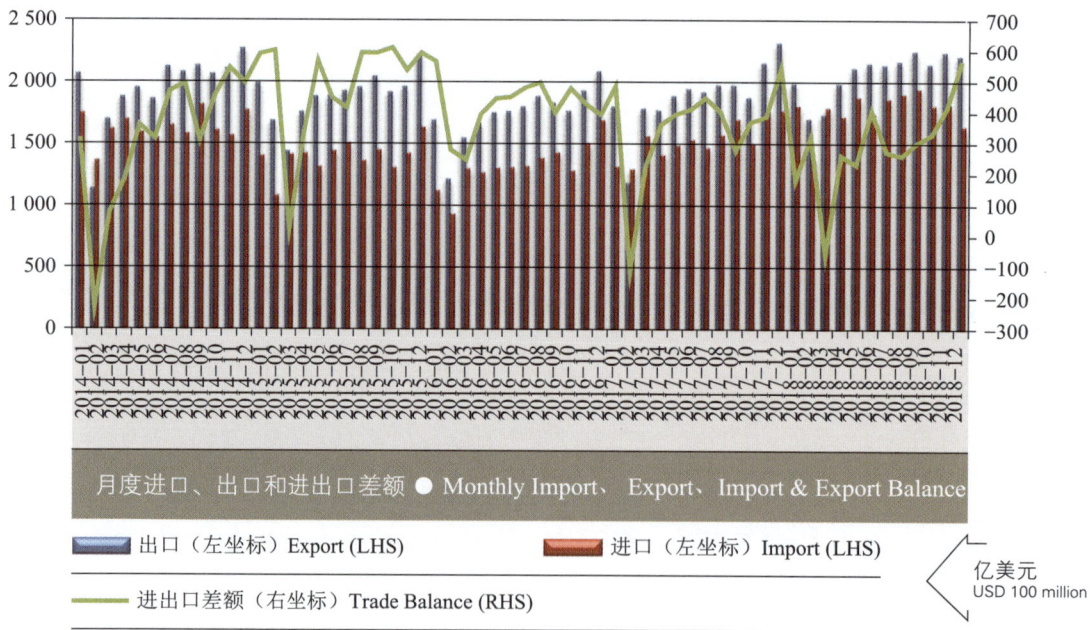

月度进口、出口和进出口差额 ● Monthly Import、 Export、 Import & Export Balance

■ 出口（左坐标）Export (LHS)　　■ 进口（左坐标）Import (LHS)

── 进出口差额（右坐标）Trade Balance (RHS)

亿美元
USD 100 million

按贸易方式分类进出口

Import & Export by Trading Forms

单位：百万美元
Unit: USD million

贸易方式 Trading Forms	2008	2009	2010	2011	2012	2013	2014	2015	2016	2017	2018
进口 Import	1 133 086	1 005 555	1 394 829	1 743 458	1 817 826	1 950 289	1 960 290	1 681 951	1 587 921	1 840 982	2 135 637
一般贸易 Ordinary Trade	572 677	533 872	767 978	1 007 464	1 021 819	1 109 718	1 109 513	923 188	899 013	1 082 759	1 273 925
国家间、国际组织间无偿援助和捐赠的物资 Foreign Aid and Donation by Overseas	49	43	22	16	27	21	38	15	19	3	5
其他捐赠物资 Other Donations	58	136	185	266	338	11	10	48	8	5	69
来料加工装配贸易 Processing and Assembling Trade	90 162	75 993	99 295	93 635	84 459	87 543	97 537	91 569	85 261	84 614	91 729
进料加工贸易 Processing with Imported Materials	288 243	246 345	318 134	376 161	396 710	409 447	426 843	355 434	311 432	346 607	378 653
寄售代销贸易 Goods on Consignment	2	2	2	2	1	0	0	0	0	2	0
边境小额贸易 Border trade	8 975	7 196	9 634	14 448	15 289	14 065	9 856	7 160	7 019	8 883	9 216
加工贸易进口设备 Equipment Imported for Processing & Assembling	2 859	953	1 212	885	912	969	687	635	463	750	1 062
租赁贸易 Goods on Lease	6 932	3 448	5 628	5 459	6 760	8 656	10 212	9 041	2 860	1 967	4 074
外商投资企业作为投资进口的设备物品 Equipment or Materials Imported as Investment by Foreign-invested Enterprises	27 677	15 176	16 312	17 508	13 429	9 835	9 059	6 161	4 067	4 450	3 443
出料加工贸易 Outward Processing Trade	160	78	126	73	236	252	307	300	265	327	300
易货贸易 Barter Trade	1	8	1	2	0	1	3	3	8	97	0
免税外汇商品 Duty Free Commodities on Payment of Foreign Exchange	6	5	10	13	26	28	20	15	22	21	25
保税监管场所进出境货物 Customs Warehousing Trade	57 277	54 392	61 099	79 658	83 969	84 844	99 870	88 705	96 773	115 485	150 008
海关特殊监管区域物流货物 Entrepot Trade by Bonded Area	73 739	64 259	109 241	140 831	185 132	218 448	186 689	182 004	158 044	171 264	196 306

单位：百万美元
Unit: USD million

续表 (Continue)

贸易方式 Trading Forms	2008	2009	2010	2011	2012	2013	2014	2015	2016	2017	2018
海关特殊监管区域进口设备 Equipment Imported into Export Processing Zone	3 118	2 113	3 994	4 741	6 094	3 993	5 133	6 544	4 894	6 441	8 512
其他 Others	1 150	1 535	1 957	2 296	2 624	2 458	2 950	9 510	15 542	15 372	15 828
出口 **Export**	**1 428 546**	**1 201 663**	**1 577 932**	**1 898 600**	**2 048 935**	**2 210 042**	**2 342 747**	**2 274 950**	**2 097 637**	**2 263 522**	**2 487 401**
一般贸易 Ordinary Trade	662 584	529 833	720 733	917 124	988 007	1 087 553	1 203 682	1 215 697	1 131 043	1 230 090	1 400 992
国家间、国际组织间无偿援助和捐赠的物资 Foreign Aid and Donation by Overseas	231	291	294	471	551	456	478	493	472	539	717
其他捐赠物资 Other Donations	2	8	3	11	2	8	6	6	6	2	7
补偿贸易 Compensation Trade	0	0	0	0	0	0	0	0	0	0	0
来料加工装配贸易 Processing and Assembling Trade	110 520	93 423	112 317	107 653	98 866	92 479	90 692	84 097	76 040	79 825	87 823
进料加工贸易 Processing with Imported Materials	564 663	493 558	628 017	727 763	763 913	768 337	793 668	713 692	639 557	679 007	709 346
寄售代销贸易 Goods on Consignment	4	6	1	2	4	1	0	0	0	0	0
边境小额贸易 Border trade	21 904	13 667	16 408	20 203	24 216	30 929	37 207	30 465	26 407	29 920	31 118
对外承包工程出口货物 Contracting Projects	10 963	13 357	12 617	14 923	14 782	16 011	16 326	16 132	13 304	15 391	16 988
租赁贸易 Goods on Lease	189	117	145	166	562	305	327	265	192	158	151
出料加工贸易 Outward Processing Trade	118	46	185	198	196	199	235	205	221	206	225
易货贸易 Barter Trade	16	1	1	1	1	2	3	2	2	15	0
保税监管场所进出境货物 Customs Warehousing Trade	28 404	26 793	35 366	43 294	42 477	46 510	53 288	49 246	38 408	41 148	42 688
海关特殊监管区域物流货物 Entrepot Trade by Bonded Area	23 937	21 476	36 502	49 655	94 819	141 990	110 395	109 580	94 289	100 007	121 082
其他 Others	5 011	9 088	15 343	17 135	20 540	25 262	36 438	55 069	78 212	87 213	76 265

按企业类型分类进出口

Import & Export by Type of Enterprises

单位：亿美元
Unit: USD million

企业类型 Type of Enterprises	2008	2009	2010	2011	2012	2013	2014	2015	2016	2017	2018
进口 Import	**11 331**	**10 056**	**13 948**	**17 435**	**18 178**	**19 503**	**19 603**	**16 820**	**15 879**	**18 410**	**21 356**
国有企业 State-owned Enterprises	3 538	2 885	3 876	4 934	4 954	4 990	4 911	4 078	3 608	4 374	5 474
外商投资企业 Foreign-funded Enterprises	6 200	5 452	7 380	8 648	8 712	8 748	9 093	8 299	7 705	8 616	9 321
中外合作 Sino-foreign Contractual Joint Ventures	88	66	74	86	82	83	87	62	43	45	44
中外合资 Sino-foreign Equity Joint Ventures	1 818	1 586	2 095	2 561	2 748	2 842	2 858	2 461	2 238	2 451	2 610
外商独资 Foreign Investment Enterprises	4 294	3 799	5 212	6 002	5 883	5 823	6 149	5 776	5 424	6 119	6 666
集体企业/私营企业 [1] Collective Enterprises/Private owned Enterprises	289	265	349	407	353	4 368	4 475	4 116	4 179	5 013	6 117
其他 Other Enterprises	1 304	1 454	2 343	3 445	4 158	1 397	1 124	326	375	406	445
出口 Export	**14 285**	**12 017**	**15 779**	**18 986**	**20 489**	**22 100**	**23 427**	**22 749**	**20 976**	**22 635**	**24 874**
国有企业 State-owned Enterprises	2 572	1 910	2 344	2 672	2 563	2 490	2 565	2 424	2 156	2 312	2 573
外商投资企业 Foreign-funded Enterprises	7 906	6 722	8 623	9 953	10 227	10 443	10 747	10 047	9 169	9 776	10 360
中外合作 Sino-foreign Contractual Joint Ventures	183	146	165	177	162	157	136	114	99	93	98
中外合资 Sino-foreign Equity Joint Ventures	2 269	1 824	2 376	2 731	2 873	3 009	3 055	2 825	2 542	2 635	2 774
外商独资 Foreign Investment Enterprises	5 454	4 752	6 082	7 046	7 193	7 277	7 556	7 109	6 529	7 047	7 488
集体企业/私营企业 Collective Enterprises/Private owned Enterprises	547	405	499	554	509	8 633	9 547	9 738	9 148	10 044	11 405
其他 Other Enterprises	3 260	2 979	4 314	5 807	7 190	534	958	541	503	504	536
差额 Balance	**2 955**	**1 961**	**1 831**	**1 551**	**2 311**	**2 598**	**3 825**	**5 930**	**5 097**	**4 225**	**3 518**
国有企业 State-owned Enterprises	−966	−975	−1 532	−2 262	−2 391	−2 500	−2 346	−1 654	−1 452	−2 062	−2 901
外商投资企业 Foreign-funded Enterprises	1 706	1 270	1 243	1 305	1 515	1 695	1 654	1 748	1 465	1 160	1 040

① 2013 年起该项下的数据由集体企业调整为私营企业。Data of Collective Enterprises was replaced by that of Private Owned Enterprises from 2013.

单位：亿美元
Unit: USD 100 million

续表 (Continue)

企业类型 Type of Enterprises	2008	2009	2010	2011	2012	2013	2014	2015	2016	2017	2018
中外合作 Sino-foreign Contractual Joint Ventures	95	80	91	91	80	74	49	52	56	48	54
中外合资 Sino-foreign Equity Joint Ventures	451	238	281	170	125	167	197	364	304	184	164
外商独资 Foreign Investment Enterprises	1 160	953	870	1 044	1 310	1 454	1 407	1 333	1 105	928	822
私营企业/私营企业 Collective Enterprises/Private owned Enterprises	258	140	150	147	156	4 265	5 072	5 622	4 968	5 030	5 288
其他 Other Enterprises	1 956	1 525	1 971	2 362	3 032	−863	−166	214	128	97	90

2018 年按贸易方式分类的进口构成
Components of Import by Trading Forms in 2018

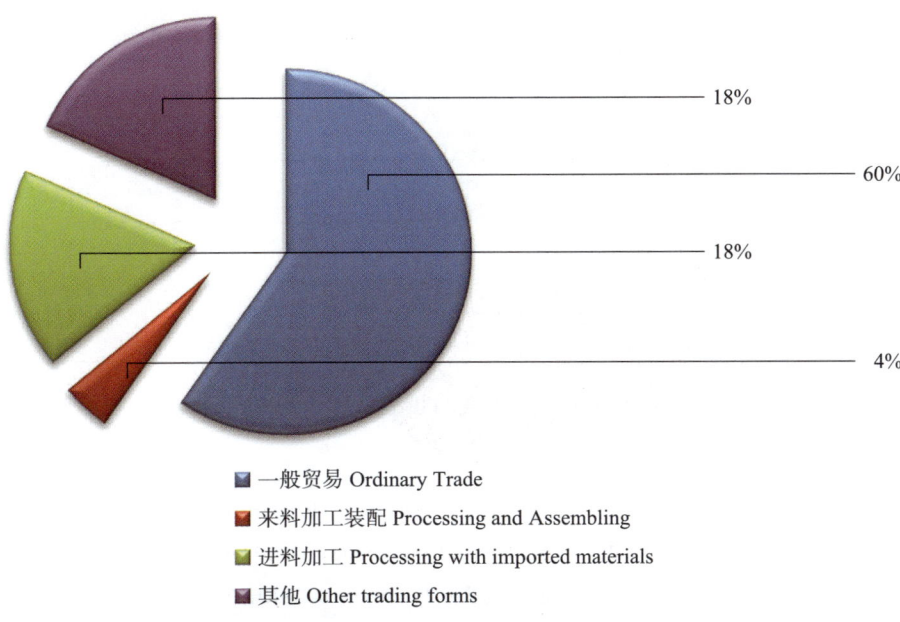

18%

60%

18%

4%

■ 一般贸易 Ordinary Trade
■ 来料加工装配 Processing and Assembling
■ 进料加工 Processing with imported materials
■ 其他 Other trading forms

2018 年按贸易方式分类的出口构成
Components of Export by Trading Forms in 2018

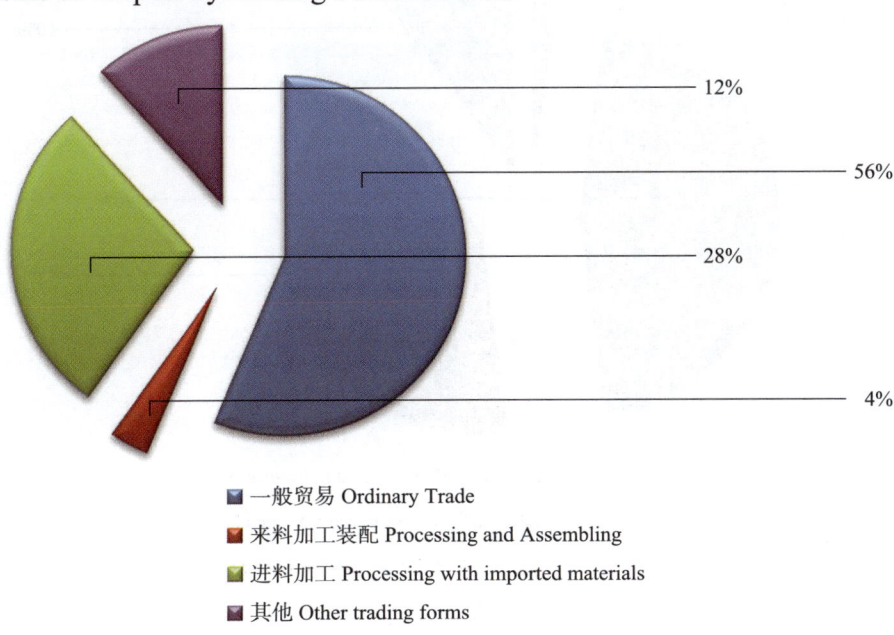

12%

56%

28%

4%

■ 一般贸易 Ordinary Trade
■ 来料加工装配 Processing and Assembling
■ 进料加工 Processing with imported materials
■ 其他 Other trading forms

2018 年按企业类型分类的进口构成

Components of Import by Type of Enterprises in 2018

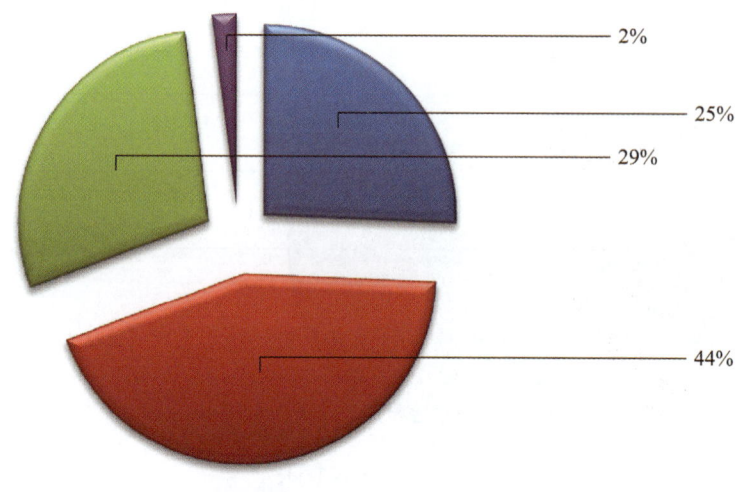

2%
25%
29%
44%

■ 国有企业 State-owned Enterprises
■ 外商投资企业 Foreign-funded Enterprises
■ 私营企业 Private owned Enterprises
■ 其他 Other Enterprises

2018 年按企业类型分类的出口构成

Components of Export by Type of Enterprises in 2018

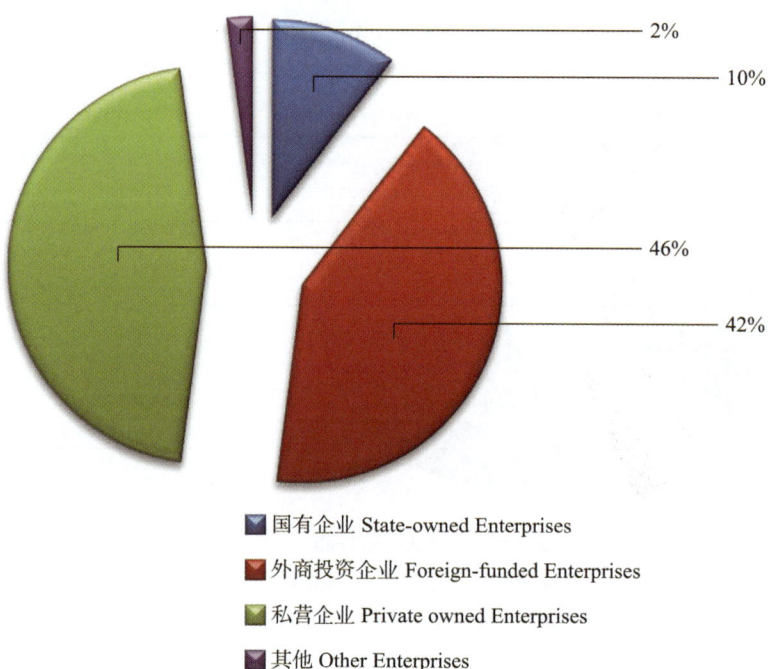

2%
10%
46%
42%

■ 国有企业 State-owned Enterprises
■ 外商投资企业 Foreign-funded Enterprises
■ 私营企业 Private owned Enterprises
■ 其他 Other Enterprises

2018 年进出口按贸易方式分类

Import & Export by Trading Forms in 2018

单位：亿美元
Unit: USD 100 million

贸易方式 **Trading forms**	进口 Import		出口 Export		进出口差额 **Import & Export Balance**
	金额 Value	同比（%） Increase	金额 Value	同比（%） Increase	
总值 Total Value	**21 356**	**16.0**	**24 874**	**9.9**	**3 518**
一般贸易 Ordinary Trade	12 739	17.6	14 010	13.9	1 271
加工贸易 Processing Trade	4 704	9.1	7 971	5.0	3 267
来料加工装配 Processing and Assembling	917	8.4	878	10.0	−39
进料加工 Processing with imported materials	3 787	9.3	7 093	4.5	3 306
其他贸易 Other trading forms	3 913	19.7	2 893	5.4	−1 020

2018 年进出口按企业类型分类

单位：亿美元
Unit: USD 100 million

Import & Export by Type of Enterprises in 2018

企业类型 **Type of Enterprises**	进口 Import		出口 Export		进出口差额 **Import & Export Balance**
	金额 **Value**	同比（%） **Increase**	金额 **Value**	同比（%） **Increase**	
总值 Total Value	**21 356**	**16.0**	**24 874**	**9.9**	**3 518**
国有企业 State-owned Enterprises	5 474	25.1	2 573	11.3	−2 901
外资企业 Foreign-funded Enterprises	9 321	8.2	10 360	6.0	1 039
私营和其他企业 Private Owned and other Enterprises	6 561	21.1	11 941	13.2	5 380

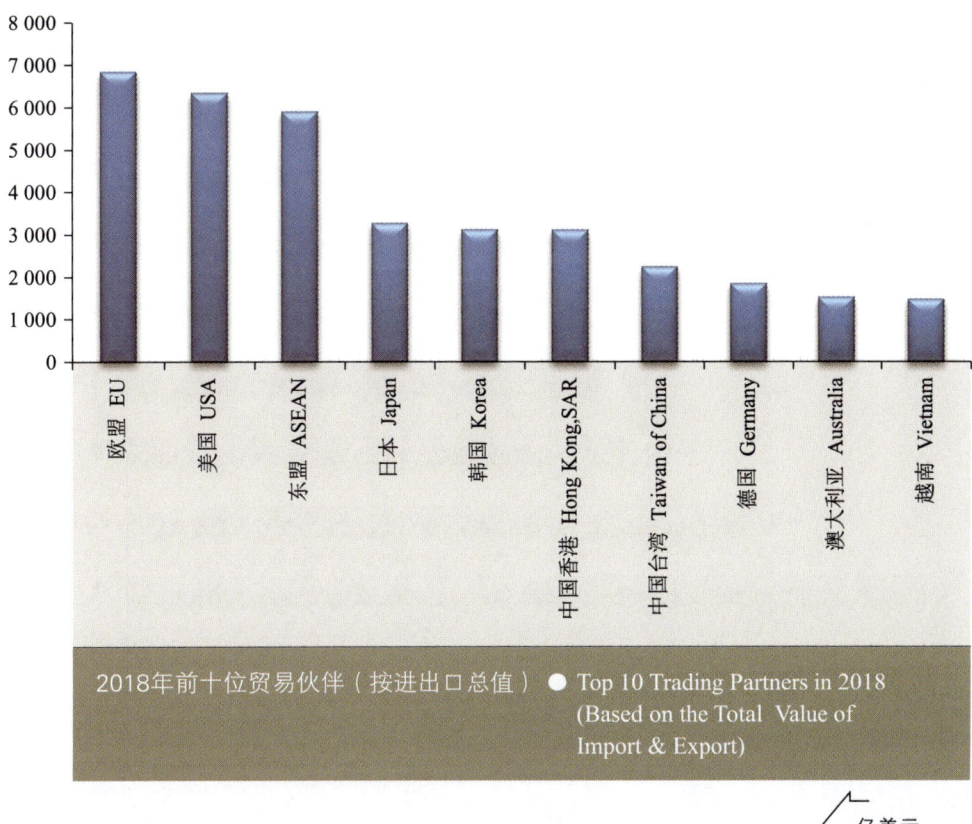

2018年前十位贸易伙伴（按进出口总值）● Top 10 Trading Partners in 2018 (Based on the Total Value of Import & Export)

亿美元
USD 100 million

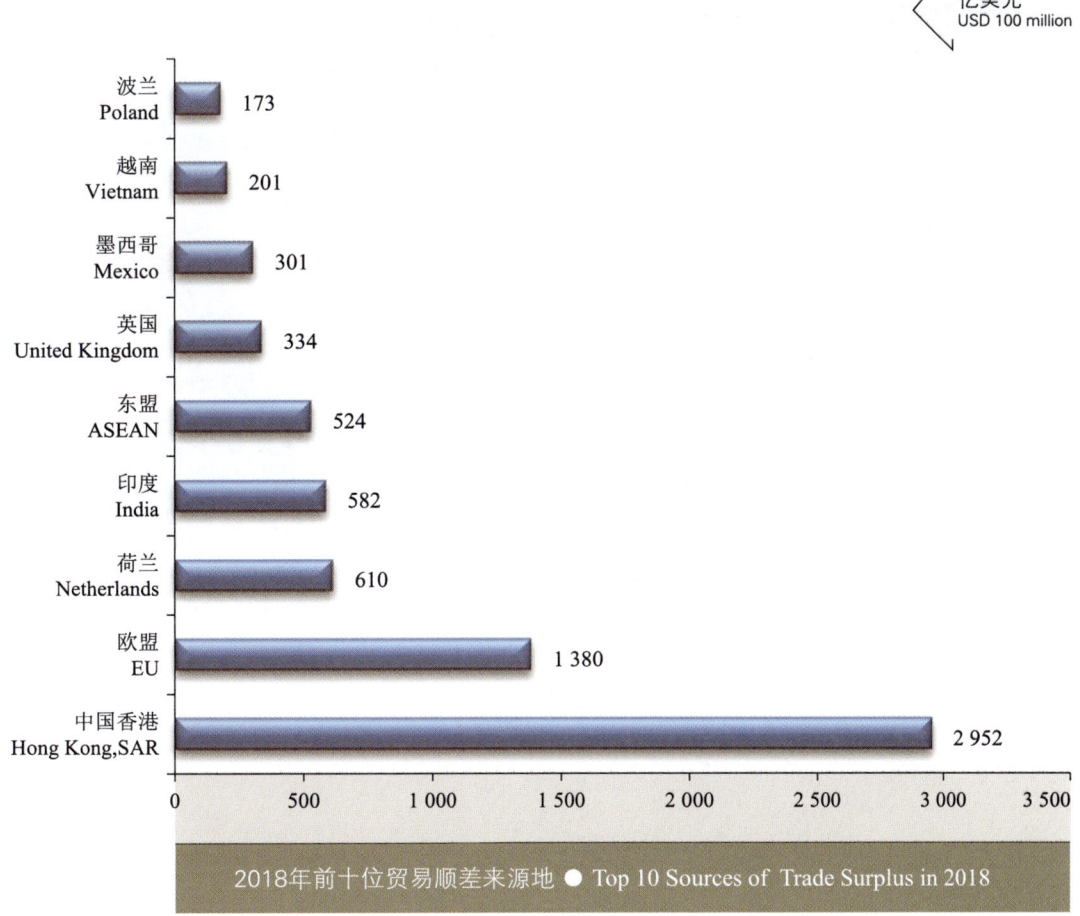

2018年前十位贸易顺差来源地 ● Top 10 Sources of Trade Surplus in 2018

亿美元
USD 100 million

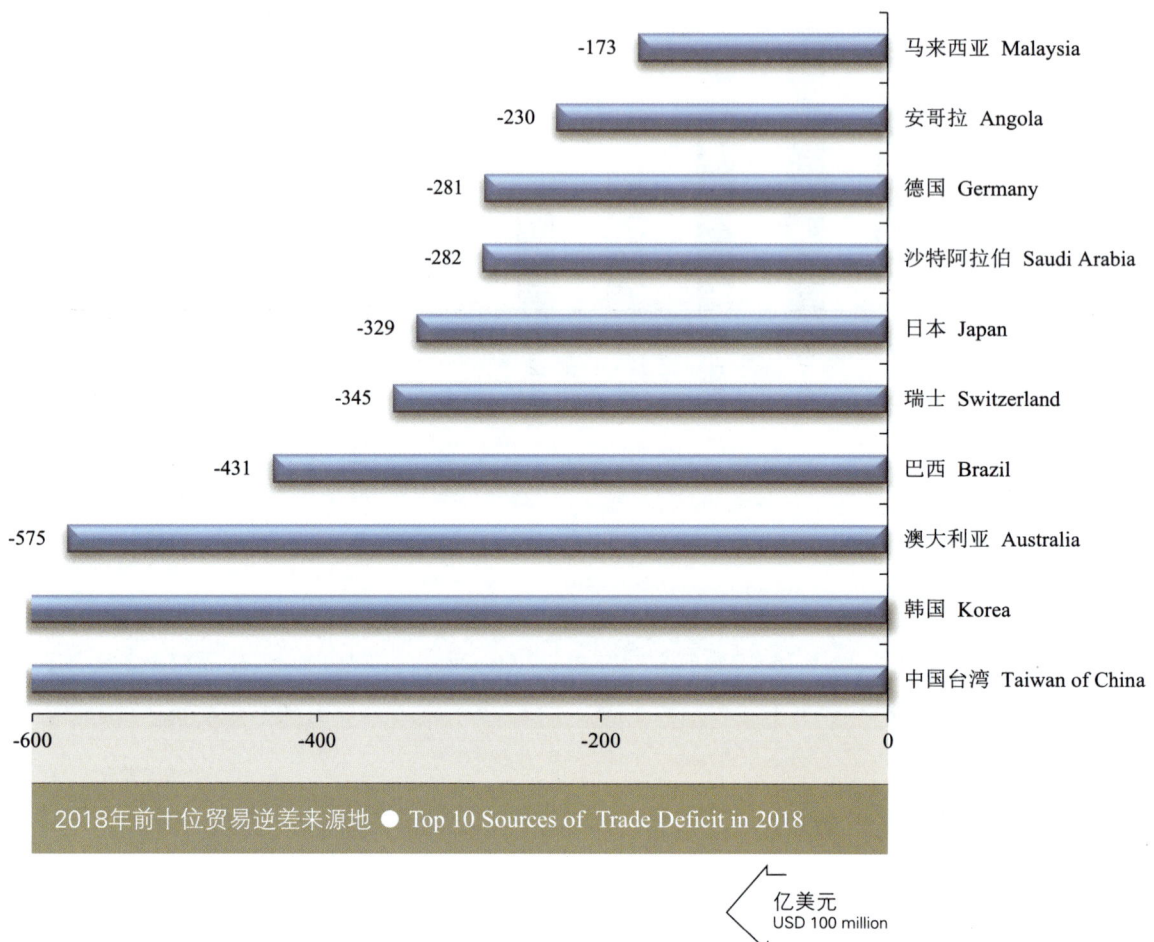

-173	马来西亚 Malaysia
-230	安哥拉 Angola
-281	德国 Germany
-282	沙特阿拉伯 Saudi Arabia
-329	日本 Japan
-345	瑞士 Switzerland
-431	巴西 Brazil
-575	澳大利亚 Australia
	韩国 Korea
	中国台湾 Taiwan of China

2018年前十位贸易逆差来源地 ● Top 10 Sources of Trade Deficit in 2018

亿美元
USD 100 million

三、外汇市场和人民币汇率 ①
III. Foreign Exchange Market and Exchange Rate of Renminbi

人民币对美元交易中间价月平均汇价

人民币元/100美元
RMB per 100 USD

Monthly Average Transaction Mid Rates of Renminbi against US dollar, 1980—2018

月份 Month	1980 年	1981 年	1982 年	1983 年	1984 年	1985 年	1986 年	1987 年	1988 年	1989 年
1 月 /Jan	149.37	154.87	176.77	192.01	204.12	280.88	320.15	372.21	372.21	372.21
2 月 /Feb	150.05	161.06	181.74	196.03	205.72	282.51	320.70	372.21	372.21	372.21
3 月 /Mar	155.12	162.80	183.79	197.80	206.08	284.51	321.20	372.21	372.21	372.21
4 月 /Apr	155.70	166.20	185.19	198.72	208.91	284.11	320.61	372.21	372.21	372.21
5 月 /May	149.06	172.27	180.97	198.52	218.21	284.75	319.44	372.21	372.21	372.21
6 月 /Jun	146.50	176.05	189.70	198.95	221.22	286.25	320.35	372.21	372.21	372.21
7 月 /Jul	145.25	175.98	192.36	198.88	229.39	287.38	363.82	372.21	372.21	372.21
8 月 /Aug	147.26	179.52	193.87	198.00	236.43	290.23	370.36	372.21	372.21	372.21
9 月 /Sep	146.81	175.01	195.04	198.14	253.26	296.26	370.66	372.21	372.21	372.21
10 月 /Oct	148.03	175.05	198.22	196.17	264.00	306.73	371.64	372.21	372.21	372.21
11 月 /Nov	151.73	173.46	199.41	198.90	266.16	320.15	372.21	372.21	372.21	372.21
12 月 /Dec	154.19	173.78	193.99	198.69	278.91	320.15	372.21	372.21	372.21	423.82
年平均 Annual Average	**149.84**	**170.50**	**189.25**	**197.57**	**232.70**	**293.66**	**345.28**	**372.21**	**372.21**	**376.51**

① 资料来源：国家外汇管理局。
Source: SAFE.

人民币对美元交易中间价月平均汇价

Monthly Average Transaction Mid Rates of Renminbi against US dollar, 1980—2018

续表 (Continue)

月份 Month	1990 年	1991 年	1992 年	1993 年	1994 年	1995 年	1996 年	1997 年	1998 年	1999 年
1 月 /Jan	472.21	522.21	544.81	576.40	870.00	844.13	831.86	829.63	827.91	827.90
2 月 /Feb	472.21	522.21	546.35	576.99	870.28	843.54	831.32	829.29	827.91	827.80
3 月 /Mar	472.21	522.21	547.34	573.13	870.23	842.76	832.89	829.57	827.92	827.91
4 月 /Apr	472.21	526.59	549.65	570.63	869.55	842.25	833.15	829.57	827.92	827.92
5 月 /May	472.21	531.39	550.36	572.17	866.49	831.28	832.88	829.29	827.90	827.85
6 月 /Jun	472.21	535.35	547.51	573.74	865.72	830.08	832.26	829.21	827.97	827.80
7 月 /Jul	472.21	535.55	544.32	576.12	864.03	830.07	831.60	829.11	827.98	827.77
8 月 /Aug	472.21	537.35	542.87	577.64	858.98	830.75	830.81	828.94	827.99	827.73
9 月 /Sep	472.21	537.35	549.48	578.70	854.03	831.88	830.44	828.72	827.89	827.74
10 月 /Oct	472.21	537.90	553.69	578.68	852.93	831.55	830.00	828.38	827.78	827.74
11 月 /Nov	495.54	538.58	561.31	579.47	851.69	831.35	829.93	828.11	827.78	827.82
12 月 /Dec	522.21	541.31	579.82	580.68	848.45	831.56	829.90	827.96	827.79	827.93
年平均 Annual Average	**478.32**	**532.33**	**551.46**	**576.20**	**861.87**	**835.10**	**831.42**	**828.98**	**827.91**	**827.83**

人民币元/100美元
RMB per 100 USD

续表 (Continue)

月份 Month	2000 年	2001 年	2002 年	2003 年	2004 年	2005 年	2006 年	2007 年	2008 年	2009 年
1 月 /Jan	827.93	827.71	827.67	827.68	827.69	827.65	806.68	778.98	724.78	683.82
2 月 /Feb	827.79	827.70	827.66	827.73	827.71	827.65	804.93	775.46	716.01	683.57
3 月 /Mar	827.86	827.76	827.70	827.72	827.71	827.65	803.50	773.90	707.52	683.41
4 月 /Apr	827.93	827.71	827.72	827.71	827.69	827.65	801.56	772.47	700.07	683.12
5 月 /May	827.77	827.72	827.69	827.69	827.71	827.65	801.52	767.04	697.24	682.45
6 月 /Jun	827.72	827.71	827.70	827.71	827.67	827.65	800.67	763.30	689.71	683.32
7 月 /Jul	827.93	827.69	827.68	827.73	827.67	822.90	799.10	758.05	683.76	683.20
8 月 /Aug	827.96	827.70	827.67	827.70	827.68	810.19	797.33	757.53	685.15	683.22
9 月 /Sep	827.86	827.68	827.70	827.71	827.67	809.22	793.68	752.58	683.07	682.89
10 月 /Oct	827.85	827.68	827.69	827.67	827.65	808.89	790.32	750.12	683.16	682.75
11 月 /Nov	827.74	827.69	827.71	827.69	827.65	808.40	786.52	742.33	682.86	682.74
12 月 /Dec	827.72	827.68	827.72	827.70	827.65	807.59	782.38	736.76	684.24	682.79
年平均 Annual Average	**827.84**	**827.70**	**827.70**	**827.70**	**827.68**	**819.42**	**797.18**	**760.40**	**694.51**	**683.10**

人民币对美元交易中间价月平均汇价

人民币元/100美元
RMB per 100 USD

Monthly Average Transaction Mid Rates of Renminbi against US dollar, 1980—2018

续表 (Continue)

月份 Month	2010 年	2011 年	2012 年	2013 年	2014 年	2015 年	2016 年	2017 年	2018 年
1 月 /Jan	682.73	660.27	631.68	627.87	610.43	612.72	655.27	689.18	642.74
2 月 /Feb	682.70	658.31	630.00	628.42	611.28	613.39	653.11	687.13	632.05
3 月 /Mar	682.64	656.62	630.81	627.43	613.58	615.07	650.64	689.32	631.74
4 月 /Apr	682.62	652.92	629.66	624.71	615.53	613.02	647.62	688.45	629.67
5 月 /May	682.74	649.88	630.62	619.70	616.36	611.43	653.15	688.27	637.13
6 月 /Jun	681.65	647.78	631.78	617.18	615.57	611.61	658.74	680.19	646.51
7 月 /Jul	677.75	646.14	632.35	617.25	615.69	611.67	667.74	676.54	671.25
8 月 /Aug	679.01	640.90	634.04	617.08	616.06	630.56	664.74	667.36	684.53
9 月 /Sep	674.62	638.33	633.95	615.88	615.28	636.91	667.15	656.34	685.33
10 月 /Oct	667.32	635.66	631.44	613.93	614.41	634.86	674.42	661.54	691.95
11 月 /Nov	665.58	634.08	629.53	613.72	614.32	636.66	683.75	661.86	693.75
12 月 /Dec	665.15	632.81	629.00	611.60	612.38	644.76	691.82	659.42	688.31
年平均 Annual Average	**676.95**	**646.14**	**631.25**	**619.32**	**614.28**	**622.72**	**664.23**	**675.18**	**661.40**

2018 年 1—12 月人民币市场汇率汇总表

美元、港币、日元、欧元、英镑、澳元、新西兰元、新加坡元、瑞士法郎、加元 10 种币种单位为人民币元 /100 外币，其他币种单位为外币 /100 人民币
USD、HKD、JPY、EUR、GBP、AUD、NZD、CHF、CAD Unit: foreign currency per 100 RMB Other Currency unit:renminbi per 100 foreign currency

Transaction Mid Rates of Renminbi in the First Half of 2018

月份 Month	币种 Currency	期初价 Beginning of period	期末价 End of Period	最高价 Highest	最低价 Lowest	期平均 Period Average	累计平均 Accumulative Average
1 月 Jan	美元	650.63	628.41	652.63	628.41	642.7413	642.7413
	港币	120. 065	124. 296	124. 296	119. 709	121. 561	121. 561
	日元	1 731.06	1 734.96	1 742.06	1 711.31	1 724. 906	1 724. 906
	欧元	779.91	784	791.55	777.21	783.99	783.99
	英镑	879.11	890.32	901.61	876.48	885.9261	885.9261
	澳元	508.01	509.15	513.62	507.73	510.8474	510.8474
	新西兰元	462.34	465.68	472.54	460.61	466.6039	466.6039
	新加坡元	486.53	478.79	488.81	478.79	485.9665	485.9665
	瑞士法郎	667.52	674.55	676.72	663.51	668.5765	668.5765
	加元	518.55	510.2	523.53	510.2	516. 803	516. 803
	林吉特	160.65	161.03	163.22	160.65	162.3274	162.3274
	卢布	885.18	893.4	893.4	867.69	879. 923	879. 923
2 月 Feb	美元	629.69	632.8	634.71	626.49	632. 046	637.7667
	港币	124.08	123. 557	124. 611	123. 107	123.6274	122.5221
	日元	1 735.8	1 684.06	1 746.21	1 670.37	1 704. 669	1 715. 493
	欧元	783.7	772.3	791	768.4	779.9415	782. 107
	英镑	894.03	869.57	894.03	869.26	879. 739	883.0484
	澳元	504.52	493.35	504.52	491.94	497.8585	504. 806
	新西兰元	464.28	456.76	469	456.37	462.1425	464.5288
	新加坡元	481.27	477.51	484.44	472.64	478.8265	482.6456
	瑞士法郎	679.57	669.77	687.82	663.8	676.1125	672.0816
	加元	513.28	493.07	513.28	493.07	502. 192	510.0072
	林吉特	161.36	161.47	163	159.77	161. 527	161.9551
	卢布	887.55	889.26	925.51	880.06	899. 038	888.8137
3 月 Mar	美元	635.65	627.26	635.65	626.85	631.7368	635.7258
	港币	123. 081	125. 016	125. 016	123. 081	124.0005	123.0225
	日元	1 670.31	1 692.58	1 695.71	1 656.7	1 677.57	1 702. 658
	欧元	775.7	772.68	783.51	772.68	779. 255	781.1417
	英镑	872.26	880.02	891.67	871.3	881.1664	882.4114
	澳元	492.07	482.36	498.38	481.77	490.1764	499.8545
	新西兰元	459.72	454	463.86	453.12	458.3968	462.4534
	新加坡元	480.39	478.39	482.13	478.39	480.3645	481.8735
	瑞士法郎	674.72	656.95	675.92	656.95	666.1155	670.0623
	加元	494.98	486.36	494.98	483.24	488.6323	502.7726
	林吉特	161.74	162.29	162.82	160.85	161.7791	161.8955
	卢布	892.77	909.64	916.28	887.2	903.1268	893.6582

2018 年 1—12 月人民币市场汇率汇总表

Transaction Mid Rates of Renminbi in the First Half of 2018

续表 (Continue)

月份 Month	币种 Currency	期初价 Beginning of period	期末价 End of Period	最高价 Highest	最低价 Lowest	期平均 Period Average	累计平均 Accumulative Average
4 月 Apr	美元	124. 928	123. 904	125. 145	123. 764	124. 555	123.3967
	港币	1 685.34	1 726.08	1 728.55	1 685.34	1 707. 832	1 703. 921
	日元	772.4	766	777.04	766	772.7305	779.0878
	欧元	881.92	867.73	896.37	867.73	884. 181	882.8435
	英镑	481.09	479.16	488.13	478.34	483.9538	495.9717
	澳元	453.48	447.63	463.61	446.91	456. 309	460. 953
	新西兰元	478.29	477.53	480.49	475.74	478.3581	481.0151
	新加坡元	657.02	639	659.09	639	649.9533	665. 152
	瑞士法郎	486.1	492.96	500.43	486.1	494.5619	500.7677
	加元	162.49	161.42	162.99	161.2	161.9067	161.8983
	林吉特	914.51	980.27	1 002.42	909.87	965.8743	911.2923
	卢布	633.25	640.96	641.75	633.25	637.1278	634. 854
5 月 May	美元	123. 922	122. 338	123. 922	122. 223	123.1079	123.3358
	港币	1 734.29	1 697.24	1 740.93	1 694.19	1 720. 653	1 707. 452
	日元	766	749.41	766	740.37	752.6674	773.5128
	欧元	860.89	849.3	863.96	848.63	855.3622	877.0447
	英镑	479.16	484.09	484.87	473.84	479.3765	492.47
	澳元	447.63	448.37	448.37	437.81	442. 867	457.1367
	新西兰元	474.81	479.08	479.13	472.4	475.6396	479.8808
	新加坡元	635.41	650.13	650.13	632.19	638.7965	659.5907
	瑞士法郎	492.8	494.57	498.98	491.74	495.0561	499.5625
	加元	161.42	160.96	161.61	160.11	160.7461	161.6551
	林吉特	980.27	971.75	990.88	958.47	974.9574	924.7262
	卢布	641.8	661.71	662.35	638.5	646.5124	636.7373
6 月 Jun	美元	122. 141	118. 435	122. 768	118. 357	121.2696	123. 002
	港币	1 705.33	1 670.36	1 726.95	1 666.21	1 701. 811	1 706. 541
	日元	748.21	773.21	773.21	739.99	754.6881	770.4719
	欧元	852.73	873.79	873.79	849.57	857.0614	873.8166
	英镑	485.1	490.06	490.06	476.89	484.52	491.1858
	澳元	447.92	448.11	451.23	444.77	448.7033	455.7744
	新西兰元	479.49	485.44	485.44	475.58	479.2867	479.7848
	新加坡元	649.4	667.58	667.58	641.53	652.8076	658. 495
	瑞士法郎	495.6	503.81	503.81	486.05	492.4267	498.4098
	加元	161.26	163.75	163.75	160.02	161.5905	161.6447
	林吉特	968.09	945.05	987.2	945.05	970.0143	932. 042
	卢布	666.32	680.38	681.02	661.23	671.2473	641.7322

美元、港币、日元、欧元、英镑、澳元、新西兰元、新加坡元、瑞士法郎、加元 10 种币种单位为人民币元 /100 外币，其他币种单位为外币 /100 人民币 USD、HKD、JPY、EUR、GBP、AUD、NZD、CHF、CAD Unit: foreign currency per 100 RMB Other Currency unit:renminbi per 100 foreign currency

续表 (Continue)

月份 Month	币种 Currency	期初价 Beginning of period	期末价 End of Period	最高价 Highest	最低价 Lowest	期平均 Period Average	累计平均 Accumulative Average
7 月 Jul	美元	117. 564	115.06	118. 555	115.06	116.7841	122. 102
	港币	1 661.82	1 639.79	1 686.77	1 628.49	1 658. 751	1 699. 624
	日元	773.03	796.8	797	772.68	784.3668	772. 483
	欧元	871.78	887.19	891.58	869.49	879.9682	874. 707
	英镑	487.6	506.52	506.52	487.6	496.8227	492.0016
	澳元	446.36	464.15	465.58	446.36	455.7205	455.7666
	新西兰元	486.58	499.51	500.12	485.57	492.3127	481.5981
	新加坡元	670.48	686.91	688.94	664.57	674.8559	660. 863
	瑞士法郎	505.25	523.01	523.01	504.18	511.1164	500.2489
	加元	164.85	167.29	167.74	163.76	165.6627	162.2263
	林吉特	948.96	917.6	953.66	912.45	934.3632	932. 378
	卢布	681.54	683	693.3	680.18	684.5265	647.3566
8 月 Aug	美元	114. 909	114.865	115. 361	113. 168	114.5751	121.1128
	港币	1 635.6	1 625.05	1 636.26	1 596.34	1 620. 664	1 689. 246
	日元	796.33	792.35	798.33	781.04	790. 607	774. 865
	欧元	892.04	883.07	892.04	870.66	879.1487	875.2907
	英镑	504.88	491.77	506.98	491.77	501.4174	493.2391
	澳元	463.55	452.01	463.55	451.7	456.5743	455.8727
	新西兰元	500.4	497.63	502.25	497.63	499.9413	484.0089
	新加坡元	686.83	704.78	705.82	685.82	692.77	665.0565
	瑞士法郎	524.02	523.77	528.36	520.75	524.99	503.5006
	加元	167.54	166.14	168.89	165.52	167.1448	162.8727
	林吉特	923.41	986	996.76	922.9	968.7365	937.1565
	卢布	682	686.8	688.8	682	685. 333	651.2516
9 月 Sep	美元	114. 998	113. 948	114. 998	113.39	114.2851	120.4125
	港币	1 627.28	1 654.8	1 654.8	1 619.29	1 633. 712	1 683.55
	日元	792.01	796.83	807.39	790.51	798.9605	777.3364
	欧元	876.41	891.38	905.86	875.08	891.7715	876.9811
	英镑	491.94	496.63	498.71	487.68	493.6505	493.2813
	澳元	450.53	455.39	457.75	447.03	452.1225	455.4881
	新西兰元	497.12	502.49	503.46	496	499.7735	485.6258
	新加坡元	703.46	699.18	714.9	699.18	707.5585	669.4157
	瑞士法郎	520.85	532.07	532.07	517.98	525.836	505.7914
	加元	165.05	165.89	166.3	164.51	165.462	163.1383
	林吉特	995.27	954.29	1 027.68	951.29	985.1865	942.0827
	卢布	686.8	697.37	697.37	686.8	691. 953	655.5458

2018 年 1—12 月人民币市场汇率汇总表

美元、港币、日元、欧元、英镑、澳元、新西兰元、新加坡元、瑞士法郎、加元 10 种币种单位为人民币元 /100 外币，其他币种单位为外币 /100 人民币
USD、HKD、JPY、EUR、GBP、AUD、NZD、CHF、CAD Unit: foreign currency per 100 RMB Other Currency unit:renminbi per 100 foreign currency

Transaction Mid Rates of Renminbi in the First Half of 2018

续表 (Continue)

月份 Month	币种 Currency	期初价 Beginning of period	期末价 End of Period	最高价 Highest	最低价 Lowest	期平均 Period Average	累计平均 Accumulative Average
10 月 Oct	美元	113.935	112.374	114.089	112.374	113.2109	119.6527
	港币	1 658.15	1 618.46	1 667.18	1 610.92	1 629.242	1 677.821
	日元	796.83	788.8	800.4	788.8	794.7713	779.1758
	欧元	891.19	884.65	907.31	879.42	895.983	878.9859
	英镑	496.63	494.6	496.63	489.08	493.0761	493.2597
	澳元	455.39	455.76	457.02	446.22	453.313	455.2586
	新西兰元	500.58	503.19	503.19	496.57	501.3804	487.288
	新加坡元	698.04	691.29	700.27	691.29	695.9013	672.21
	瑞士法郎	535.81	530.04	535.81	528.59	531.5978	508.5141
	加元	165.81	166.6	166.86	165.53	166.3161	163.4735
	林吉特	945.41	943.09	974.23	937.68	950.3709	942.9571
	卢布	692.05	695.58	696.18	688.94	693.7527	659.0481
11 月 Nov	美元	113.101	112.321	113.423	112.321	112.79	119.0236
	港币	1 627.01	1 628.96	1 644.18	1 620.63	1 633.114	1 673.722
	日元	789.33	786	794.82	780.77	787.9445	779.9796
	欧元	896.63	886.75	907.96	883.65	893.3586	880.3034
	英镑	498.17	507.26	508.04	498.17	502.8459	494.1384
	澳元	459.84	477.09	477.09	459.23	470.0714	456.6165
	新西兰元	502.72	506.83	506.83	500.97	504.4127	488.8578
	新加坡元	690.53	696.21	699.54	686.33	693.0482	674.1202
	瑞士法郎	528.85	523.03	528.85	521.85	525.3436	510.0568
	加元	165.48	166.13	166.35	165.03	165.6755	163.6754
	林吉特	947.65	959.57	977.42	944.34	956.6614	944.2133
	卢布	687.98	687.55	690.77	683.43	688.3086	661.4024
12 月 Dec	美元	113.489	113.805	114.081	113.009	113.5543	118.5836
	港币	1 650.38	1 592.09	1 650.64	1 592.09	1 628.369	1 670.073
	日元	781.13	786	786.63	775.01	782.45	780.1784
	欧元	876.64	877.25	878.67	864.17	871.5767	879.6012
	英镑	506.93	484.1	506.93	481.85	493.3519	494.0751
	澳元	476.94	461.48	476.94	460.07	469.2562	457.6334
	新西兰元	502.98	504.36	504.36	500.53	501.9929	489.9146
	新加坡元	689.36	700.3	700.3	685.01	693.6738	675.6935
	瑞士法郎	521.24	504.14	521.24	504.03	511.6052	510.1814
	加元	165.06	166.28	166.28	164.23	164.9219	163.7757
	林吉特	964.95	1 008.34	1 009.54	961.54	980.0681	947.0982
	卢布	650.63	628.41	652.63	628.41	642.7413	642.7413

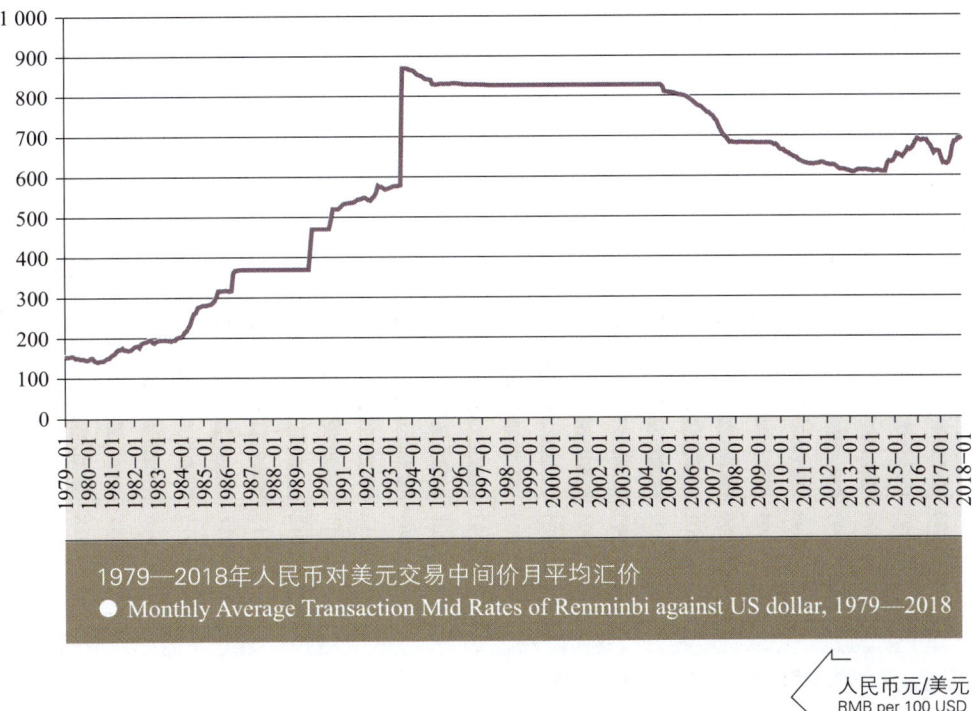

1979—2018年人民币对美元交易中间价月平均汇价
● Monthly Average Transaction Mid Rates of Renminbi against US dollar, 1979—2018

人民币元/美元
RMB per 100 USD

四、利用外资 ①
IV. Foreign Investment Utilization

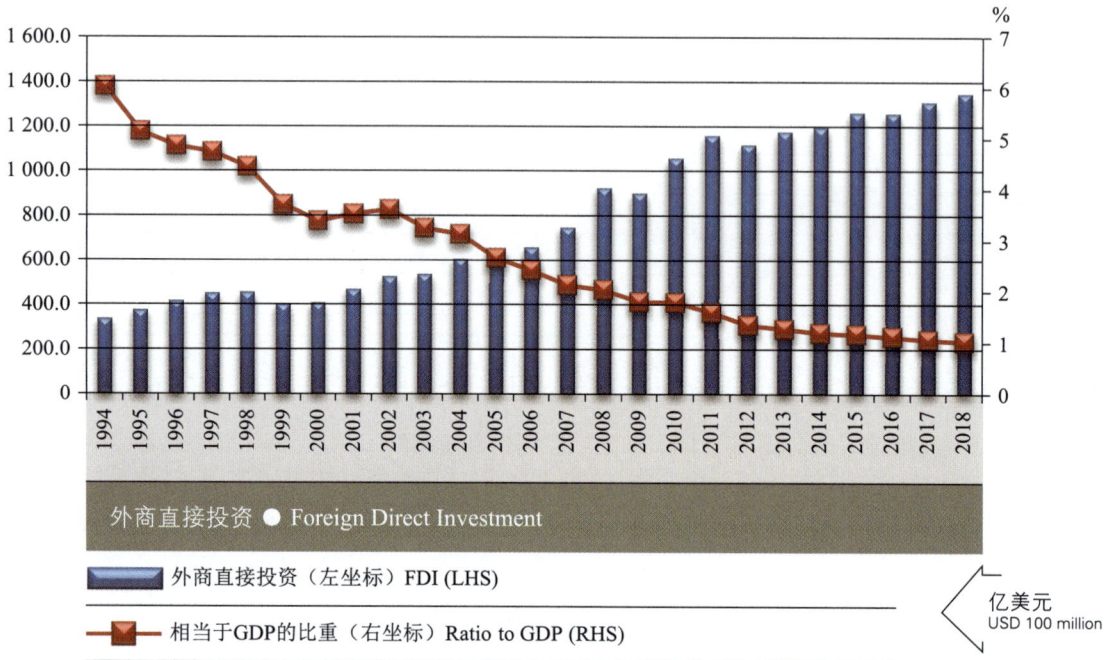

外商直接投资 ● Foreign Direct Investment

外商直接投资（左坐标）FDI (LHS)

相当于GDP的比重（右坐标）Ratio to GDP (RHS)

亿美元
USD 100 million

---

① 资料来源：商务部。
Source: Ministry of Commerce.

2018 年利用外资

单位：亿美元
Unit: USD 100 million

Foreign Direct Investment in 2018

利用外资方式 Mode of Foreign Investment Utilization	本年批准外资项目数 Approved Foreign Investment Programs		本年实际使用外资 Actual Utilization of Foreign Investment	
	本年累计 Accumulative in This Year	同比增长（%） Increase	本年累计 Accumulative in This Year	同比增长（%） Increase
总计 Total	60 533	69.8	1 349.7	3.0
一、外商直接投资 Direct Foreign Investment	60 533	69.8	1 349.7	3.0
中外合资企业 Sino-Foreign Equity Joint Venture	10 170	21.6	344.9	16.0
中外合作企业 Sino-Foreign Contractual Joint Venture	107	-13.7	7.7	-4.1
外资企业 Foreign Investment Enterprise	50 106	85.5	893.97	-2.1
外商投资股份制 Stock-Holding by Foreign Investment	129	3.2	82.99	28.2
合作开发 Cooperation Exploitation	1	-50.0	11.93	1.1
二、外商其他投资 Other Foreign Investment	0	0.0	0	0.0
对外发行股票 Issue Stocks to the Outside	0	0.0	0	0.0
国际租赁 International Tenancy	0	0.0	0	0.0
补偿贸易 Compensative Trade	0	0.0	0	0.0
加工装配 Processing & amp; Assembling	0	0.0	0	0.0
其他 Others	0	0.0	0	0.0

注：统计数据为非金融领域。

Note: The data is subject to non-financial sectors.

五、外债 ①
V. External Debt

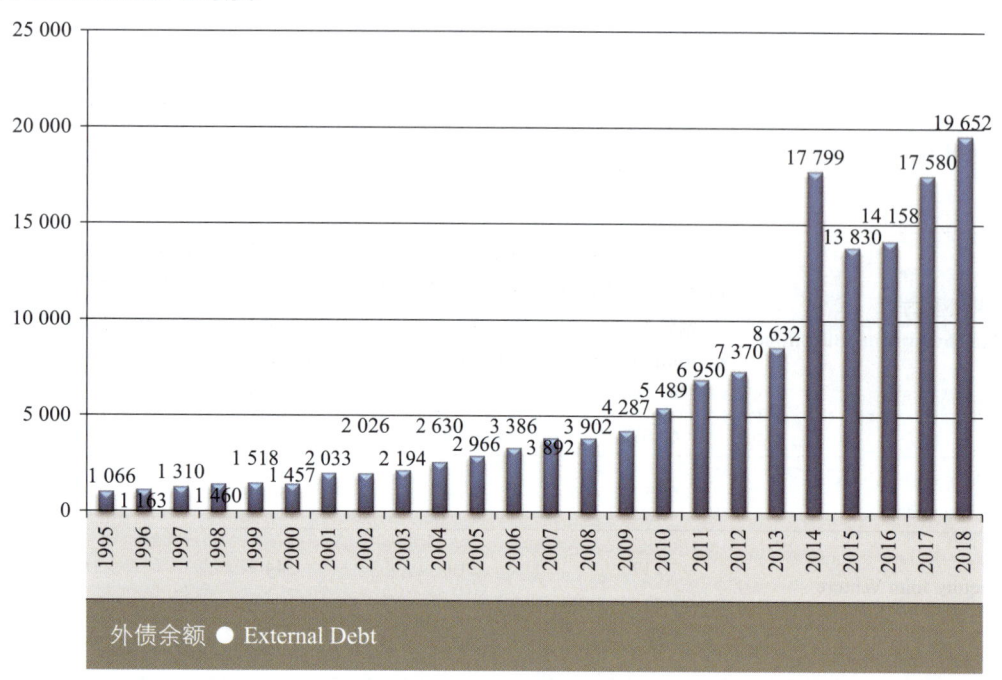

外债余额 ● External Debt

亿美元
USD 100 million

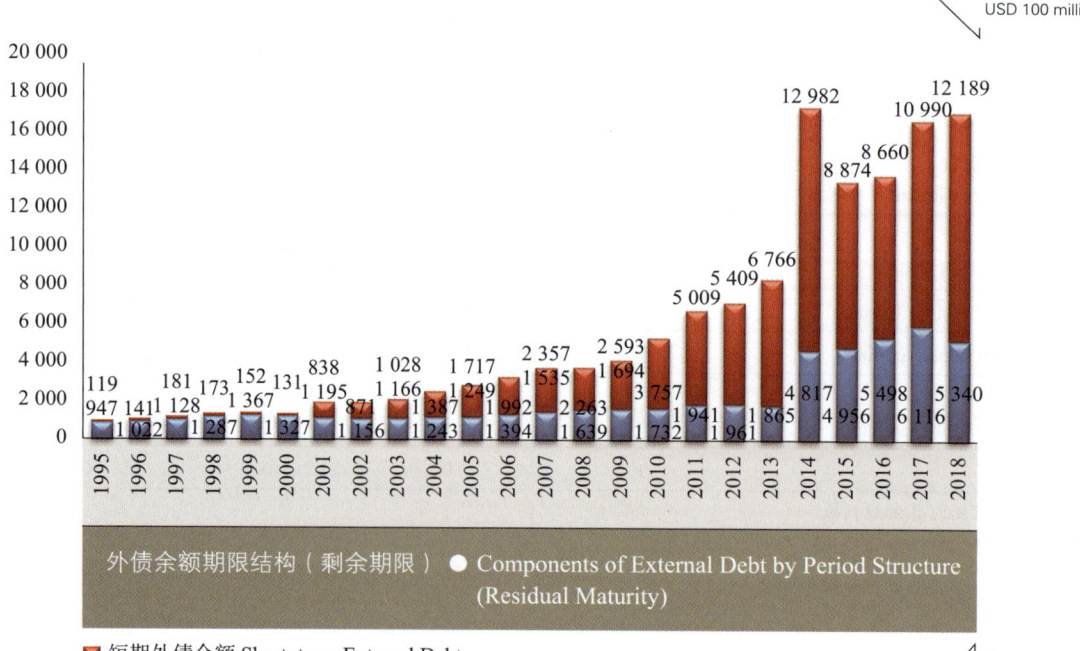

外债余额期限结构（剩余期限） ● Components of External Debt by Period Structure (Residual Maturity)

■ 短期外债余额 Short-term External Debt

■ 中长期外债余额 Long-and-medium-term External Debt

亿美元
USD 100 million

① 资料来源：国家外汇管理局。
Sources: SAFE.

2018 年末外债余额期限结构（剩余期限）
Components of External Debt by Period Structure (Residual Maturity), End-2018

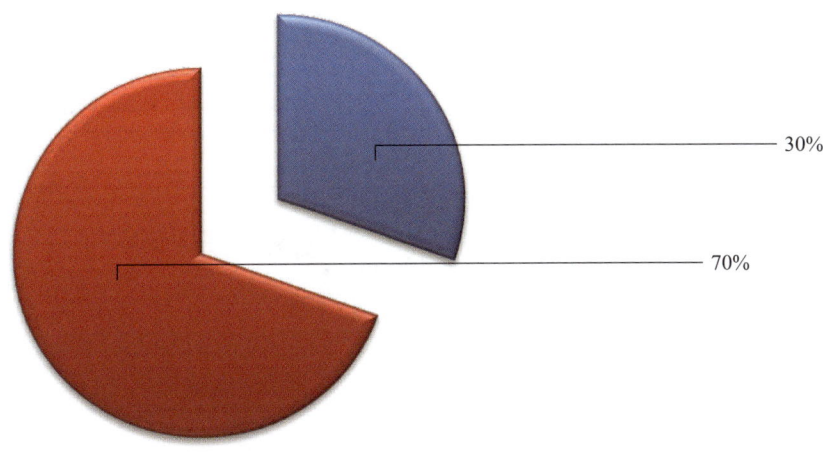

30%

70%

■ 中长期外债余额 Long-and-medium-term External Debt
■ 短期外债余额 Short-term External Debt

2018 年末登记外债余额主体结构
Components of Registered External Debt by Type of Debtor, End-2018

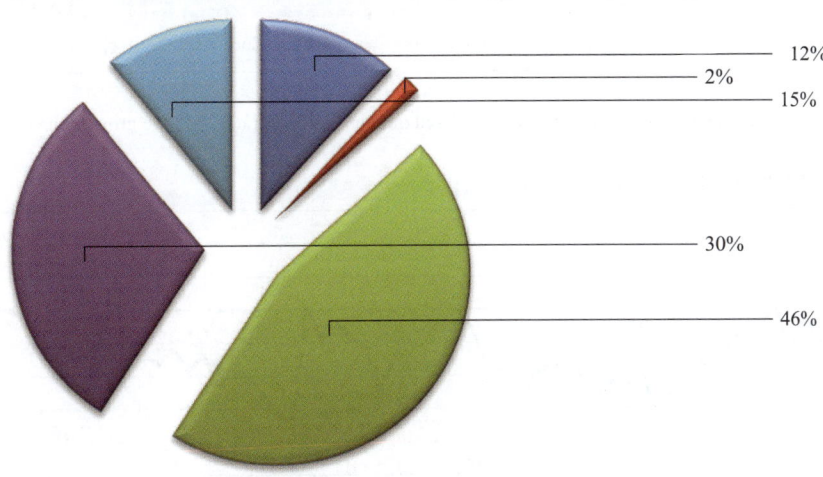

12%
2%
15%

30%

46%

■ 广义政府 General Government
■ 中央银行 The Central Bank
■ 其他接受存款公司 Other Deposit taking Company
■ 其他部门 Other Institutions
■ 直接投资：公司间贷款 Direct Investment:Inter Company Loans

六、世界经济增长状况 [①]
VI. Growth of World Economics

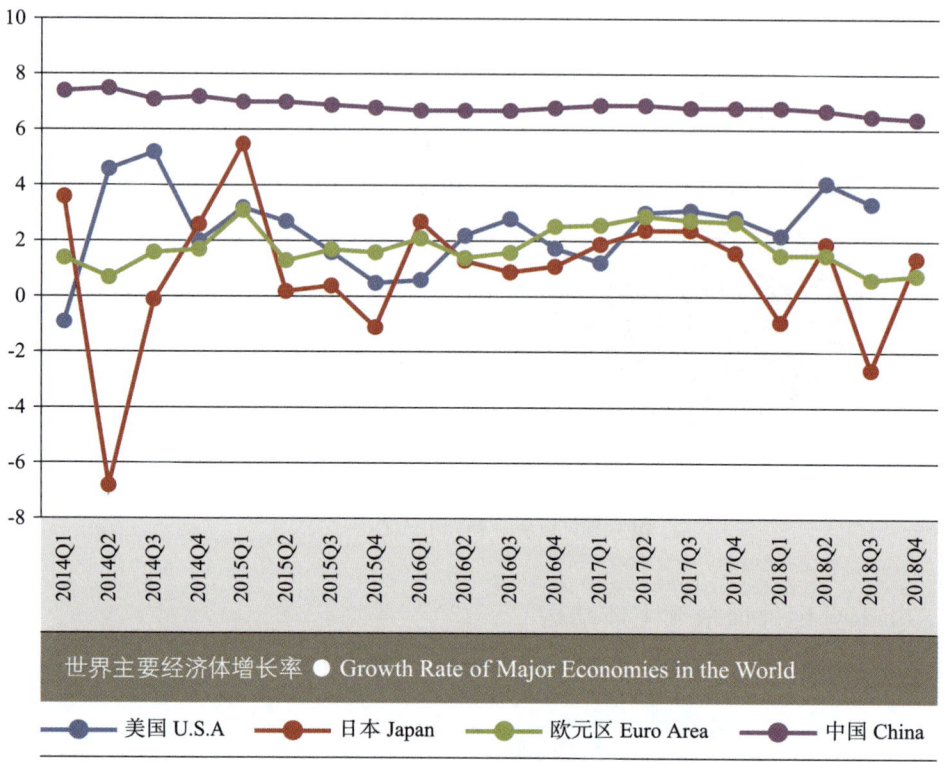

世界主要经济体增长率 ● Growth Rate of Major Economies in the World

━●━ 美国 U.S.A　━●━ 日本 Japan　━●━ 欧元区 Euro Area　━●━ 中国 China

注：美国、日本和欧元区是实际GDP季比折年增速，中国为年比增速。

The growth rates of U. S, Japan and Euro Area are the annualized quarterly growth rates, and the growth rate of China is the year-on-year quarterly growth rate.

居民消费价格指数（CPI）

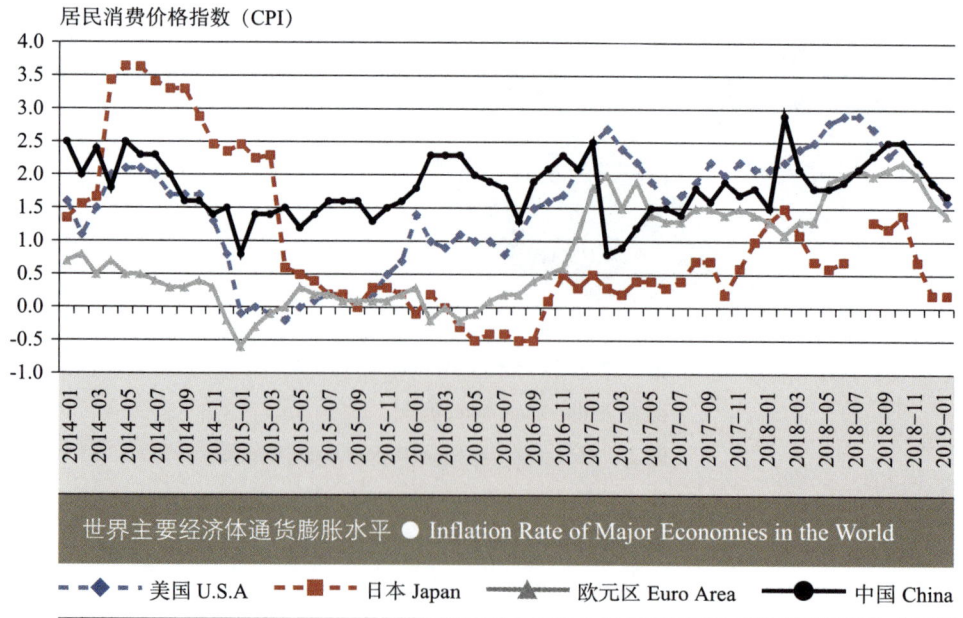

世界主要经济体通货膨胀水平 ● Inflation Rate of Major Economies in the World

━◆━ 美国 U.S.A　━■━ 日本 Japan　━▲━ 欧元区 Euro Area　━●━ 中国 China

[①] 资料来源：彭博资讯；CEIC 亚洲数据库。
　　Sources: Bloomberg; CEIC Asia Database.

失业率 Unemployment Rate (%)

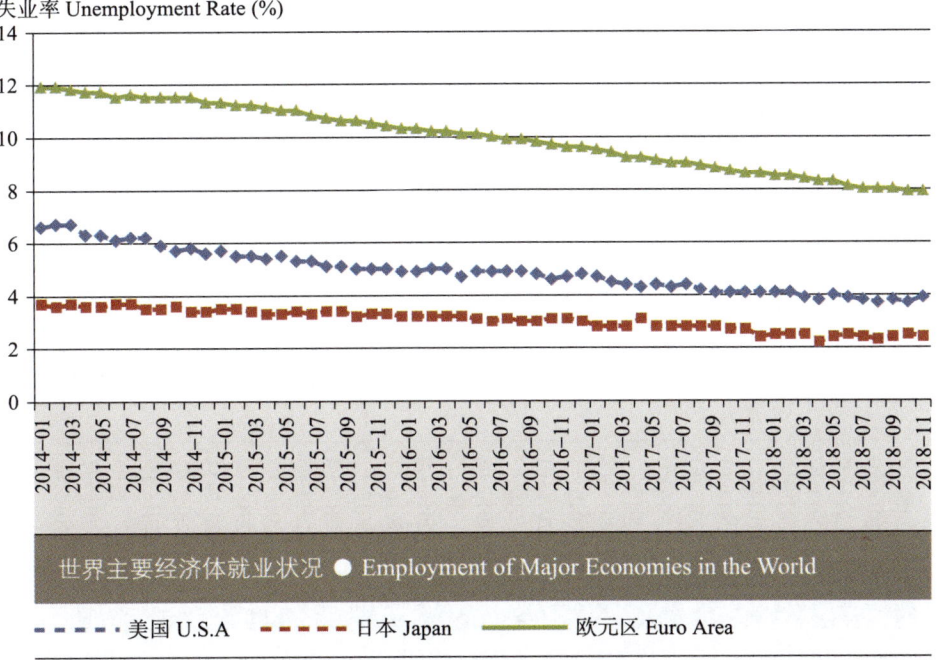

世界主要经济体就业状况 ● Employment of Major Economies in the World

- - - - 美国 U.S.A　　- - - - 日本 Japan　　——— 欧元区 Euro Area

七、国际金融市场状况 [①]
VII. International Financial Market

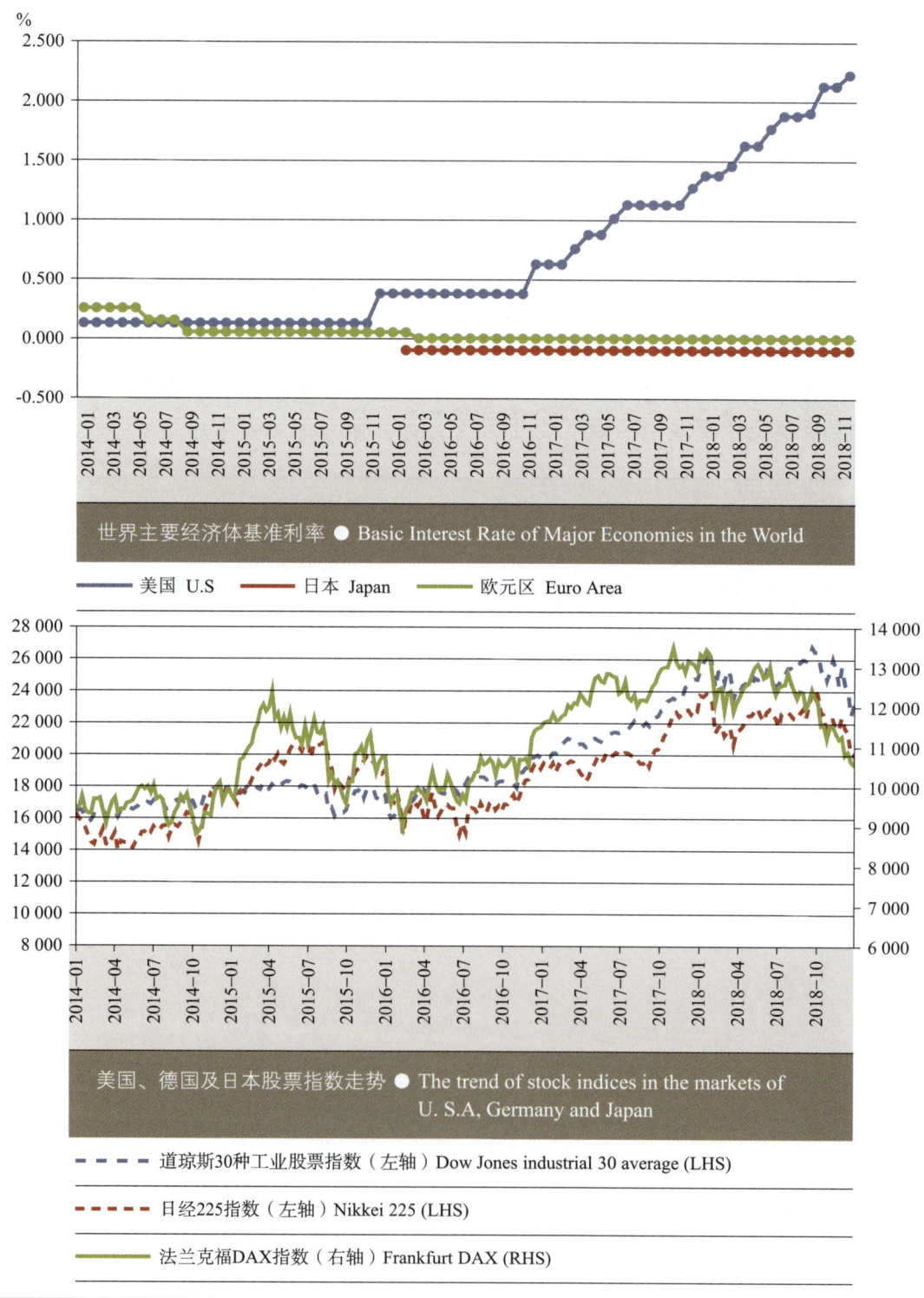

世界主要经济体基准利率 ● Basic Interest Rate of Major Economies in the World

美国 U.S　　日本 Japan　　欧元区 Euro Area

美国、德国及日本股票指数走势 ● The trend of stock indices in the markets of U. S.A, Germany and Japan

- - - - 道琼斯30种工业股票指数（左轴）Dow Jones industrial 30 average (LHS)
- - - - 日经225指数（左轴）Nikkei 225 (LHS)
──── 法兰克福DAX指数（右轴）Frankfurt DAX (RHS)

---

① 资料来源：彭博资讯。
Source: Bloomberg.

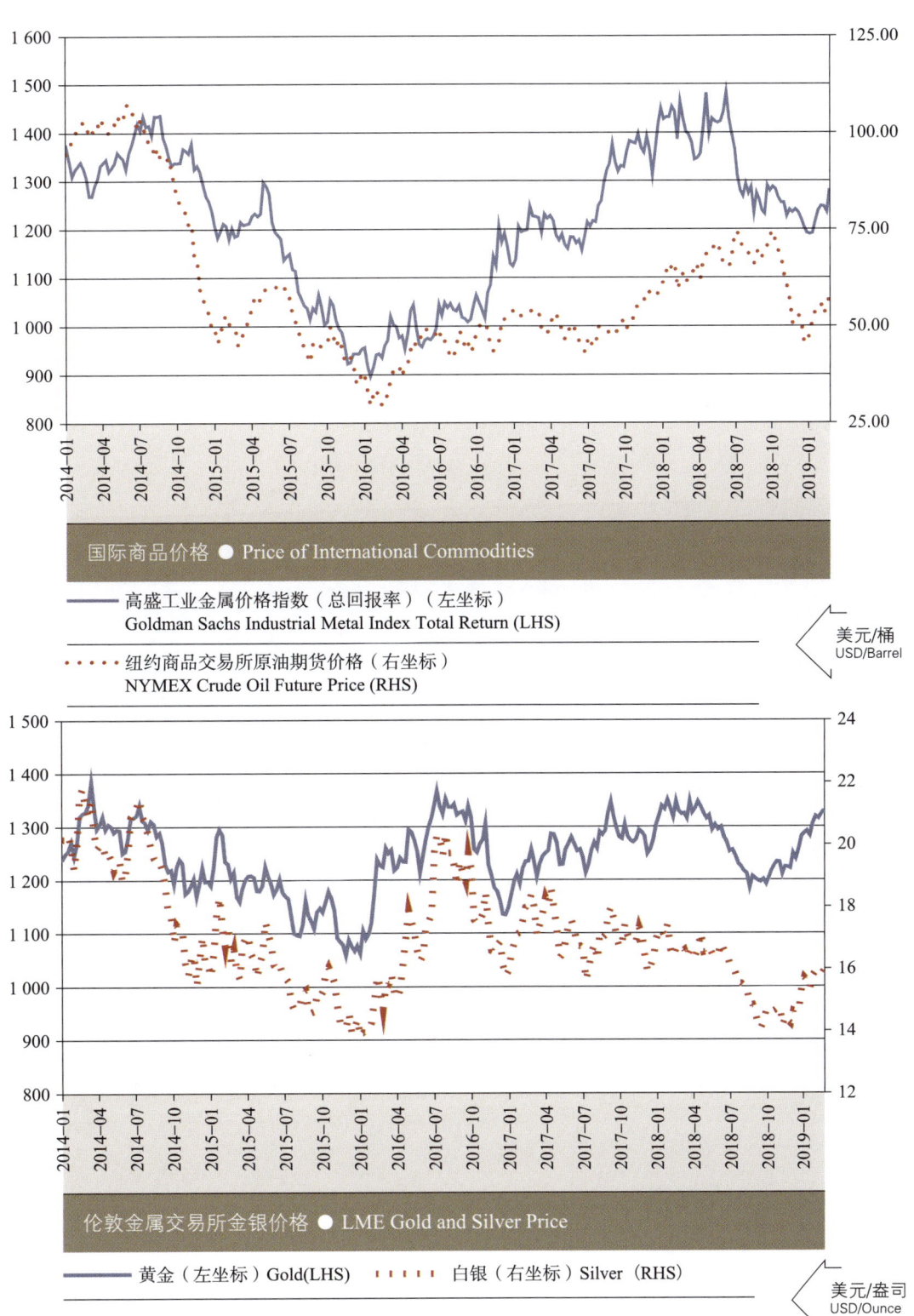

国际商品价格 ● Price of International Commodities

——— 高盛工业金属价格指数（总回报率）（左坐标）
Goldman Sachs Industrial Metal Index Total Return (LHS)

········ 纽约商品交易所原油期货价格（右坐标）
NYMEX Crude Oil Future Price (RHS)

美元/桶
USD/Barrel

伦敦金属交易所金银价格 ● LME Gold and Silver Price

——— 黄金（左坐标）Gold(LHS)　·····　白银（右坐标）Silver（RHS）

美元/盎司
USD/Ounce